Peter Batt was born,
dren, on a borrowe
East London in 1933. At the age of twenty-
he decided one morning to give up working on the building sites to get a proper job; later that day he was working for the *Daily Mail*. He has since worked as a columnist for most British daily and Sunday national newspapers, and was named 1973 Sportswriter of the Year.

'Extremely readable and profoundly moving . . . [A] superbly written book . . . it has taken him a lot of courage to write with such honesty'

Independent

'A brutal self-analysis of one of the great characters of Fleet Street who gambled like an idiot, drank like a fish and wrote like an angel . . . [a] desperate, compelling and ultimately triumphant story'

Sun

'A funny and moving book . . . I hope it sells a million'

Mail on Sunday

'Undisputed world champion of self-destruction . . . Crammed with great stories . . . it is more than a rollicking one-sitting read'

Daily Mail

'King of the column and sultan of sozzle in the good old days that have gone for ever. There has been a spate of books filling the sports shelves about the evils of booze . . . this tragic-comic book is worth 200 of them'

Guardian

BATTY

The Life and Wild Times of the Guvnor of *FLEET STREET*

PETER BATT

HEADLINE

First published in 2000
by HEADLINE BOOK PUBLISHING

First published in paperback in 2000
by HEADLINE BOOK PUBLISHING

10 9 8 7 6 5 4 3 2 1

ISBN 0 7472 6385 X

Typeset by Palimpsest Book Production Limited,
Polmont, Stirlingshire
Printed and bound by
Mackays of Chatham plc, Chatham, Kent

HEADLINE BOOK PUBLISHING
A division of Hodder Headline
338 Euston Road
London NW1 3BH

www.headline.co.uk
www.hodderheadline.com

CONTENTS

ACKNOWLEDGEMENTS

For Heidi

The great thing is to last and get your work done; and see and hear and understand; and write when there is something that you know; and not before; and not too damned much after.

Ernest Hemingway
Death in the Afternoon

CHAPTER ONE
MARILYN MONROE

Marilyn Monroe made me the man I am today. Without ever being remotely aware of it, this most divine of 20th-century sex goddesses opened the door to a life of fantasy, fulfilment, tragedy and transformation which I still barely believe actually happened to me.

When we 'came together', she was minding her own business on the front page of the *Daily Mail* and I had been wasting my days as a navvy on a building site and my nights as a snooker hall layabout. It was in the austere 1950s, and I was in my early twenties. The Cold War was in its infancy and Ban the Bomb marchers were tramping out daily reminders of what a dismal world we all inhabited.

For macho young males, however, the lighter side of life was on the up. Elvis was tuning us in, the Busby Babes were making our hair stand on end and Marilyn was turning us on big time. The one cloud on my personal horizon was that my dear old mum was nagging the daylights out of me. Her daily grouse was, 'When are you going to settle down and get yourself a proper job, boy?' As a young gambling man, my standard reply was: 'I've got to settle up first, Mum.'

But I could not deny that her disappointment in me was understandable. Only a couple of weeks earlier, she had been forced to endure the shame of seeing me appear in her street on a horse and cart, waving a handbell and shouting 'Any old rags.' So, one fateful morning, prompted by a mixture of shame for what I was doing to my mum and regret for the long-stifled ambition I had once nursed for myself, I phoned the *Daily Mail* in response to their advertisement for a shorthand telephone reporter for their foreign room. My old army boots were still covered in wet concrete from the building site when I made that call.

In those days of full employment, a CV was as futuristic a concept as the idea of fabulous Fleet Street decamping for Wapping. So all I had to do was sit a shorthand typing test that same afternoon and convince them I had what it takes. I hurried home, washed the sand and cement off, changed into a suit and presented myself before Mr Curtis, the foreign editor.

To say I rated my chances of getting the job as upwards of a thousand to one would be an understatement. My 'form lines' were ancient history. When I left school at 15, I had spent two years as a messenger boy in an official shorthand-writers' establishment and I had attended Pitmans' College for shorthand and typing lessons, but for the past six years my dormant brain had occupied itself as a plumber's mate, a steel erector, a factory hand, a foundry worker, a National Service soldier, a brewery worker, a hod carrier and, of course, as the aforementioned rag and bone man. My fingers had not touched a typewriter in all that time and the only need I had had for a pen was for writing out illegal betting slips.

All I remember about Mr Curtis 45 years on is his walking stick, his kind face and his twinkling eyes. And it must have been that twinkle in his eye I had to thank for the stroke of luck I received when instead of droning out some heavy political diatribe from Nikita Khrushchev as I dreaded he would, this benign, elderly editor asked me to take down a nice light, fluffy piece about Marilyn Monroe, which was that day's offbeat 'centre kicker' story that the *Mail* always featured in the middle of its otherwise very serious broadsheet front page. God knows how I managed it but I swear that, in a sudden fit of desperation to better myself, I put that article to memory. After all, along with millions of other young men around the world, I had conjured up the most tactile fantasies about Marilyn often enough, although touch typing her was the last thing I had had in mind.

As he painstakingly read the transcription of my mixture of half-remembered shorthand outlines and hopeful guesses of what his esteemed reporter had been on about, Mr Curtis frowned frequently, sending my spirits on a downward spiral towards that sadly familiar low point of tearing up the betting slip. Then, after poring over my sweat-stained pages for what seemed longer than the time needed to read *War and Peace*, he suddenly looked me straight in the eye and asked one challenging question: 'How much do you want this job, young man?'

As luck would have it, my ad-libbed response turned out to be inspirational. 'More than I would want a night with Marilyn Monroe,' I only half lied. And when he proffered a congratulatory handshake, I could only assume that it was more in approval of my foot-in-the-door 'front' than an assessment of my stenography skills.

The upside of this blind, against-all-odds optimism of my youth was that this unlikely interview was to be the initial step of a fantastic journey which took me around the world, all expenses paid, brought me into close contact with some of the most memorable personalities of the second half of the 20th century and gave me a free seat at almost every major sporting event on earth. It was today's equivalent of winning the lottery. But there was a downside to my unrealistic expectations, too. Nothing ever seemed to be enough. For me, the grass was always going to be greener, at the next newspaper office, in the next pub, on the next racecourse, at the next dog track, in the next house, the next town or the next country.

Given that attitude, I was inevitably doomed to lose the lot – including my sanity and my soul.

CHAPTER TWO
WAR BABE

When the first, spine-chilling air raid warning of the Second World War rang out over southern England, putting the future of every man, woman and child on hold, I was strolling along the sea front at Brighton. Nearly 60 years on, I can still feel, if I so choose, the echoes of that wailing noise which ran through my body from head to toe as if it had been struck with a tuning fork of fear.

One of a little group of cockney evacuees, I was six years old and instinctively glanced at my older brother, Jim, for guidance. He shouted 'Run!' and we all took off, with pounding hearts, in an aimless dash to we knew not where. As the youngest kid of the bunch, I was soon trailing behind and pleading: 'Where are we going?'

Jim looked back over his shoulder and shouted: 'Fuck knows – just keep running.'

As it turned out, my big brother was describing my future more accurately than any fortune teller on Brighton pier could ever hope to have done. A child of my times,

I was born into the big-boys-don't-cry syndrome. Even worse, in the slums of the East End of London, little boys were not allowed to cry either. If you came indoors whingeing that you had come off worst in a street scuffle, your old man simply stuck the toe of his boot up your arse and sent you back out there.

Having been taught those tough laws of survival at such an early age, I have since often asked myself why it is, then, that the predominant memories of my childhood are full not of courageous battle cries but of unknown, unidentified emotional fears of a recurring nature that have interrupted my sleep and interfered with my daily actions throughout my adult life. I suspected that these uncomfortable recollections had something to do with being evacuated and separated from my mother several times over, but I never dreamed of using it as an excuse until – at the age of 59, no less – I found myself being put to bed with a teddy bear in an alcoholic recovery clinic and being instructed by psychotherapists to 'find my inner child'. To my dismay, the inner child I eventually discovered pissed the bed most nights and missed his mum like mad most days.

I can still visualise my mother coming to see me in Brighton. She was wearing a hat with a veil, had padded shoulders in her coat, and her shoes were covered with sacks to prevent her slipping on the ice and snow. Nothing of that visit stays in my mind except her arrival and departure, and that as she slithered away out of my sight, I thought she had gone for ever.

Yet it could not have been all bad in Brighton. I can smile when I remember Jim forming an evacuees' band which, as a mouth organ player, he led, while I played paper and comb. Tough guy Jim, who went on to become a 'minder' in later life, found his vocation when he was forced to look after me in those early days. Six years older than me, he dished out more cuffs round the ear than encouragement as he bullied me to cock my leg over the crossbar of a bike and taught me how to tell the time. And the only time I ever saw him attempt to back down from a confrontation in his entire life came when he and I were waylaid on some waste ground by a few local kids one day and challenged to fight. They were much older than me and older even than my big brother, and I distinctly remember thinking we were done for when I disbelievingly heard my hero Jim say to them: 'It ain't fair. You've got long trousers on!'

With so little heart for the fray, Jim soon found himself getting the worst of it from their leader, who was by now squatting over him on the ground and demanding, 'Give in, give in.' In desperation, I picked up a handy half house brick and clonked Jim's assailant over the head with it. This did the trick. As the rest of his cronies backed off, their bully boy leader soon found the tide of battle turning as an inspired Jim gave him a hiding and put the whole gang of them to flight. I felt 10 feet tall.

I was not so full of myself, however, when I was moved from Brighton to Horsley in Surrey. Until my evacuation, I had never seen a blade of grass outside of Victoria Park in Bethnal Green, so Horsley was another world. And in this world lived a witch, called Granny McCourt. At least that's what I imagined she was as she brushed her long silver hair in front of the fire every night. There was no big brother to watch over me this time. Jim had insisted on going back to London and taking his chance with the bombs. I am sure most of us kids would have preferred to have been blown to smithereens than separated from our loved ones the way we were, but my misguided mum wanted to make sure her baby stayed safe and sound in the countryside.

Dear old Granny McCourt obviously wanted the same thing for me too, as she demonstrated by sprinkling holy water over my head whenever a plane droned over her cottage – no matter if it was one of theirs or one of ours. Sadly, that holy water never prevented me from catching ringworms and having my head shaved so that it resembled an egg shell and I was forced to cover my shame by wearing a cap. One of a crowd of local kids snatched it off me one day and flung it into the branches of a tree. He and his mates formed a circle round me, jeering 'Chekker, Chekker, Baldhead' over and over again. It is still among the worst memories of my life. Sometimes, in convoluted nightmares, I still charge those cruel faces one by one, but my fists bounce off them and they just keep grinning at me.

Still, as so often happens, good came out of bad when my mum decided to take me back to London. I was soon to be on the move again, though, when we were 'bombed out' during the Blitz. The house which Hitler wrecked was number 83 Grosvenor Street in Stepney, London E1. I first saw the light of day there on 7 June 1933 on what I was told later was a borrowed mattress. It was a tiny terraced house with no front garden where in summer, men and women often sat in chairs on the pavement, children constantly played street games and, occasionally, a husband and wife could be seen having a stand-up fist fight with each other on the cobbles.

One feature that firmly fixed it in its place and time in social history was that like all the other houses thereabouts, it was never locked and, indeed, there was always a front door key tied to a piece of string hanging behind the letter box, for neighbours and friends to let themselves in with. There was nothing worth stealing anyway in those hard times, so the residents really did literally live according to the lyrics of that old music hall song, 'Come Round Any Old Time And Make Yourself At Home'. And I was assured by older relatives later, who remembered those times more accurately than I did, that none of us ever felt a sense of deprivation either. We were exceedingly poor but we were proud and cheerful, and most of the children in the area were well educated at church schools.

I was the youngest of seven children – four boys and three girls. All my brothers and sisters are dead now but one brother, George, lived long enough for me to let him know that I was planning to write about those days of innocence and he told me about the day I was born. He was 12 years old. 'It was stifling hot,' he recalled. 'I was on my way out to school when Mum stopped me and told me to go round to Duckett Street and borrow a mattress from a relative of ours.'

George said he remembered carrying the mattress on his head for what seemed like miles and claimed he was 'sweating buckets' by the time he reached home. He told me: 'Mum wrote me a note for the teacher explaining why I was late and said that when I got back from school that evening, she might have a nice little surprise for me. Well, that surprise turned out to be you.' George was 75 when he told me this story just before his death, and he grinned as he said: 'I didn't even know Mum was pregnant. In fact, I honestly think I still believed that babies grew under gooseberry bushes until the day you arrived.'

My father, Jack to his wife, Johnny to his mates and miserable old bastard to his kids, was a drunkard (we had not yet heard of the term 'alcoholic') and because of this we all grew up to hate him bitterly. I now realise, of course, that he was not alone – the Stepney slums must have been full of them. What else could a man do in those days of monster-size families, with a tiny house full of kids and no room to swing the cat round in, but go down to the pub in the evening? The trouble with my old man was that he was rarely out of the boozers – morning, noon or night. My mum reckoned she never saw him sober in 40-odd years.

A veteran of the First World War, during which he was machine-gunned charging the enemy trenches, he had a withered left arm and was invalided out of the infantry. As a result, he was extremely lucky to get himself a reasonably well-paid job as a porter in Billingsgate fish market while most of his mates were still in France. He did not need two arms for that work as he carried the boxes of fish on his head.

Theoretically, a good job should have meant a good living for the Batt family, but what my dad did not spend in the bar, he squandered at the races courtesy of free transport from his taxi driver mate, Johnny Pimm. So while his brood struggled along literally on the breadline, old Jack Batt led the life of Riley. Market pubs in London opened at the crack of dawn and the old git was having a livener as early as 4am every working day.

My long-suffering mum, Louisa, who rarely drank, was a strong-willed, passionate, fiery-tempered woman who railed against her husband's drinking throughout their long life together. Consequently, ours was not a happy household. All of us children grew up with volatile personalities, presumably because we thought arguments, quarrels and conflicts were the norm. One of my earliest memories is of the old man coming home from hospital with a bandaged head after the 'old lady', as we boys affectionately called her, had 'crowned' him with a candlestick, splitting his skull open. Mum and I were quivering with fear when he came in, wondering what sort of violent revenge he would wreak on her. Instead, the old sod shook her hand and said: 'Congratulations, I never knew you had it in you.'

At weekends, while the old man was drinking his wages away, Mum let us kids stay up late to play cards for peanuts. We used to dread the sound of his key in the front door. The old man invariably came in singing his favourite song, 'Bye Bye Blackbird', which included the line: 'Make my bed, light the light, I'll arrive late tonight . . .' Ritualistically we would all chorus: 'Don't bother.' If he was in a good mood, he would just grin and stagger up to bed. But as often as not, our cheek would cause him to kick the table, cards and peanuts up into the air as a signal for him and Mum to go at it hammer and tongs verbally, at times with a spot of fisticuffs thrown in.

Later in life, my old man lived to regret those nights when every one of my brothers was forced, at one time or another, to exact physical revenge on him. When we grew up and asked him to explain his actions, he said it was the norm for husbands to knock the wives into shape in those days and he boasted that Grandma Batt, his Scottish mother, who wore a man's cap and regularly visited the pub for a jug of stout, could knock skittles of shit out of his six-footer father in their regular street fights.

Nine out of ten cockney kids dropped their aitches, said 'fink' and 'fought' instead of 'think' and 'thought', and had acquired an encyclopaedic knowledge of swear words by the age of 10 at the very latest. Not my mum's first born, Louise, though. Something must have interfered with her voice box in the womb because Louise's very first words were uttered in an unfamiliar posh accent, and she spoke that way until the day she died 74 years later. My old mum always reckoned that Louise's gentility was in her genes – passed on by my maternal grandmother, who was the daughter of a Swedish sea captain. Whatever, my big sister – she was 16 years older than me – went to Sunday school from an early age, married the curate of our local church, St Dunstan's, an upper-crust young man named Jack Weatherston, graduated to university and became an officer in the WAAFs in the war.

After Louise, children arrived at two-yearly intervals until I popped out as an afterthought six years later than Jim. My mum told me years later that she never even had a pram until the fourth one arrived. She would go shopping, apparently, with a baby cradled in one arm, a shopping bag in the other hand and a couple of toddlers dragging at the hem of her skirt. Then, of course, she would go home to keep the little house spotlessly clean and do the washing and mangling by hand, as all the women did in those days.

Friday night was by tradition bath night in our neighbourhood. The Batt brood took turns in the tin tub in the living room. The fact that Dad used to bring home live eels and kill them by bashing their heads on the side of that same bath seemed to us to be of no concern whatever. Mum was also a dab hand at lighting fires. She had learned that little knack in her childhood days just after the turn of the century when Jewish neighbours paid Gentile kids a farthing to light their fires on the Sabbath. In contrast, her husband claimed he did not know how to put a penny in the gas meter or mend a light fuse.

The height of the old man's indolent chauvinism was a little family ritual at six o'clock every evening when he would put down his *Daily Herald* and attempt to tune into the evening news before sloping off to the pub, where he indulged himself by pontificating on current affairs and was known to his cronies – according to Mum, anyway – as 'Mr Right'. He would twiddle the knobs of his little radio, spluttering, 'How the bleedin' 'ell do you get the Home Service on 'ere?' And that was the signal for one of the kids to find the right spot on the dial for him a bit sharpish.

How my mother managed to live to the ripe old age of 94 defies belief. But the fact that she outlived the old man by 30 years must have had more than a little bit to do with the virtues of the work ethic.

Eldest brother John was the brainbox of the family. Like Louise, he, too, passed matriculation and qualified for university, but at the outbreak of war he joined the navy at the age of 17. Next brother, George, was the joker in our pack – the song and dance man at the famous Batt family knees-ups which were a regular occurrence when we all reached maturity. George followed John to war when he was 18, as did my next sister, Violet, who became a WAAF like her sister. Sister Irene had died in early childhood, so this left just Jim and me to cope with our feuding parents until he, too, joined the army later in the war and I found myself as an 'only child'.

The biggest favour my old man ever did the three of us – Mum, Jim and me – was to become a special policeman during the Blitz, which meant that we hardly clapped eyes on him for a couple of years. Even with constabulary duties to be done, however, he never missed too many sessions in the pub. Ironically, he was out firefighting when his local took a direct hit and he had to help dig what was left of his drinking pals out of the debris. They say the devil looks after his own, don't they?

I must confess that, even as I wrote that last sentence,

I found myself apologising under my breath to my long gone but not forgotten old dad. Attempting to make light of the Blitz deserves the same response as I got half a century later when I tried to laugh off my alcoholism in one of the many detox units I was to encounter where, before I opened my mouth to say anything, I was ordered by the therapist, on every occasion, to recite to the group: 'This is a killer illness and not a joke.'

And there were similarities in the two situations. For, of all the tension-filled, alcohol-fuelled emotional peaks I have teetered on during my adult life, few could compare with the sense of powerlessness which the night sky offered during an air raid. On the odd occasion when the siren's alert was a bit late, we would go stumbling off to the street shelter while our eyes were being hypnotised with the sights and sounds of the spectacular aerial conflict. Tracer bullets, search lights and flaming incendiary bombs made you feel both scared out of your wits and incredibly alive at one and the same time.

My only understanding, since, of what the hell Jim and I were doing back in London while the enemy bombs were falling, was that the authorities had boobed by sending us evacuees away, too early, during the 'phoney war' of late 1939 and early 1940, because most of us had drifted back home by the time the real action started later.

As we lived so close to the docks, the inevitable eventually happened when we emerged from the communal shelter one morning to find that our house had been demolished. The next clear memory I have is of me sitting in the back of a big lorry with the remnants of several other families. I say remnants because the men of military age were all away fighting in the war. I can still hear my mum and the other women trying to cheer themselves up by telling each other that they would have the luxury of inside lavatories and constant hot running water in the new homes we were headed for. There was talk, too, of green fields and hedgerows, but I now realise that this was just collective whistling in the dark. All the occupants of that lorry were terrified to be leaving the familiarity of their beloved East End. And no wonder. My mum would recall how, in her courting days, she would promenade with her straw-hatted suitor, Jack Batt, up and down the Mile End Road, which in those days was a wide boulevard lit with gas lamps and not the tatty thoroughfare for monstrous huge lorries that it is now.

Our disembarkation point turned out to be a place called Enfield Lock, and Jim and I hated the place on sight. We were dumped on a new estate in the middle of a field, which had been filled with East Enders like us. The older men, most of them dockers, were found jobs in the nearby Royal Army Ordnance factory, where they manufactured Lee Enfield rifles for the British infantry. The factory was just a short walk from our new home so it meant that my old man never had to travel more than a few hundred yards to either his work or the pub for the rest of his life.

This estate was surrounded by gypsy encampments which made it resemble a Western film set, and some of the pub fights which occurred thereabouts made anything that John Wayne got up to on screen look like wimps' night out by comparison. Over the years, with all the unsettled youths who had been uprooted and plonked down in what we regarded as this 'wilderness', nearly every one of my near neighbours wound up in either borstal or prison.

I went back to visit Enfield Lock after more than 40

years recently and to my astonishment, it is very much 'upmarket' these days. The old munitions factory has been converted into a luxury riverside housing complex and the pub, The Tavern, which was to play such a central part in my family's immediate post-war life, is now a fashionable night club called 'Rifles'. Perched on the banks of the River Lea, it had the practically foreign postmark of 'Middlesex' in my youth but is now part of Greater London.

All the cherished boyhood pursuits such as fishing, birds nesting and tree climbing were on offer, but the trauma of living with Granny McCourt in the green belt of Surrey must have ruined my appreciation of country life. I did try it again for the sake of my three children later, but was eventually compelled to return to London like a homing pigeon.

My childhood took a turn for the worse when Jim and I started running wild for a while. My mum took a job as a cook in a local working men's cafe so we became the equivalent of today's latchkey children. Jim engaged his entrepreneurial streak by encouraging me to skip my new school – which I hated anyway – and strong-armed me into helping him to chop firewood, which we then sold door-to-door to finance his frequent long bus and train trips back to his old pals in Stepney.

Mum was fanatical about keeping us clean and tidy and she demanded what she called 'instant obedience', which she was quick to enforce with the physical help of the punishment she often dished out and described as 'more kicks than ha'pence'. If she had known we were both playing truant on an almost daily basis we might have fared worse than our brother George had done when, in a rage, she once threw a fork at him which stuck in his leg. But another wartime tragedy was soon to drastically change my way of life yet again.

I was suffering from a cold one day and would probably rather have gone to school than chop firewood anyway when Mum, who despite her occasional wallopings spoiled me rotten, decided I could help her at the cafe near the factory instead. It was 1944 and I would have been approaching my eleventh birthday by then, but what made this year another horribly memorable one in the annals of British history was not only the D-day invasion but the fact that Hitler was bombarding us again – this time with his new V1 rockets, known to us as 'doodlebugs'. At night, these monstrosities were even more terrifying than the bombs in the Blitz had been. Lying in the shelter, you could hear them roaring overhead. Then they would cut out, making you hold your collective breath and causing you to say your prayers a bit sharpish. For we had learned to understand that when the rocket cut out completely, the long silence while it fell to earth would be followed by a deadly explosion. And the scariest part was that you nearly always imagined that this killing machine was directly over your head. During the daytime, you could not only hear the awful droning noise, you could clearly see the flames spouting out of the rocket's tail.

This was the awesome sight which greeted us as we all rushed out of that cafe one lunchtime to watch a doodlebug which was obviously much too close for comfort. Down it came and 'scored' a direct hit on my Chesterfield Road junior school, killing two teachers and injuring many pupils.

My mum responded by having me packed off to my sister in Ashington, Northumberland. Louise had left the air force by now and joined her husband, the one-time

Stepney curate Jack Weatherston, as the vicar's wife in this Geordie mining community, which became famous for being the birthplace of those illustrious footballing brothers, Sir Bobby and Jack Charlton.

In many ways, this turned out to be an even worse move for me. As I said earlier, my sister had always been a very posh young lady and she set out now to turn me into a little Lord Fauntleroy. If I had suffered a culture shock in Enfield, imagine my puzzlement when on the first day at school, I asked one of the local kids the time and he replied with words which sounded like, 'I devent nare, kiddo,' which translated as 'I don't know, mate.'

Louise had inherited her mother's penchant for iron discipline, so there was no chance of me playing the hop any more. There was to be no chance of me getting a decent education either, because all the comings and goings led to me missing the 11-plus exams.

CHAPTER THREE
BOYHOOD

But I did read my first book in Ashington. Louise bought it for me as a birthday present. I can still remember how it began: 'Boom, boom, went the cannon . . .' Not the best of introductions, admittedly, but those magical words gave me a lifelong taste for literature, which has proved to be one of the greatest pleasures that existence has had to offer.

This book was all about Hernando Cortez and his conquistadors in South America – a part of the world I myself was to visit as a 'conquering hero' – in my own eyes, at least – many years later as *The Sun*'s number one football writer for the Mexico World Cup in 1970.

Louise and Jack also introduced me to Jesus and He, of course, made a much more lasting impression than Cortez. There was a luminous crucifix in my bedroom on the mantelpiece in the vicarage which glowed green every night and frightened me considerably more than the bombs and doodlebugs had done. I was pretty pissed off with Jesus, too, when Jack made me get up at the crack of dawn every morning to serve at the altar for his communion service for the miners and their families. Yet, love Him or loathe Him, once Jesus had entered my consciousness, I was never able to shake him off, especially after Jack later arranged for me to be confirmed at St Paul's Cathedral, on St Patrick's Day, by the Bishop of Willesden.

Being a useful footballer helped me to survive among the soccer-crazy Geordie kids, but I was never able to live down the embarrassment of being known as the posh kid who lived in the vicarage. So I cussed and swore at every opportunity. One person I never swore in front of, though, was my mother. So when it came to persuading her to rescue me from my Professor Higgins of a sister, there was nothing else for it but to turn on the waterworks. I found the perfect opportunity to do this when the old lady came to help Louise with the birth of her first child and my first niece, Susan Jane. I remember Louise wringing her hands in despair as I tearfully begged our mum to take me away from my new friends in the north, even if it was only back to north London and not our beloved East End.

So it was 'home' to an elementary education at Albany Boys' School in Enfield. Within weeks, Jim was off to join the Army and I remember he had Mum and me in fits of laughter when he played the piano, in our front room, with his great big bunch of banana fingers and his impersonation of Noel Coward singing, 'I'll see you again, whenever spring breaks through again.'

The war meant that I was not going to see any of my brothers and sisters for a few years, so I had to get used to being the only child. This involved trying to keep the peace between Mum and Dad and my most searing memory of that unhappy period is of gripping a poker and creeping up behind the old man with the intention of smashing it over his head to put an end to him. Thank God, my courage failed me at the last moment and thankfully, too, around that time my old man suddenly seemed to age and he became more morose but less violent.

My dear old mum, I now realise, spent this period of her life by unconsciously using me as her counsellor. She never seemed to tire of telling me stories about her trials and tribulations, which were colourfully recounted and obviously gave me a taste for story telling. But she inadvertently instilled a deep sense of guilt and worthlessness in me by 'dumping her emotional rubbish' onto an impressionable young schoolboy who could do absolutely nothing to rescue her from her ogre. She always said that the worst thing that could happen to me was that I would turn out to be a drunkard like my father. I agreed with her and took a vow never to drink, which, at that age, was not hard to keep. Especially whenever I peeped through the window of The Tavern and saw my dad and his mates guzzling pints of cold beer in the depths of winter and wondered why on earth they wanted to freeze their gullets that way.

I took refuge from my parents' problems by playing football and cricket for the school teams and by making a fortnightly pilgrimage to the home games of Millwall. It was a mildly astonishing thing for a 13-year-old boy to do – to travel alone to and from Enfield Lock and the ground in Cold Blow Lane on wartime transport. It involved a mile walk to the station, a 40-minute steam train journey to Liverpool Street and then a couple of different tube trains to New Cross Gate before the excited walk to the infamous 'Lions' Den'.

The Lions, so called because of the red lion on the

white pockets of their royal blue shirts, had been the love of my life ever since my old man and my elder brothers had spun yarn after yarn about their favourite team's exploits during my earlier childhood. In his cups, my old man had a penchant for telling tales of derring-do about his exploits in World War One or for climbing onto his socialist soap box. His other favourite topic of conversation was Millwall. Ironically, for such an absentee father, it was a passion he somehow managed to pass on to his sons.

The older male members of my family talked about Millwall so much, and in particular about the heroic way they had been the first ever Third Division side to reach the semi-final of the FA Cup, that I had a mental picture of most of their players long before I saw Millwall for the first time myself, when they were in the old Third Division South and their ranks were full of famous 'guest players' from the Armed Forces. They even included an exotic foreign import in their line-up by the never to be forgotten name of Frank Soo. Although I had never seen them in the flesh, I felt an affinity with the stars of that famous 1937 Cup run, men such as centre-forward Dave Magnall and England amateur winger JR Smith. According to the older members of the Batt family, the Lions were unluckily beaten 1–0 in the semi-final by a star-studded Sunderland team which featured the great Raich Carter and which went on to beat Preston North End 3–1 at Wembley. Not only could I recite the names of that particular history-making Millwall team off by heart, I also had a kind of photographic memory with which I could unerringly put names to the faces of the hundreds of footballers which adorned cigarette cards in those days, and which I collected from the discarded fag packets that I used to comb the streets searching for.

My old man might have been a nasty piece of work but he could also be a very funny old git in a self-deprecating kind of way. He claimed that the reason he supported Millwall was because they were the only team in the country who kicked off at 3.15pm on a Saturday instead of the traditional starting time of 3pm – and that meant they never interfered with his drinking time. He was not joking because the pubs south of the river stayed open until three o'clock in those days as against 2.30 elsewhere and as the bulk of the Millwall fans were dockers, who had already done a morning's work, the club would never dream of kicking off before the pubs closed.

Since then I have been in countless football stadiums the world over and I have never encountered fans who were more passionate about their team than those Millwall followers of my boyhood. They loved my heroes like Tommy Brown, Jimmy Constantine, Willie Hurrell, Ernie Forrest, Ted Smith and the Fisher twins as if they were their own sons.

But it was a gruff, hard-bitten brand of love which most of those genuinely macho dockers could only express in a fond, piss-taking way. They gently barracked their own players endlessly, but woe betide any visiting fan who attempted to do the same. And for that matter, woe betide any opposition player who had the temerity to foul one of their own. As referees down the ages will be only too willing to testify, the Millwall supporters hold the undisputed world record for the number of times their ground has been closed by the authorities for unruly fan behaviour – and many of these bans occurred long before the modern football hooligan was even a gleam in his grandfather's eye.

I have nothing but fond memories of those old-time Millwall fans. They were extremely volatile, but they could be very funny with it. It was their banter, as much as the action on the field, which made my long, lonely journeys so irresistible. I was in attendance at two of those ground closure matches and I could not have been a closer eye witness to the events which sparked off both of them. On the first occasion, a burly docker standing next to me became so enraged with the referee that he said to his mate: 'Bill, open up that sack of King Edward potatoes, will yer?' And when Bill's knife had performed that little task on the said potato sack, which they had no doubt smuggled through the dock gates that same morning, my big neighbour began hurling the King Edwards in the direction of the referee, scoring several direct hits on that official's bald head.

The second occasion was only a few weeks later and not long after the ground had just been reopened. Not unusually, the home fans were totally dissatisfied with the standard of refereeing on offer. Consequently, I heard a conspiracy being cooked up which went along the lines of, 'We don't want the ground closed again, so we'll 'ave to do this bleedin' ref outside the premises.'

Gleefully, I hung around later to watch the action. And, sure enough, as the departing referee passed the tea stall outside the ground, he was showered with cups and saucers. The twisted logic of that little demonstration still has me chuckling, because whenever they were in a rare good mood with their team, those fans would greet a misplaced pass with sympathetic cries of 'Ne'mind, son, well meant!' And from this biased fan's point of view, nothing was more 'well meant' than the show of disapproval towards authority that my old compatriots indulged themselves in that day.

I did become more than a mite unfaithful to the Lions later when, mainly for geographical reasons, my brothers and I deserted earthy Millwall for the more urbane appeal of Tottenham Hotspur. The geography was simple. We now lived a mere half an hour's trolleybus or train journey from Tottenham's ground at White Hart Lane as opposed to the two-hour trek to Millwall. My new life as a diehard Spurs fanatic only started after the war when my brothers returned from the forces, but I did put in one or two little wartime dummy runs, when the Lions were away from home, to watch either Spurs or Arsenal, who were forced to share White Hart Lane then because the Gunners' ground at Highbury had become a site for anti-aircraft operations during the war.

It was on one such occasion that I experienced my first ever skirmish with a sports star. I was autograph hunting at White Hart Lane with a bunch of schoolmates when we suddenly spotted Denis Compton approaching the players' entrance in uniform. He had probably just stepped off a trolleybus – that was the way players travelled to matches in those austere times and they continued to do so for several spartan years after the war.

Now in those days, autographs did not come any bigger than Denis Compton's, even though his greatest triumphs as an Arsenal and England winger and one of the all-time greats of world cricket were still a few years away. I found myself at the head of the pack of young pursuers and when we reached our quarry, I stupidly blurted out: 'Can I have your autograph please, Compton?'

There was a smidgin of an excuse for my inexcusable rudeness in that when the cry of 'There's Compton' had gone up from us kids earlier, I wasn't sure which Compton it was – Denis or his older brother Leslie, who also played football for Arsenal and England and cricket for Middlesex.

I was soon left in no doubt, though, when Denis stopped in his tracks, fixed me with a stern gaze and then, making me feel two feet tall in front of my mates, slowly said: 'Don't you mean Mr Compton, son? Or Denis, perhaps?'

'Yeah, sorry, Mr Denis,' I blushingly mumbled. Then, after the great man had signed my book, flashed me a warm smile and ruffled my hair, I knew how it felt to be famous for a moment as my companions chorused: 'Blimey, he spoke to you, Batty. Denis Compton actually spoke to you!'

'He bollocked me, you mean,' I replied in an attempt to regain my composure. I was to sit in many a press box beside Denis in later life when he wrote for the *Sunday Express*, but I never plucked up the courage to remind him of that invaluable lesson in manners.

When the famous, fabulous, Russian Red Army team Moscow Dynamos arrived on these shores shortly after the war, they were greeted by the newspapers, the radio and the public at large as if they were visitors from outer space. This was long before the era of European Cup matches which did not take place in Britain until after Sir Matt Busby invaded the Continent with his Busby Babes many years later. Suitably awestruck, I turned up at 10 a.m. clutching my paper bag containing a cheese sandwich and bottle of school milk. The Dynamos were at White Hart Lane to play a star-studded Arsenal representative team which, if memory serves me, included the one and only Stanley Matthews. Some 70,000 of us were packed into the ground that sunny midweek afternoon and, as was traditional then, I, along with hundreds of other schoolboys, had been passed over the heads of adult spectators to a prime place near the touchline fence.

Never have I heard such a resounding collective groan

of disappointment as that which arose from those massed ranks when a blanket of patchy fog descended almost as suddenly as a lightning flash about half an hour before the scheduled kick-off time. This match was taking place long before the advent of floodlights, of course. All I can remember of it are the photographers' flashlight bulbs as the goals went in – four for Arsenal, I believe, and three for Moscow Dynamos. Nobody saw a thing for more than a minute or two when the mist momentarily thinned, but nobody left the ground, either. That is how starved of top-class entertainment we had become during the grim war years.

As for getting a bus home afterwards, there was absolutely no chance of that as you literally could not see a hand before you in the famous pea-soup London fogs we used to endure every year. It was not for nothing, then, that London got nicknamed 'The Smoke'.

CHAPTER FOUR
TEENS

Considering the poverty I have been pleading you would be entitled to wonder how it was that I could afford these boyhood sporting treats I have been going on about.

The answer is that now that my old man was helping to make Lee-Enfield rifles for a living instead of humping fish around, he no longer had the early morning market boozers to frequent, so his factory wages were not taking such a belting as in the old days. His only source of drunken mischief then was 'Workers' Playtime' in the lunch hour and his regular nightly and weekend stints in The Tavern. As he got older, he could not cope with the same amount of booze that he used to put away, either. This meant that Mum could raid his pockets on a regular basis while he slept and that I could tap him from time to time if I sensed the atmosphere was congenial enough. Sadly, I was to forfeit this privilege in much the same careless way as I was to go on to lose so many plum jobs in journalism.

My early material demise came about on one of the first post-war Derby days. The old man had been going on for months about this 'unbeatable' three-year-old called Prince Simon and had backed the colt at all prices down to odds-on favourite. I borrowed a shilling off him and told him I was having a tanner (sixpence) each way on his horse to bring him luck. The old sod had so much on the Prince's nose that, counting his chickens, he took a rare Wednesday afternoon off to listen to the commentary on the radio.

Now even at that embryonic stage of my gambling career, I was old enough to work out that two bob at 10–11 was not going to make me rich, so I craftily had his loan on French horse Galcador at 100–9. Yes, you've guessed it. Prince Simon blew up and as that great old radio commentator, Raymond Glendenning, roared my horse home first, I could not resist letting out a roar of triumph. The next thing I knew, the cat was flying head first off the old man's lap and into the living room wall, and I had only managed to get a few inches out of the starting blocks before his boot connected with my arse. Needless to say, that was the end of my 'poncing' money. Or as the old man himself put it: 'Dolly had definitely done effing dancing around 'ere!'

When I began writing this book, I thought I still hated my dad. But the more I dredge my memory, the more amusing he becomes. Perhaps distance does lend enchantment, after all, even to an old 'Alf Garnett' type of git like him. As late as my twenties and thirties, whenever my life took a slight turn for the worse and I was looking for scapegoats, I would start conversations with mates in the boozer about dads in general and theirs and mine in particular. Those who had a good loving relationship with their father always struck me as having much more self-worth than I did, which meant I felt justified in blaming the old man for most of my character defects. But now I find myself chuckling fondly at some of those weird sayings he came out with. One had me baffled until many years later when I discovered its origins. Whenever he had a little 'tickle' himself on the horses, he would tuck the cash away underneath his socks in a drawer in the little box-room-sized bedroom to which he had now been banished by Mum while she slept with my sister Vi. One day I sidled up behind him while he was performing this little task, without him knowing I was there. I heard the old sod chuckling triumphantly and saying aloud to himself: 'I'll stow this little lot away from boilers.'

It was not until years later that I learned that down at the London docks, where most of his pals worked, certain goods on each ship were marked with a message which proclaimed: 'Precious cargo – stow away from boilers.'

I had precious little to stow away from boilers myself, and this lack of funds meant that I had to abandon spectating in favour of playing. I managed to do this successfully enough to captain my school team, which was the best in the district. It was not that I was the best player, but simply that I nagged the other players more than anyone else did.

By the time I was 13, I started to enjoy the green fields of Enfield Lock at last because they enabled me to play football in winter and cricket in summer every evening until nightfall. My mates and I also fished and swam in the River Lea, but the water rats were never ideal swimming companions. And when my brothers eventally came home from the war, we all played for different Sunday morning soccer teams then had a ritualistic sing-song accompanied by a couple of crates of beer, with my sister Vi on the piano, in the front room all afternoon.

I had started to enjoy life to the full now, but there was one great source of worry. Jim had fallen victim to a rare form of face cancer which was assumed to be incurable. He spent a couple of years in the military hospital at Roehampton where he endured a total of 14 operations which involved the removal of his cheekbone, his upper palate and teeth, which meant that he needed a piece of bone removed from his hip and grafted into his mouth. This not only left him horribly scarred but meant he had to learn to speak all over again.

Jim, a well-built six-foot plus, had been a handsome young man and his facial disabilities weighed heavily on him, although he never showed it except in the hitherto uncharacteristic vicious streak which crept into his otherwise extremely likeable personality. The result of this was that when he did eventually rejoin the rest of the family, he became a hard man and earned his living as a 'minder' with his old East End mates, who by now were some of the top names in the London underworld.

Jim's excuse for his lifestyle was that it was the only way you could get your name up in lights in those days. And while I cannot pretend that his was a noble career, it did require tremendous physical courage to pursue a life of professional violence knowing as he did that just one blow to the face could have killed him. At my impressionable age, this made my big brother an even bigger hero to me than he had been in childhood. And although we were to fall out from time to time, it stayed that way until, defying all the odds, he managed to survive until past his 60th birthday before he died during his umpteenth operation.

But it was this hero worship that was to blow my own life drastically off course. Part of me wanted to ape and mimic Jim, but I never had it in me to become a first division tearaway like him, and by the time I found my own path via that Marilyn Monroe interview, it could and should have been too late for me to escape from my self-inflicted scrapheap.

However, mine was a scrapheap of my own making. For when I left school at 15, I had been given a dream chance to 'make something of myself' by my headmaster, who had arranged with one of his friends to fix me up as a messenger boy with Saxon Snell and Son, Official Shorthandwriters, of Middle Temple Lane, Fleet Street. How many headmasters would intervene in a boy's life to such an admirable extent today, I wonder? He took the trouble to send for my mum and tell her that I was potentially the most intelligent pupil he had yet encountered. I did not know whether to laugh or cry when she told me this, because I spent half my time pleasing my mates by playing the two-bob tearaway and the other half admitting to myself that I secretly loved English, history and drama. Although it seemed to me, judging from the amount of woodwork and metalwork classes we attended, that our school's main aim was to turn out law-abiding factory fodder, there was still the opportunity to learn from the dedicated teachers who had just fought for six years for our freedom.

A couple of these strict but very likeable men, Mr Wilson and Mr Williams, discovered that I had what they considered to be a rare talent for acting and writing, and pressed the headmaster to find some way for me to express myself in later life. The first thing he did was to arrange for me to join the famous Italia Conti school of acting. But back then, every actor and actress spoke with a plum in their mouth and my old man and brothers simply fell about laughing at the prospect of me pronouncing 'How now, brown cow' properly. So much so that I swallowed it, only to see contemporaries of mine like Michael Caine and Anthony Newley make the cockney accent so acceptable and even fashionable a few years later.

When, as a second choice, the headmaster contacted his friend at the shorthandwriters' office and informed me that a job there would necessitate me attending Pitmans College in Holborn for shorthand and typing lessons, the Batt men laughed even louder and began calling me Missy. But Mum begged me to take the job and I signed up for a two-year stint at £2 50 shillings a week, half of which had to go for my keep at home – even though my brothers and I slept two to a bed and four to a bedroom – and the other half on train fares.

After I left school, my biggest source of discontent was that all my mates in our local estate football team were rolling in money from their well-paid labouring jobs on building sites and their bits and bobs of 'tea-leaving'. And we were all beginning to realise that there were other, more expensive things in life than football – like girls and clothes. And this was precisely where Pitmans College started to drive me mad. As part of my contract, I went every morning and it was better than being let loose in a sweet factory. I was the only male in the class and as someone who had previously attended boys-only schools, I began to find it increasingly difficult to keep my mind on the football training in the evenings, as it kept wandering back to the sights and scents I had been enjoying only a few hours earlier. In those days, the idea of going Dutch was unheard of and the first requirement for dating girls was 'readies', even if it was only enough for a couple of seats in the back row of the cinema. So I knew then that no matter how well I progressed as a shorthandwriter, the moment my contract was up at 17, I would be compelled to jack it in and start what I foolishly imagined to be 'living'.

Ironically, I became an excellent shorthand typist. In addition to running messages around London in the afternoons, I was allowed into the world-renowned Law Courts opposite our quaint little office to take verbatim notes of the proceedings there and I thoroughly enjoyed doing it.

When I say Saxon Snell's office was quaint, there was no other word for it. Nor for the ancient Saxon himself, who wore a tail coat and spats to work. To me, the boss looked as old as the office, which happened to be the very room in which Pepys wrote his historic London diary. More significantly for me, our office was located off Fleet Street and I became so entranced by those poetic old pavements and the grand newspaper offices which bestrode them like ancient fairytale castles that I vowed then that I would one day find a way to storm their battlements and become a newspaper reporter myself. This turned out to be like wishing for the moon when on my seventeenth birthday I quit Saxon Snell's and, as far as Fleet Street was concerned, sank without trace for the next six formative but fragile years.

No one was angrier than Jim over my decision to leave. He gave me the mother and father of a bollocking and told me that I was tossing my life into the dustbin. Considering that one of the main secret motives behind my move was so that I could get myself a more macho image like his, I was astonished at his reaction. But I have since learned that tough guys like my big brother, the world over, have a more than sneaking respect for 'men of letters', as I was to find out years later.

My first working day as a potential tough guy ended in the most wimpish fashion imaginable and was all over by lunchtime. I had got myself a job as a plumber's mate and found myself working on the roof of the Science Museum in Kensington. I had not been up there for more than 10 minutes when it dawned on me that my technical skill was nonexistent and as my new 'master' started to explain why we were embarking on the welding job which awaited us, my eyes glazed over and my brain went into neutral.

I soon discovered that this was the kind of work where you needed your wits about you, if for no other reason than self-preservation. As I clumsily moved about, handing my superior the various tools and bits and bobs he required, I kept standing on the hot metal wastage from his welding actives. I was wearing a pair of suede, crepe-soled shoes, and consequently the soles of my feet were red raw from burns as the scorching metal seared through the bottom of my shoes. Never one to blame myself, I quickly told the plumber where to put his welding iron and crawled home beaten before I'd even got started.

The piss-taking indoors became so unbearable that I decided I would have to leave home at the earliest opportunity. This came via an older guy who lived on our estate named Denny Saunders. A man in his mid twenties, Denny was a proud 'spiderman', or steel erector. I remembered him as 'King of the Kids' when, already in his teens, he used to play sword fencing games and such like with younger boys like me. Being a 'spiderman' suited Denny down to the ground, even if it meant that he spent his life balancing on steel girders in mid-air most of the time. 'Spidermen' needed a head for heights, the balance of a cat and the temperament of a Hollywood stuntman.

So when Denny offered me a job, to say – using the

vernacular – that my arse fell out would be an understatement. But, determined not to show my fear, I joined him on an excursion to Austin Motor Works at Longbridge, Birmingham, where we were to carry out repairs to girders in the roof while the car workers were on their annual holiday.

Within three days, the third member of our team, another big husky guy called Lenny, found himself hanging, head down, by his toes, which were trapped between two steel girders high above the empty factory floor. I rushed to get a ladder to try and help but found my arms turning to jelly as I listened to poor Lenny's screams.

Eventually, Denny and I managed to rescue our mate and my last day as a steel erector was spent at Lenny's hospital bedside where, after having his toes amputated and still feeling the beneficial effects of the painkilling drugs, he kept looking at his bandaged foot and repeating that old nursery rhyme: 'This little piggy went to market.'

As for this little piggy, he decided to take the bull by the horns and go for the most macho job of all: hod carrying. This involved scaling up and down ladders with really heavy hod-fulls of bricks and cement on your shoulder, and it nearly broke a skinny teenager like me in half. But I stuck at it in an effort to build up my muscles and earn myself the 'walking about money' which I craved. But I must confess that it came as something of a relief when I was called up for National Service a couple of weeks before my eighteenth birthday.

CHAPTER FIVE
SOLDIER

The least said about my ignominious military career, the better. Shamefully, I proved to be such an indisciplined soldier that I was posted all over the country until I ended up in Bicester, Oxfordshire, as an 'undesirable'. Eventually, I was sent to Egypt, from where I was not to be demobbed until several months after my original release date, because of the many days I had spent in the glasshouses (army prisons) – and all those days were added to the requisite two years.

My problem was that I would not do as I was told quickly enough or often enough – a fault which puzzled me when I recalled my mother's demands for 'instant obedience'. I could not even keep out of the nick on the troop ship taking us to Egypt. On Christmas Eve, 1952, we were given a few hours' shore leave in Malta, where a mob of us got drunk down the infamous alleys known to generations of British troops as 'The Gut'. After a running battle, which delayed the ship several hours, the military police finally used their truncheons on us, flung us onto launches and somehow got us up the Jacob's ladder and into the brig, where we were imprisoned for the rest of the voyage.

Characteristically, it could all have been very different if I had conformed and not childishly attempted to do things my own way. For when the army first discovered that I was that extremely rare animal, a young man who possessed verbatim shorthand skills, they were ready to make me a sergeant in the Royal Army Service Corps and post me to Paris, to the Supreme Headquarters Allied Forces in Europe, where, I was told, I would even be allowed to wear civilian clothes on duty. I refused point blank, saying that I did not want a 'big gel's blouse' job and insisting that they treat me as one of the lads. This they did by bunging me into the Royal Army Ordnance Corps and designating me to perform 'general duties', which was another way of describing a good-for-nothing dogsbody.

Life as a soldier would not have been so bad if I could still have played football but, at the age of 17, the cartilages in both my knees had been ruined by primitive, old-fashioned surgery.

Still, one of the consolations of Egypt was that I learned to play a decent game of tennis, wearing ugly old elastic protective kneebands, but that was the only plus point to come out of what, up to then, had been far and away the worst years of my life. Back in 'civvy street', I, like a good many other disgruntled young National Servicemen, felt that the army had left me fit for nothing – that was my excuse, anyway, for turning into the brain-dead layabout I soon became.

At least, during the year preceding the spell in the army, I and a team of young pals had gone dancing at the Tottenham Royal a couple of nights a week. I say 'gone dancing' but in those big band days, the Royal was really the venue for big bust-ups, too, between the rival gangs of teenagers from many of the north and east London districts. I distinctly remember that was the venue where Ronnie and Reggie Kray first earned their growing reputations as the toughest kids on the block. If you managed to avoid getting a black eye or a split lip, you had the dubious chance of walking one of the virginal young Doris Day-type girls home for a quick snog up against the back fence of her parents' house or flat. But the walk home, after the trolleybuses had finished running at about 11.30, could take hours. That was called 'living it up' back in the early fifties.

The idea of work did not get a look-in during the first few months after my demob. So the biggest problem was getting the necessary 'readies' to fuel my already addictive gambling habit. It was possible to win money on yourself at snooker providing you were shrewd enough to negotiate the right amount of black balls per frame as a start in the unofficial handicapping system we employed. But since I was nowhere near the best in our district, let alone London, I often found myself playing for and losing vital pieces of clothing, such as my overcoat in the depths of one cold winter. You could also have side bets on the best hustlers and indulge in the illegal dice games and card schools which went on in the inner sanctum at most of the old snooker halls in those days. But, as it was simply a case of dog eat dog, I found myself having either to start 'tea leaving' – which, thankfully, I had a built-in aversion to – or finding a job.

Getting work in that era was a doddle. Keeping in work, though, what with the combination of my rebellious nature and 'lazyitis', was a different matter. So I sampled dozens of different occupations on a strictly short-term basis and with the specific intention of building up a gambling 'tank'. These jobs included navvying on building sites again, working in local factories, becoming a foundry worker at the local sweat shop known as the Enfield Rolling Mills, collecting old rags and scrap metal and working at the Guinness Brewery. It was while cleaning a vat out there that I truthfully first heard that old old chestnut of a joke about the workman who was drowned in a vat of beer. And, apparently, when the boss went to inform his widow and she asked if her husband had suffered much, the boss replied: 'No, I don't think so, my dear. I'm told he got out three times for a piss.'

When I was not going dog racing or playing snooker, I was being persuaded by my more macho mates to join them in 'looking for bovver' in the boozers most Saturday nights. The truth was, as some of us later admitted to each other, that most of us in our gang did not really want to be anywhere near this kind of action, especially as it often involved pitting ourselves against much older and harder nuts who, as often as not, gave us a real seeing to. The trouble was that our team, as I suspect most others in the various London neighbourhoods did, contained a couple of psychopaths who called the shots and rather than lose face by backing down, the rest of us would risk life and limb too. I say life and limb, but thankfully we did not use knives in those days and there was an unspoken code of honour whereby the odds had to be fairly even, unlike today when packs of kids attack just one or two victims.

I was lucky enough to have my big brother Jim's reputation to fall back on, and by putting his name up as a 'frightener' I did not appear on the casualty lists as often as I might otherwise have done. Sometimes a mere word in the ear was not enough of a deterrent, however, as it proved one night in Edmonton when me and my mucker Ronnie Sedgley, a wonderful young footballer and the uncle of Steve Sedgley who played for Spurs, were picked on in a late night cafe by three much older 'professional' hard cases for no other reason than they appeared to want a fun ending to their night out on the piss. With quaking knees, Ronnie and I reluctantly accepted their invitation to come outside. I had noticed Jim sitting at the other end of the same cafe with a couple of his cronies and silently prayed that he might come to my assistance.

My problem was that my big brother had refused to speak to or even acknowledge me for the past year or so because he was so disgusted at my generally flash and objectionable demeanour of late. The film *Guys and Dolls* was all the rage then and the boys I ran around with were all dressing and behaving like Sky Masterston and Nathan Detroit.

Thank God, though, blood turned out to be thicker than water and as I stepped out of that cafe door and into the rainy night, I felt a gust of wind as Jim swept past me. He had hands like shovels and for a big man had deceptively quick hands and feet. I have never seen three guys hit harder or with more finality than those nasty bastards were. The resounding crack as fist hit bone bounced back off the walls as the first two went down and out, and as the third attempted to leg it, Jim caught up with him and with another single shot sent him flying sideways over a wall while he was still in the act of running.

Neither Ronnie Sedgley nor I had moved a muscle during this whirlwind fracas and we sheepishly slunk off into the night not knowing what to say to Jim or anyone else in the inevitable crowd which had gathered to witness the bloody aftermath of the action.

It was still to be some weeks yet before Jim deigned to speak to me and then it was only to say, 'The old lady has got enough to worry about with me, let alone you,' before he knocked me from the top to the bottom of the iron staircase behind a snooker hall in Ponders End, after he had been wrongly informed that I had been stealing lead and copper at night from local building sites.

Why I ever wanted to live Jim's kind of lifestyle, I never figured out – unless it was the diet of Western films and gangster movies we were fed on back then. But it was not long after this incident that some inner force compelled me to grow up at last and apply for that life-changing newspaper job. Incidentally, when I told my pals that I had got a job on the papers, they assumed I meant selling them and most of them continued to think that until I got my first by-line. The most immediate reward from that 'date' with Marilyn Monroe, though, was that it earned me Jim's much-needed approval, and we were buddy boys from that day on.

CHAPTER SIX
COPYTAKER

My proud kinship with Jim was to provide me with some embarrassing moments in my new career when his name and our address started to appear in the newspapers. But first things first.

My stint on the *Daily Mail* for Mr Curtis turned out to be fairly brief and decidedly fraught. I was required to take shorthand notes of dictaphone messages and copy directly from the telephone from some of the most distinguished foreign correspondents of the day. This turned out to be heavy duty material for someone with such a flimsy grasp of politics and diplomacy as I then possessed, and I soon began casting my eye around the place for something more stimulating.

After asking around among the other copytakers on Associated Newspapers, it did not take me long to work out that life in the newsroom would be more lively and interesting, or that day work would be preferable to the unsocial evening and night shifts I was working. Early morning stints on the *Mail*'s sister paper, the London

Evening News, was the obvious solution, so I applied for a job in the *News*'s news room, which was situated in the same building, New Carmelite House in Carmelite Street. This was a huge imposing building housing not only the *Mail* and the *News* but the *Daily Sketch* and a Sunday paper, too. It was located off Fleet Street and was only a stone's throw away from my boyhood home with Saxon Snell in the Middle Temple.

I was delighted when I got this new job and I enjoyed almost every minute of it for the next couple of years. There were a dozen or so of us copytakers and we operated on an old-fashioned switchboard where we took turns at answering the incoming calls by flicking one of the switches in front of us. A mischievous mob, we would sometimes entertain ourselves by deliberately connecting the industrial correspondent with the theatre critic, and the sports reporter with the court reporter, and so on, and I soon learned that however erudite these 'posh' journalists happened to be, when they were annoyed and frustrated they could swear as loudly and colourfully as anyone on a building site or in a snooker hall.

Crime, even the petty variety, was still big news in those days of broadsheet papers and gargantuan circulations – the three London evening papers' sales ran into millions then, as opposed to the few hundred thousand the capital's lone evening, the *Standard*, sells today. The lively early morning editions were crammed with accounts of robberies, car chases, gangland feuds and all the other titbits of metropolitan mayhem. As for murder stories and the subsequent inquiries, they made front page news on a sometimes daily basis and would run for days on end, unlike the few paragraphs they are often afforded in these celebrity-obsessed modern times.

And crime was where Jim came into the equation for

me. I had to take down running stories about illegal goings-on which I knew he was currently involved in. Worse, his name actually appeared several times as a defendant in copies of court cases which I had to hand in to the news editor. My boss, news editor Frank Starr, just happened to be as formal, respectable and law-abiding an executive as you could find anywhere in a city which was still bristling with men who sported pinstripe suits, bowler hats and brollies. He was so autocratic that even hard-boiled veteran reporters were required to call him 'Sir', and he would have had me run off the premises if he had twigged that the sheets of copy he was reading carried accounts of my brother being banged up in prison. Thankfully, he had much more serious affairs with which to concern himself than playing spot-the-black-sheep-brother games, and I was left to immerse myself in purple-prosed telephone accounts of 'slouch-hatted' gangsters like 'Jack Spot' Cromer, Billy Hill and Albert Dimes violently sorting out their territorial differences.

Later, I was privy to some off-the record, eye-witness colour stuff from Jim. And one of his little black humour anecdotes which still gives me a guilty giggle even now concerned the last few days of one of his 'stretches' when, because he was nearing release, he was classed as a trusty and detailed to accompany a 'screw' on the nightly 'cob of bread and mug of cocoa' round. Upon entering the cell of one young man who had just been sentenced to 15 years that same morning, Jim and the screw were greeted by the sight of the prisoner sitting with his head in his hands and moaning: 'Fifteen years – I'll never do it . . . I'll never do it.' Whereupon the kindly screw patted him on the back and said: 'Ne'mind, son. Do as much as you can.'

Not all the copy I took was as entertaining as the crime

and sports stuff, however, and I developed a mysterious talent for taking down reams of stuff about an industrial dispute or a night at the ballet while my mind's eye was studying the trap draw for the racing at Walthamstow that evening or fretting about team selection for the next Spurs match. Yet still my copy was as often as not word perfect. I don't make that last claim boastfully, but simply to point out that Frank Starr would have had my guts for garters if it wasn't.

By far the most enjoyable task I undertook at that time was to volunteer for overtime to act as telephone runner for reporter Monty Court, who was later to become the editor of *The Sporting Life*. Monty became one of the earliest Fleet Street 'ghosts' when he was detailed to write running copy for the legendary cricketer Sir Len Hutton, who had just been signed up by the *News* to give his considered verdicts on the current Test matches. Monty employed the then fashionable staccato style of writing which was littered with dots and dashes and could not have been more different to Sir Len's languid speech pattern, which was, naturally, delivered in a broad Yorkshire accent.

I shall never forget racing to the phone box to telephone the following sizzling sentence back to the office on Sir Len and Monty's behalf: 'This match will long be remembered for one of the most superlative slip catches it has ever been my privilege to witness . . .'

For even as I spoke, Sir Len's real words were ringing in my ears. They were: 'It's a wonder t'fielder saw t' ball – let alone bloody catch it.'

I would one day be doing similar things to Joe Hulme's prose for the *Sunday People*. In the 1960s, dear old Joe, who was once an England winger and also the manager of both Spurs and Arsenal, 'wrote' football reports which, as a staff man, I ghosted for him. As a relative new boy to the writing game then, I was inclined to go a bit over the top with some of the phrase making and I would often sense old Joe creeping up behind me, whisky in hand, as I was dictating his pearls of wisdom from the press box. He would invariably start tutting and protesting: 'Don't make it too flowery, son, or my friends will think I've gone stark raving mad.'

My idyllic sojourn on the *Evening News* was about to be interrupted in the most unexpected way imaginable. For when the infamous Suez crisis erupted in 1956, I, one of the lousiest soldiers in the British Army, received my call-up papers. One morning a brown envelope popped through the letter box of the family home, 10 Arnold Avenue East, Enfield Lock, with a typewritten card inside it which instructed me to report for duty the following Thursday.

CHAPTER SEVEN
SUEZ

Of all the many nonsensical decisions Her Majesty's various governments have made down the years, none was more illogical than to command me to partake in the British invasion of Suez.

As a serving soldier, I had been about as much use to the Armed Forces as an ashtray on a motor bike, and as a reluctant, unpaid reservist, I had already been publicly promised that I would be left in peace. Consequently, I felt as disbelieving and disorientated as a character out of Kafka as I turned up at a displaced persons camp in deepest Hampshire to be greeted by a quartermaster sergeant who began stuffing boots, bedding and khaki shorts into my arms. And when I was told to stand in line, roll up my civilian shirtsleeves and prepare for a series of injections against tropical diseases, something in my brainbox snapped and I broke ranks and pissed off home.

Solace and sanity eluded me there too, though. John and George were married off by now and Jim was also a guest of Her Majesty, albeit in less noble circumstances than mine. As soon as I walked through the door with the intention of clearing my spinning head, the old man was on me like a ton of bricks. This was a Thursday evening and he never stopped nagging until I crawled back to the army with my tail between my legs the following Monday morning. In reply to my whining complaint that every sergeant-major I had ever served under had victimised me, Dad crushingly replied: 'I suppose it couldn't have been anything to do with you, boy.' And then he launched into a tirade about no deserter ever being allowed to take refuge under his roof. Ironically, although as a diehard socialist he was dead against the Suez invasion, he was also a king and country man of the old school.

When I reported back, I was inevitably put on a charge and accused of desertion. Asked to explain my actions, I told my commanding officer that, as a romantic, I would much rather fight for the Hungarians, who were being overrun by Russia at that time, than bully the poor old Egyptians over a few barrels of oil. He, predictably enough, was so furious with me that the veins stood out on his temples. He had in front of him by now my military record, which he said was more like that of an animal than a romantic. Then he sentenced me to 28 days' imprisonment at a proper army camp a few miles down the road.

I was 23 years old and considered myself a more than streetwise man of the world, yet here I was being held prisoner by a bunch of teenage regimental policemen. They felt too sheepish to get too heavy with me, so my only consolation was to take money off them at cards most nights.

While I was banged up, the invasion had not only taken

place, it was all over. And in addition to all their other embarrassments over the whole sorry affair, the army was left with a lone prisoner at a normal camp that was in no way connected with Suez. They chose to ignore this particular problem completely and simply left me there to rot. They were gracious enough to let me out of the nick after 28 days, but from then until they eventually got round to releasing me five months and three Elvis Presley hit songs later, I was left more or less to my own devices as a misbegotten misfit.

The man I held most responsible for this bizarre episode was Frank Starr at the *Evening News*. My argument was that the army were not entitled to call me up in the first place and that he should tell them so immediately. But when I first showed him the dreaded call-up papers, he had coldly said: 'You must be a paid reservist, so you won't get a penny in wages from us while you're away.' I protested that this was definitely not the case, but none of this managed to penetrate Mr Starr's consciousness, which was, understandably, too full of headlines and stories about this 'monumental', Sir Anthony Eden-inspired national crisis.

So I found myself back on the pittance of army pay living out a total nightmare, going on parade every morning then doing a variety of odd jobs which included cleaning the piss off the urinals with a razor blade. The only stroke I managed to pull during this whole episode was to replace that 'lost' overcoat I mentioned earlier by getting credit for a new one which I knew would be written off by the authorities because of the extreme circumstances of my call-up.

But it was more than a new overcoat I needed now – it was a new job. For if the army had unsettled me originally, it had positively unhinged me now. All of a sudden, because of those hellish five months, I was a young man in a bigger hurry than ever. I kept telling anyone who would listen that I wanted to become a real live reporter instead of a telephone one. The general reply was that I had more chance of winning the pools. For starters, Fleet Street newspapers would not be queuing up to employ uneducated cockneys like me, and on top of that I was also in the wrong trade union.

The best I could do was to con my way onto a local weekly paper somewhere for much less money than I was earning now, and for that I had almost certainly left it too late in life already. In those days of closed shops, this would mean belonging to the National Union of Journalists, and as a copytaker I had automatically been enrolled into the clerical union, NATSOPA.

The good news was that I knew that in reality – if not in theory – the kind of training I had received on the *News* was as good, if not better than that I would have received as a 'cub' reporter. I had been drilled in the kind of journalese which would be required of me by absorbing it into my brain every day from every kind of reporter under the sun. Frank Starr had also made his copytakers more than just telephone reporters. He had virtually turned us into sub-editors by instructing us to query writers' copy if we thought it was inaccurate or unwieldy, no matter how famous they were or how much it irritated them.

So I spent the next year or so nagging the Father of my Chapel, the newspaper version of a shop steward, into helping me to become a probationary member of the NUJ. When this hurdle was crossed, I replied to an advertisement for a reporter on the *Richmond Herald* by writing a tissue of white lies to that esteemed newspaper, which I believe is now owned by the Dimbleby family, telling them what an experienced reporter I was and that they should not miss this big opportunity to recruit me.

Meanwhile, I had to find a way to let the *News* know that I intended to leave them. This I did in my customary over-the-top fashion by refusing to do a Saturday football copy-taking shift for the old 'classified' edition on the grounds that I felt compelled to see that Welsh wing wizard, Cliff Jones, make his debut for Spurs after his £30,000 transfer from Swansea a couple of days earlier.

The *News* said the choice was mine and that it was either them or the Spurs. When I chose the Lilywhites, they promptly sacked me thereby making my departure much less complicated than it might have been.

CHAPTER EIGHT
LOCALS

My sojourn on local newspapers could be described as not so much a career as a manic caper. My plan, if any of my crazy, impetuous actions could come under such a sensible heading as a plan, was to make it back to Fleet Street almost immediately, if not sooner. My ambition knew no bounds and, luckily, my energy level was sky high. But my judgement of how to survive and prosper was as always extremely suspect, to say the least.

All this, with the help of a push or two in a backwards direction from some disillusioned editors, meant that in little more than three years I managed to work on no fewer than five separate titles. They were, in chronological order, the *Richmond Herald*, the *Windsor, Slough and Eton Express*, the *Romford Times*, the *Walthamstow Guardian* and the *Stratford Express*.

Thanks to the excellent grounding I had received at the *Daily Mail* and the *Evening News*, I took to the role of reporter like the proverbial duck to water. But although

I seemed to have found my niche in life professionally speaking, I was still something of an ugly duckling on a social level. Dog tracks, pubs and snooker halls were still my favourite recreational venues and I was not impartial to the odd fling with the opposite sex providing it did not interfere too much with my drinking and gambling.

Throughout my stints on all these papers I found lodgings in the various districts I worked in, but I was still heading back to the boozers in north London and the East End at every opportunity. (In the case of Romford, Walthamstow and Stratford, I did not have far to travel, of course.) I soon built up a reputation which was to stick with me for the next 30 years or more – that of a good reporter and writer and a nice guy when sober, but trouble when drunk. And as a potential alcoholic – a fact of which I was blissfully unaware at the time – I could not have chosen a more dangerous lifestyle.

As this was long before the days of tape recorders, my verbatim shorthand was a tremendous help, especially for the court cases and local council meetings I had to attend on a regular basis. Richmond, I soon discovered, was much too sophisticated a place for my working-class tastes, so it was only a matter of months before I landed a job on the *Windsor, Slough and Eton Express*, because I had heard on the grapevine that Slough was a particularly lively area for crime and hard news stories. What I had no idea I would enjoy so much, however, was the 'posher' end of that particular market, which soon had me reporting on rave-ups at the luxury home of Diana Dors down by the Thames riverside in Maidenhead. As the leading British sex bombshell of her time, actress Diana's name was rarely out of the papers, so I was filing freelance pieces about all her celebrity guests to the nationals and consequently making a nice few bob on top of my normal weekly pay, which was little more than a tenner a week with a few shillings and pence expenses on top.

Another unexpected development stopped me in my tracks, however, when my old man died. His death was not unexpected by any means, but my reaction to it was. The booze and the fags did for him at the age of 64. Along with my brothers and my mum and sister, I was at his bedside in that little boxroom and we heard the death rattle when he passed away.

Before he became ill with a stroke and hardened arteries, he had started coming over almost soppy and sentimental with me on the few occasions I popped home, and he was as proud as could be that I had become a real live journalist. Strangely, as the old lady closed his eyelids and probably said a silent prayer of gratitude to be free of the old sod at last, I experienced a feeling of despair and depression which stayed with me for months afterwards.

I must have been thinking how different it all could have been if he had not been such a piss artist, and I remember feeling sickened at the wasted, meaningless life that was expiring in front of me. Yet my sense of emptiness was tinged with respect for the fact that he had worked hard all his days, even if it had been to put more beer and whisky down his gullet than food on his family's table.

It was the long hot summer of 1959 and I remember that I had backed the Derby winner, Parthia, at 10–1 on or around my birthday, which always fell during Derby and Oaks week. We buried Dad on a stifling hot day in August and I found that for some weird reason I did not want to go on with the career I had been so mad keen on. Never really understanding why, I quit my job, came home to live with mum and my sister for a while and returned to the old layabout's way of life in the snooker hall. Neither of these two lovely ladies was too happy about having me on their hands again, but my old mum killed me with kindness by saying: 'You do exactly what you want to do with your life from now on, boy.' It was probably the best intentioned but the very worst single piece of advice I could ever have received from anyone.

Having been thus encouraged to regard myself as the centre of the universe, I sank into a pit of self-pity and lethargy before eventually emerging from this 'black dog' depression at a dog track, of all places. And what a delightful old dump of a dog track it was – Hackney Wick Stadium, which to the best of my knowledge never had a lick of paint on it in more than 50 years and where racing took place every Thursday afternoon. It was there, some 18 months earlier on a bitterly cold February day, that I had experienced the biggest shock of my life to date. Between races, the dreadful news of the Manchester United Munich plane crash began coming through via the radio in the bar. As the enormity of the tragedy unfolded, hardened old cockney punters and villains had tears coursing down their cheeks, and no one had the heart to have a bet. I had been in the crowd at Highbury only a few days earlier to see the Busby Babes win their last match before they made that fateful journey to Belgrade and, like almost everyone else in the country, had been captivated by their youthful zest and brilliance. Before that, my brother Jim and I had made a big thing of going across the water to watch a midweek match at Charlton when Bobby Charlton, who was a still a teenager at the time, scored two spectacular goals to herald his arrival as a future superstar.

On this afternoon, a year and more after Munich, the

particular bunch of fellow layabouts that I happened to be standing with on the dog track terraces began recalling that terrible day and the shocking demise of those gifted young men who had so much to live for. It turned out to be the psychological kick up the arse I needed, and I vowed there and then to get my own life back on the rails and not waste the little bit of talent I had been endowed with. Within days I had talked my way into a job on the *Romford Times* and this time I decided to experiment with football reporting, too. The main reason for this was that the paper's local football team were managed by an ex-Spurs centre-half, a bow-legged giant of a man named Jack Chisholm. I had seen Jack playing against my older brothers back in his amateur days and he was a bit of a hero of mine. It was not long before he and I were meeting on an almost daily basis.

By this time, however, sportswriters were no longer the household names they had been at the time of the Munich disaster. Then, with televised football still in its infancy in terms of audience, it was the newspapermen who were the media maestros. When the Manchester-based *Daily Express* football writer Henry Rose was buried after Munich, his funeral stopped the traffic in that city. And his protegé, Desmond Hackett, became even more famous than Henry, courtesy of the promotion the *Express*'s four million circulation figure afforded him. In those days, Hackett and the *Daily Mirror* sports columnist Peter Wilson were as big in the celebrity stakes as Des Lynam is now. One of the reasons for this was that the newspapers then did not plaster their pages with by-lines and pictures of their own writers as they do now. For better or worse, they made one or two men star performers and the rest of us had to get our seats warm for at least a year or more before we could expect to get a head-turning by-line on top of our report. As for seeing our pictures in the paper, that was more than our old mums could conjure up for us in their wildest dreams.

Anonymously, then, I cut a swathe through the local paper jungle of East London and Essex, an area which was to produce a whole string of well-known Fleet Street sportswriting contemporaries such as Brian James, the late Peter Lorenzo, Norman Giller, the late Harry Miller, Michael McDonnell, Trevor Bond and Jeff Powell, who still works for the *Daily Mail* today. But apart from wanting to rub shoulders with ex-spur Jack Chisholm, which I did for a while at Romford, I decided that a sportswriting career was not for me yet.

The twin reasons for this were, firstly, that as a fanatical Spurs supporter I would not give up my Saturday afternoons at White Hart Lane for anything, and secondly, because I nursed dreams of becoming a star foreign correspondent like James Cameron and Vincent Mulchrone, who still filed fantastically well-written, history-making 'I flew over the wreckage' pieces before live television did for them too.

My own actions around that time were already making me something of a legend in my own lunchtime and the result was that it did not take me long to get fired from both the *Romford Times* and the *Walthamstow Guardian*. Insanely, I saw my behaviour as simply playful and high-spirited, and refused to believe for a moment that booze had anything whatever to do with my manic mood swings. I found myself back on that old familiar scrapheap again, where I became in even greater need of my 'fuck 'em all' medicine in the upmarket saloon bars to which I had now graduated. But human nature being the quirky commodity which it undoubtedly is, I was able to pull another white rabbit out of the hat in the shape of Tom Bailey, editor of the *Stratford Express*. Mr Bailey was a pernickety little man whose proud boast was that he had 'resisted the call of Fleet Street' to serve his local community on London's lively eastern borders with Essex, a county which was itself now bursting at the seams with exiled cockneys. The *Stratford Express* was a sister paper to the *Walthamstow Guardian* and Mr Bailey confounded my cronies when he told them that he was taking a chance with me, despite my demise at the *Guardian*, because he was convinced he could tame me. Sadly for both him and me, he turned out to be wrong in that assumption. He even went so far as to let me report on a Spurs match at West Ham, with a by-line thrown in as a special treat for my old mum. But on a New Year's Eve celebration in the office, I slipped on yet another one of those banana skins with which I was convinced fate was deliberately strewing my path by getting so rat-arsed pissed that Mr Bailey not only sacked me, but sought the assistance of the police to have me escorted from his building.

During this next bout of unemployment, I had such a bad run at the dogs – where, being the mug punter I was, I was naturally allowed to bet on credit – that I knew it was time to scarper for a while before the bookies got too heavy with me. I can only assume that it was something in my genes – like it was for Jack London's husky canine hero 'Buck' in *The Call Of The Wild*, that classic allegory which had mesmerised me in my teens – that made me choose Scotland as a bolt hole.

My paternal grandmother had been a Cummings from Scotland and Grandad Batt had hailed from Cumberland, so I must have subconsciously assumed that I would 'find myself' in the north. I replied to an advertisement in the trade paper for a reporter on the *Scotsman* and sent them my cuttings. That esteemed publication first arranged for me to be interviewed in their Fleet Street branch office, where I was given a one-way ticket to Edinburgh and boarded a sleeper train which was to carry me to a land and people which I have loved ever since.

But wouldn't you just know it, Spurs, whom I had followed faithfully through as much thin as thick since those great push-and-run days of the 1951 Championship-winning team of Alf Ramsey and Bill Nicholson, picked that first year of my exile to go and win the League and Cup double.

CHAPTER NINE
SCOTS

I kidded myself that I was dressed to kill when I reported for my first day's duty at the imposing, almost palatial offices of the *Scotsman* on New Bridge Street in Edinburgh. And, indeed, I was told later by Eric Mackay, the distinguished-looking managing editor who greeted me, that he felt like dropping dead with shock at the sight of me as I strode purposefully across his carpeted office towards the giant desk he was sitting behind and said cheerfully: 'Morning, guv'nor.'

My scant piece of homework on the subject had told me that the *Scotsman* was miles upmarket of anywhere I had been yet in my brief journalistic career. In view of this, I had decided to get suitably suited and booted for my new life as a serious 'quality paper' scribe. With the help of a little bit of wheeling and dealing on the 'never never' hire purchase market, I acquired a Prince of Wales check suit, loud enough to frighten even the most extrovert of people I might be called upon to interview or investigate, a pair of 'with it' winkle-picker shoes with toe caps narrow enough to have crippled a Geisha girl, and had brushed my bushy hair back into a back parting which we streetwise lads called a 'duck's arse' and was based on the style favoured by Hollywood 'dream boat' Tony Curtis.

As bosses went, Eric Mackay struck me as a nice, quiet sort of bloke, and it was not until weeks later that I found out why he was so reticent, after he had told some of my new chums that he was the Scottish equivalent of 'gobsmacked' by my appearance and my broad cockney accent as I went about selling myself to him. The only clue I got as to his frame of mind came at the end of our meeting when, as I scraped back my chair ready to leave his room, he spoke these words in a soft voice: 'When you leave this building, young man, you will see a huge poster on an advertising hoarding in New Bridge Street, and you will see that same poster again and again all over this city and this country. And as that poster proclaims, "The *Scotsman* – The Voice of Scotland", I trust that this will make you understand why I am worried about your appointment.'

Happily, for both of us, his fears were unfounded. I gloried in my role as the only cockney-speaking Englishman in the entire Scottish press corps and I became a bigger stage cockney than ever. My line of chat also went down rather well with the single lasses north of the border, too, I am glad to report – although in those austere, pre-sexual-revolution late 1950s, you had very little chance of having your wicked way with them unless you could guarantee to come up with a wedding ring or, at the very least, an engagement ring. And with my gambling luck running so low, I had enough trouble getting a round of drinks in, though this problem was eased by the credit we newspapermen could always obtain, until next pay day, at the office pub.

To my delight, the features department gave me a starring role of sorts by making me their 'Englishman Abroad'. I found myself writing comment pieces about the Edinburgh Festival, various events at Edinburgh Castle, and even holding forth on matters of the Kirk. Plus I got my picture in the paper when I did a spot of menswear modelling in the new clobber I bought myself as soon as I had a touch on the dogs.

It was in Scotland that I first heard tell of a magical sportswriter named Hugh McIlvanney, who went on to become as respected and famous in our business in America as he was in Britain. Later, even though he was a few months younger than me, Hugh became my mentor and taught me most of what I was to learn about the art of sportswriting, when we both hit the 'big time' in London.

For now, though, my head was being turned when I began receiving overtures to join the Scottish *Daily Mail*. This had me dreaming of a triumphant return to where it had all started for me back on the *Mail* in London, and ruthlessly I quit the *Scotsman* to savour the more exciting and demanding role of a 'foot in the door' man on the extremely competitive Scottish news beat. They say what goes round comes round, and although I felt a sense of guilt turning my back on my saviours, I was to learn many times over that employers could be every bit as cold-hearted as employees in the harsh reality of newspaper life.

I got myself fixed up in the 'Hibs' end as opposed to the 'Hearts' end of town with an Irish landlady named Agnes, who had an ever open purse for my hard luck stories, a sociable Scottish husband named Tom and a couple of other 'respectable' lodgers, one of whom was my room-mate, a clerk from Chesterfield called Jack. While

I was an airhead inclined towards mysticism, Jack was a down-to-earth gardener, so our philosophising was never less than interesting to us both – except, of course, when I was pissed and Jack very sensibly gave me a wide berth.

Getting pissed became a much more frequent pastime after I joined the *Mail* and teamed up with three older soul-mates named Len Lord, Ian Ramsey and Ernie McIntyre, who all wore white raincoats and were never without a half bottle of whisky either in the raincoat pocket or in their desk in the newsroom. Apart from living up to the traditional hard-bitten image of newspapermen, the prime reason for this 'carry out' booze was that getting pissed was theoretically more difficult in Scotland because the boozers up there shut at the uncivilised hour of nine o'clock every evening and never opened at all on Sundays.

This was my 'Hemingway' period when we tried to write staccato, machine-gun sentences like the great Ernest and spat out a 'See you Jimmy' Scottish-style version of our hero's macho aggression in the pubs. The one thing this trio of Celtic tipplers did not share with me was my passion for dog racing, although they came to the track occasionally for a 'bevvy'. The track was the famous Powderhall Stadium, which was five minutes walk from the *Mail* office and was frequented by the same cast of colourful characters as those in London except that the slang was different, but no less entertaining for that. As for the 'bevvying', as my Scots pals called boozing, that was done not only in the pub but in the late night bar at the Press Club and also at the more grandiose Overseas Club, which was frequented by some very attractive Continental au pair girls who were, whenever any of them felt like it, very well equipped to distract my manic brain from its triple addiction to work, booze and betting.

But such was the adventure and excitement to be had by reporters on the road and in the offices and pubs that there was very little time left over for marginal luxuries like courting. My work took me all over the country, to the lowlands and the highlands, and embraced every kind of news story such as murder hunts, coal mining disasters, Gretna Green elopements, stake-outs and sieges. It even included Britain's first-ever kidney transplant operation, when I covered myself in glory by becoming the only reporter to track down and interview the anonymous donor.

The veteran Scottish news editors not only mothered me, they were patient teachers who schooled me in grammar and the usage and abusage of the English language, which I had been denied in my school days. The most surreal character of all the office eccentrics I became involved with was a *Mail* news editor called Stuart Barr. One of a well-known family of Scottish journalists, Stuart had boxed the legendary Randolph Turpin while both of them were in the navy, and he had the bull neck and barrel chest to prove it.

His combative nature was tailor-made to suit the intense inter-office rivalry, and whenever he had taken a dram or two too many, he would line his men up for a raid on the 'opposition' pubs and insist that we taunt their reporters with chorus after chorus of: 'A *Mail* man for me, a *Mail* man for me, if you're no' a *Mail* man, you're nae use tae me . . .' to the tune of that old battle anthem, 'A Gordon for me'.

Being a member of the group of foot-in-the-door men, required, I am ashamed to say, a thick skin as well as a ruthless determination to put one over on your rivals. Our lives were often full of high-speed car chases against the opposition and even included such low-life tricks as persuading relatives to hand over pictures of near and dear ones who had perished in mining accidents and the like. On reflection, it is no wonder so many of us took to drink but, unlike me, most of the others knew when to stop.

I should have sussed that my drinking was becoming problematic, I suppose, when it provided me with my most embarrassing Christmas to date. The beauty of being an Englishman in Scotland was that I had the best of both worlds during the festive season. Most Scotsmen would not give you a thank you for Christmas, so I was given time off every year to go home on the understanding that I worked at New Year instead. Needless to say, the only thing I worked at on Hogmanay was getting as high as a kite, which was not the least bit difficult to do in such hospitable surroundings.

Christmas 1960 found me in the unusual situation of having enough readies to splash out on a load of Christmas presents for my family, some of whom had children of their own by now. They were all gathering at my mum's place and I took a late train on Christmas Eve, carrying a paper bag which at the point of departure was bulging with gifts. Sadly, when I arrived home on Christmas morning, the bag had a giant hole in the bottom and was full of fresh air. No one in the Batt house believed for a moment that I had ever bought any presents. Consequently they retaliated by declining to give me any, and spent most of the afternoon taunting me with a popular seasonal ditty about 'The Little Boy That Santa Claus Forgot'.

Back in Scotland, in times of tension or trouble I always had football to console me. I followed boxing, cricket, tennis and athletics, too, and, as always, I kept the odds-layers happy by taking an all too active part in the racing game for my own good. But football was my escape and apart from that brief flirtation with reporting on the game for the East London local papers, I indulged myself with a place on the terraces every Saturday afternoon. Living in Edinburgh and using newspaper contacts, I also always managed to get a ticket for the big Murrayfield rugby internationals and then availed myself of the traditional post-match pub crawl down Rose Street which, I was informed, had more hostelries in it than any other street in Britain. So I became a regular patron of Hibs and Hearts and spent more than a few away days at Celtic or Rangers matches, too. Contrary to what a good many Englishmen may imagine, I never encountered a moment's trouble. Thankfully, my alien accent seemed more good for a laugh than a head butt, no matter which team I cheered for.

But on the subject of head butts, I never saw more of those going in on any one occasion then when I made the mistake of visiting a Glasgow dance hall one Saturday night during the start of 'Fairs' week, when almost the entire work force went on their annual holiday at the same time. I had been to Carntyne dog track and won a few quid for a change, and decided I would play up my luck by attempting pull a nice wee lassie at the local Palais. I left the track midway through the programme to make sure that I did not blow my winnings back, and this meant that I arrived at the dance hall before the pubs had closed.

As I entered the dance hall, with its welcoming twinkling lights, I thought I was in heaven. The walls were lined with beautiful girls and there were no more than a dozen men in the place. A long way from being the best dancer in the world, I had to rely on my chat rather than my footwork, so I was still busy working out the strategy of my night's work when the doors suddenly burst open and hordes of young men, some running, some staggering, some retreating before a frontal assault, flooded the place and – full of Dutch courage – proceeded to try to sweep the girls and any unfortunate males that happened to get in the road off their collective feet. I soon scarpered at the sight of all these horny 'bravehearts' and felt reasonably convinced that even such tough guy cockneys as the aforementioned Ron and Reggie Kray, the instigators of so many of those old Tottenham Royal shindigs, would have arrived at a similar decision to mine.

In all, I was to spend nearly three very happy years living and working in Scotland, but just as all good things must come to an end sooner or later, so it was with my love affair with Scotland and the Scots. Even that had to take second place to the burning ambition which insisted that I must make it back to Fleet Street before I could feel truly fulfilled.

CHAPTER TEN
HERALD

My first day's work as a reporter on the *Daily Herald* in London fell on April Fools' Day, 1962. I was numb with excitement and anticipation and spent those first hours doing very little other than gawp at all the journalistic stars I was being introduced to. As is always the way when you are having fun, the time passed as quickly as a snap of the fingers. But it was the moment when my first shift finished which turned out to be the most significant of the day and, possibly, the rest of my life, too.

As they let me get my new seat warm, barely anyone in the office had taken a moment's notice of me. I had not been ordered to chase any fire engines or, for that matter, even to set foot outside the door. So when I figured it was time to leave, I attempted to slink out of the premises in a low-key fashion. That was the first mistake of the many I was due to make from here on in.

A cold, metallic, patronising voice rang out and the icy remark 'Where do you think you're going, young man?'

hit me between the shoulder blades. It belonged to Adrian Douglas Long, a news editor who was later to climb the slippery slope to the very top of the management pile.

As I turned to face him, I could think of nothing better to mutter than 'Home.'

'Home is a place that does not exist for a news reporter,' Mr Long informed me. 'Get your arse over to the office pub and wait for us to phone you with a story.'

It so happened that, from choice rather than by command, I was to go on to spend more hours in that pub, the Cross Keys in Endell Street, Covent Garden, than almost anywhere else. And many years later, when I was scraping the barrel for scapegoats for the mess I had made of my life, Doug Long figured high on the list of people I held responsible for making me cross the invisible line from social drinker to alcoholic. Not so, of course. The man had enough troubles of his own in that he was an incurable Fulham fan. But it did strike me as ironic that I was to get the sack many times over, from many different papers, because of my boozing and its subsequent consequences.

But within weeks, all this could have been rendered irrelevant, for my world nearly came to an end on two counts when, at one and the same time, I looked like being blown to smithereens by Nikita Khrushchev and Spurs lost in the semi-final of the European Cup to Benfica of Portugal.

That fatal match took place slap bang in the middle of the Cuban Missile Crisis when John Kennedy and Khrushchev were eye-balling each other for Armageddon.

As the capacity crowd poured into White Hart Lane that night, the talk on everyone's lips was not of Eusebio and Jimmy Greaves but, literally, it centred on 'the end of the world is nigh.' At that precise moment Russian atomic missiles were cruising towards what was intended to be a permanent base for them in America's back yard – Castro's Cuba. If they reached there, which they were due to do at about half-time, Kennedy had promised the world he would unleash nuclear devastation on Russia and if that happened Khrushchev had vowed to make it a case of vice versa.

I promise you I have never known such a weird, eerie, almost mystical atmosphere as there was in that theatre of football that night. Most of us Spurs nuts were of the opinion that if we had to go to Heaven we might as well do so in the company of Danny Blanchflower and Dave Mackay who we were convinced were going to make us the first English team to win the European Cup, anyway.

As history has since recorded, of course, neither of these momentous events occurred. Khrushchev bottled it and turned back at the last moment and Jimmy Greaves had a perfectly good goal disallowed for offside in Spurs' 2–1 victory but we still lost 4–3 on aggregate. The fact that Spurs did eventually become the first English team to triumph in Europe soon after this when they won the European Cup Winners Cup was of small consolation.

By this time I had my feet under the table at the *Herald* and my toothbrush in my top pocket for a marvellous helter-skelter lifestyle when, on most days, I was greeted by Doug with the words, 'Don't bother to take your coat off,' and was then dispatched on stories anywhere and everywhere, home and abroad. This was way back in the days when we covered most stories personally rather than use the modern method of getting them via the telephone. Then it would be back to the Cross Keys and, even though it was within walking distance of Bow Street Magistrates' Court, we drank in there into the wee small hours of most mornings. Ann Hulbert, the widowed proprietress, must have had a cosy arrangement with the Metropolitan Police over the little matter of the licensing laws.

I defy any landlord to conjure up a more cosmopolitan clientele than the one which frequented the Keys and its near neighbour the Radio Arms, so nicknamed because it was such a rumour factory. There were Covent Garden porters from the flower market who drank around the clock (funny how I should follow in the footsteps of my dear old dad, eh?). There were wonderful, toothless old crones who had once presumably been beautiful flower girls like Eliza Doolittle, and who now entertained us with the occasional knees-up whenever it took their fancy. There were printers, elderly cockney tape-room messengers, newspaper van drivers and, in season, American tourists. But mostly there were journalists, who were the elite few whom Ann allowed to stay over for the after-time drinking. Ann was a particular favourite of mine because she liked an occasional night out at the dogs with some of us and kept an ever open handbag for our financial crises; as, too, did 'Mum' at the nearby Radio Arms.

They were an elite crowd, those *Herald* men and women and their drinking mates who flocked in from other Fleet Street hostelries to join them. It might have been in decline but the socialist-supporting *Herald* had once been the first paper to pass the magical two-million circulation barrier and was still much revered. You can imagine how stimulating it was for this uneducated boy from Stepney to listen to conversations between people such as that great writer James Cameron, Spanish Civil War veteran Alan Dick, diarist Alan Hall and his many and varied guests, film critic Ann Pacey, theatre critic and playwright David Nathan and, for me the most fascinating conversationalist of them all, television critic Dennis Potter, who went on to become a household name with his fabulous TV plays and films. To top all this, we had an all-night poker school in the news room which attracted players from all over Fleet Street and did not break up until the cleaners came in to kick us out just after dawn and spill us into the early morning Freemasons Arms.

Somehow I found the time to go clubbing elsewhere, too. Tommy Merrin, an outrageously colourful character on the *Daily Sketch* who was renowned for his crime and showbusiness contacts, took me under his wing and introduced me to Al Burnett, the owner of such popular Piccadilly night spots as the Stork Room and the Pigalle. My love of dog racing gave me a starting point with Al, who owned a greyhound Derby winner appropriately named Pigalle Wonder. So did my love of booze – and it was not long before Tommy had persuaded Al to let the pair of us drink as much of the stuff as we liked for free, so long as we gave him and his clubs plenty of publicity. The inevitable happened one night when Burnett stood us both to attention and addressed us thus: 'You drink like a couple of camels that have just come out of the desert and what do you put in your papers about me? Nothing! You're both sacked and what's more, you're both barred.'

The very next night, a quiet Sunday, the phone rang on my desk – I had volunteered for permanent night work at this particular time so that I could be free to go dog racing in the afternoons and play poker in the office card school every night – and it was Al Burnett on the other end, screaming: 'Batty, get round to the Stork Room this minute – I've got King Hussein of Jordan in here.'

'But you fired me yesterday,' I teased him.

'Bollocks,' said Al. 'Get your arse round here now or I'll do a lot worse than give you the bullet.'

Naturally, his Royal Highness made a nice little scoop for Merrin and me, as he told us of the efforts he was expending in finding a suitable school in Britain for the Princess with which his English wife had presented him. Understandably, the highly educated King failed to mention how he hoped to further his scholarly ambitions for the Princess by viewing the showgirls in the Stork Room with a bodyguard in tow. But there are some questions even a reporter just doesn't ask.

A big question was asked of me around this time when, via my brother Jim, the Kray twins invited me to the East End pub the Grave Maurice, which they used as an office, and Reggie politely inquired if I would like to look after public relations for 'the firm'. I very graciously declined this kind offer, but that did not stop Reggie's unmistakably chilling voice from frequently turning up on the end of my phone in the office to inform me that the publicity-conscious twins were bringing over celebrities like Judy Garland, Joe Louis and George Raft for 'charitable causes'.

When it came to celebrities, I was doing very nicely on my own account, too, although I was not always being very charitable towards them. One star name I still feel a very large pang of guilt over is singing superstar Shirley Bassey, of whom I have been a lifelong fan. She was appearing in cabaret at the Savoy Hotel one night and I was delighted when I was instructed to go and 'keep an eye on her'. The reason for the press attention Our Shirl was getting at this time was that her first marriage was going through a troubled period and, consequently, so was she. Perhaps she was not quite at her sensational best on this occasion, but she had my sympathy and that of my press colleagues when the toffee-nosed audience of diners continued to clatter glasses and crockery and even chatted during her performance. Shirley cracked and slagged them all off for being the rude mob which they undoubtedly were. And then she fled the stage and we, the press pack, caught up with her at the open gates of the lift to offer our sympathy and condolences. Unsurprisingly, we received an even worse rollicking than her audience had done, and to my consternation she accused me of being the ring leader and for one frightening moment made as if to scratch my eyes out before the lift door closed on her. I trust she forgave us next morning when we all wrote sympathetic front-page pieces about the incident.

Only one celebrity has left me absolutely speechless with awe and admiration, however, and that was the fabulous Sophia Loren. I was sent to interview her at London Airport once and could only gawp and stutter as I found myself sharing an escalator with the definitive sex symbol, who was even more desirable than Marilyn Monroe and Diana Dors. But the last impression I want to give is of a life which was simply a daily round of star-studded encounters. I kept up the habits of a lifetime by mixing with my share of low life, too. And I regularly earned the wrath of Doug Long for my cavalier attitude towards expenses. Sending me off to cover a murder investigation in Southend which ran for days and became known as the 'Lady Bountiful' case, he first informed me: 'You had better make up your mind if you want to be a reporter or a professional gambler. I won't have you treating my expenses float as a bottomless pot of gold.' Then, ignoring the fact that I and my opposition colleagues had played a prominent part in helping to solve this 'whodunnit' by pointing the police towards the local milkman as the slayer of the generous rich widow, he refused to wire me any more money with which to pay my hotel bill.

As I have mentioned before, I have invariably been lucky enough to pull a rabbit out of the hat in times of dire need and on this occasion I did so by borrowing a fiver off one of my pals, nipping down to the Southend dog track and having it on a winning dog out of trap three at 10–1. But I needed more than luck to keep me afloat in my next year at the *Herald*. For 1963 was to be the most memorable one in history when it came to the sheer volume of long-running, sensational news stories, which kept us all on our collective toes up and down Fleet Street.

That momentous year began with the death of Labour leader Hugh Gaitskell, went on to provide us with the infamous Christine Keeler saga, gave us the Great Train Robbery and then capped everything off in November with the assassination of President Kennedy.

It was also a year which was to earn me some esoteric notoriety with my involvement in what later became known in the business end of the Fleet Street boozers as the 'Nuns' Story'.

During an electric storm, a plane carrying British holidaymakers crashed in the Pyrenees. Together with another reporter and photographer from our sister paper the *Daily Mirror*, photographer Arthur Tanner and I were sent off to fly into the teeth of that same storm to report on the tragedy. Our employers, Odhams Press, had been first off the mark by hiring a small private plane, which meant that we were the only two on-the-spot British newspapers there in time to file stories from the nearby French town of Perpignan that same night.

Exhausted by our efforts and dismayed at the death of so many of our countrymen and women, the four of us went on the town to unwind. Unfortunately, as was my wont, I was the only one among us to overdo it and I crashed out fully clothed, only to be woken a few hours later by the hotel maid, who was hoovering around my prostrate body. In a panic, I vaguely remembered that we had arranged the night before to go up into the mountains that morning to record the gruesome details of the salvage operation. My colleagues, who were not as hungover as I was, had decided to let me sleep, but not before pushing a note under my bedroom door informing me of the exact location where I could catch up with them, as we had all day in which to do the follow-up story. Disastrously for me, they were hungover enough, however, to have slipped the note under the wrong bedroom door and no doubt some puzzled Frenchman wondered what the said note was all about.

I rushed out into the street and ordered the first available taxi to take me up into the mountains. I had forgotten to look in the mirror first. If I had done so I would have seen that I was in the most dishevelled state imaginable and looked worse than death warmed up. I had also neglected to check on the local weather report and the taxi driver and I were confronted with a violent storm which was so spectacular that it continued to make the news itself, with torrential flooding and the like, for days afterwards. I had not got the foggiest idea where the wreckage was and did not speak a word of French, so I just glared at the driver and pointed to the mountains. He must have thought I was stark raving mad, but he was persuaded to take a chance on me when he saw the wad of francs which I was waving under his nose. Frequently winding the window down to be sick out of it and with the incoming gale matting the vomit to my hair, I could only keep muttering, 'Fuck, fuck, fuck,' which I assume the driver mistook as the English word for rain, because he frequently glared out at the storm and said, 'Oi, very fuck, much fuck.'

Eventually, the weather became so impossible that even this brave French stalwart refused to go any further. And after extracting what was obviously an extortionate fare out of me, he ordered me out into the rain, leaving me stuck up the mountain. Luckily, it was not long before I heard footsteps and a group of local people gently guided me towards a little hamlet where some nuns began taking care of me. Word soon went out that there was one miraculous, mystery survivor of the crash, and when the rest of Fleet Street eventually turned up they were disappointed, to say the least, that the survivor only turned out to be 'Batty'. That story, I am told by colleagues, got told many times over in newspaper bars around the world and it was, more or less, the beginning of the 'nutty as a fruitcake', people-pleasing image I stupidly found myself compelled to live up to more and more.

My personal life was becoming just as 'nutty', too. I had moved down from Scotland with a pal from the Scottish *Daily Mail* named Bill Meek. Bill, who landed a job as a *Mail* reporter in London at the same time as I got my break on the *Herald*, looked and behaved like the Jack Lemmon character in the hit Neil Simon play and film, *The Odd Couple*. On a good day I might have passed for Walter Matthau, too, especially when it came to the slob stakes. The pair of us, Bill and I, teamed up as flatmates in a top-floor apartment in highly desirable Holland Park Avenue, where he did the cooking and kept the place looking spick and span for our steady stream of young female visitors. My job was the downmarket one of dish washer, dustbin man and general dogsbody. It was a job for which, I had been foolish enough to confess to him in an inebriated moment, I had been well groomed by the British army. And it was a job which nearly wrecked my career.

One of the other big stories on the go at that time was the Vassall spy saga. Civil servant John Vassall had been sentenced to a long term of imprisonment as a Russian spy and now there was a tribunal being held to investigate the whole episode. This resulted in a couple of pals of mine, Brendan Mulholland – once of the *Herald* but at this time on the *Mail* – and Reg Foster of the *Sketch*, being jailed, too, for refusing to disclose the source of their informants in the reporting of the whole sordid episode. Another pal, 'Sinister Sid' Williams of the *Herald*, had wriggled out of a similar fate by telling the tribunal that he had lost his noteboook when he was sent to the Indo-China border war and dropped it at the sight of the advancing Chinese.

Very much a bit-part player in all this, I was on my voluntary night duty throughout the whole Vassall affair and my duties consisted of coming in on a sliding shift at 2pm on Monday, 4pm Tuesday, 5pm Wednesday, 6pm Thursday and then at 9pm for the Friday night 'dog watch'. Never the best of timekeepers, I had somehow contrived to turn up late on every consecutive day, and that had managed to make Doug Long snap. My cause had not been helped by the fact that he had tumbled that while out in the office car on stories with our cockney driver, Bob Cox, I had also been interrupting my investigations by popping into the nearest dog track – and when questioned as to what the noise of barking dogs was doing wafting over the phone during my check calls to the office, I invariably fibbed that there were police alsatians in the vicinity.

So with good cause, Long was well and truly pissed off with me this particular week. So much so that by Thursday evening he had threatened me with instant dismissal if I was so much as a minute late on Friday night. I was not too disturbed by this threat for the simple reason that I figured that no sane man, nor even a nutter like me, could possibly turn up late for work at nine o'clock at night. But I had not bargained for the impulsive actions of an irate window cleaner.

When this window cleaner arrived at our flat, it must have been his last job on a fine summer's early evening and he was probably gagging for a pint. I happened to be singing quite happily in the bath at the time and when he knocked loudly at the bathroom door and demanded his money, I told him I only had enough for the fare to work and that this kind of transaction was down to Bill Meek and not me, anyway. He protested in such an aggressive fashion that I made the mistake of shouting for him to 'piss off'. What had slipped my mind during this little contretemps was that our bathroom was outside the flat on the landing, and that when the enraged window cleaner pulled our front door shut from the outside, I would be left stranded with no front door key and no clothes. And I was to remain naked, vulnerable and utterly depressed until the caretaker in the basement flat arrived home at about 9.15 that night.

When I eventually made it to the office an hour late, I was astonished to see Doug Long still sitting behind his desk instead of standing at the bar of 'The Keys'. I decided that attack was the best form of defence and waded into him verbally with stories of window cleaners and dodgy alarm clocks, and then rounded off my explanation with the pledge that I would go home to live with my old mum again if it meant getting to work on time in future.

In that icy nasal whine of his, Long replied: 'I don't give a fuck if you go and live with Vassall, you're still fired.' (Vassall, incidentally, was gay.)

It was a terrible weekend, during which I was so desperate to save myself that I deserted Bill Meek and rented a room above a shop which was next door to Covent Garden tube station and two minutes' walk from the imposing building which then housed the *Herald* and the *Sunday People*. On the following Monday, Long relented and contented himself with a written warning before giving me a punishment posting to Birmingham, for a circulation drive in which I was to have the other members of the office 'heavy mob' as companions. They were Sinister Sid Williams, Geordie Peter Moorhead, who later became a poacher turned management gamekeeper, and the big, bad Scot, Bob Adam. In charge of us was another Scottish lunatic, assistant news editor Bill McLelland. We had a fabulous, all-expenses-paid fortnight at the Midland Hotel, but there was a punishing element involved in our stint, and that was mad McLelland's mania for poker playing. Bill would spend most nights drinking in the Birmingham Press club and then return to hammer on our bedroom doors in the wee small hours, demanding that we join him for a poker session. We had no alternative but to become his reluctant opponents, because he was in charge of the 'expenses float' and the only way we could get any readies out of him was to acquiesce with his nocturnal demands on us.

Still, a far worse fate than that awaited another of our poker-playing pals when office driver Bob Cox, poor chap, collapsed and died holding kings 'back to back' one dreadful night during the *Herald* game.

Keeper of the night safe for those legendary schools was night news editor Colin Hart, who was one of the few other news men to switch to sport when he later became the very well-known boxing and athletics writer for Rupert Murdoch's *Sun*. In additon to being my guv'nor, it was Colin who determined how much desperate players like myself could draw out in advance expenses, of which he was in charge. Colin was to remain one of my very best friends for the next – at the time of writing – 38 years. And I was to have a great deal for which to be thankful to him when I hit truly desperate times in middle age.

Incidentally, Colin tells a story of his own early days as a reporter on an East London news agency which I think is well worth a mention here. It concerns a little girl who became known as the 'Limehouse Cinderella'.

It was Christmas week and one of Colin's police contacts at the local nick had phoned to give him a nice little seasonal yarn. The police sergeant said that a 13-year-old local waif named Jennifer Chiles had found a wallet full of money lying on the pavement of a busy main road and handed it into the police station unopened. Delighted, the sergeant said he thanked the girl profusely and wished her a merry Christmas. She told him that for her it would not be all that merry because 'me and me dad are skint and we ain't got no grub for Christmas dinner.'

The desk sergeant immediately invited the child to the Christmas party for the police officers' children at the local nick. Colin went straight round to Jennifer's address and discovered that it was a hovel, with no food in the cupboard and only embers in the fire grate. The girl's father turned out to be a road sweeper and a hopeless drunk, but Jennifer said she loved him dearly and she looked after him at what passed for the home they shared together.

Colin filed the story to all the papers and the *Daily Express*, who were the kings of Fleet Street at that time, immediately signed up the girl and her father. They took her to Teasy Weasy, the most famous hairdresser in the country, they bought her a fabulous ball gown and they even went to Bertram Mills circus and hired six ponies, as well as a glass coach, a pumpkin and a fairy godmother to take Jennifer to the party at the nick. The story and the pictures were syndicated all round the world and Jennifer and her old dad became instant celebrities for about a week. Offers flooded in from people wanting to adopt her, but Jennifer insisted she wanted to stand by her dear old dad.

Sadly, however, the local council eventually stepped in and took the weeping child away from her father, rightly saying that she was in need of care and protection. Colin and I still wonder how little Jennifer's life turned out.

To go from one extreme to the other, most of us now know how Jack Profumo's life turned out. He was the War Minister who nearly brought down Harold Macmillan's government and the husband of one of the country's leading actresses, Valerie Hobson. And he spent the latter years of his life in virtual anonymity working for a charity in the East End of London. The story of Profumo's dangerous liaisons with call girls Christine Keeler and Mandy Rice-Davies, and of Keeler's involvement with a Russian spy, has been told too many times to need repeating here. But one fascinating aspect of it that has never been told was the 'kiss over dinner' reunion Profumo had with Valerie, which I got as an almost impossible exclusive, but which wasn't used.

For weeks on end, I had been staked out near the

Profumos' Regents Park home awaiting his return after he had 'disappeared'. During that time, I had been plying the butler with drink because newspaper readers were holding their collective breath, wondering whether or not Valerie would ever forgive him. On the night Jack finally returned, his house was besieged by news and picture men, but my mate the butler filled me in with the most intimate details of the reunion scene and the conversations that took place in the house. Randolph Churchill, son of Sir Winston, was the dinner guest and Valerie gave Jack a forgiving kiss. When I filed all this to the *Herald* desk just before midnight, I thought I was going to be a hero. But the night news editor on duty, another late mate, Mick Rhind, went all the way up the *Herald*'s line of command to Lord Sidney Jacobson at the very top. And his Lordship killed my sensational piece because he said he did not want a 'peeping Tom' story on his front page. Just like the fisherman who has seen a big one get away, I was more than a little peeved when I led the follow-up questioning of Randolph on his doorstep next day.

But the time when I became an unwitting peeping Tom myself is still etched on my mind as having one of the funniest pay-off lines of all the countless escapades I was involved in during those laugh-a-minute Fleet Street nights. Ann Pacey, our paper's film critic, was the definitive blonde bombshell of that period. With her hair cropped into a fashionable urchin cut, she tottered around in high-heeled shoes to show off her shapely ankles and wore low-cut blouses which barely concealed her ample bosoms. Like many a roving-eyed male before him, bachelor Jack Wood, who had just joined us from the *Mail* as a boxing writer, was smitten by the sight of our Annie when he first clapped eyes on her in 'The Keys'.

On being told she was single and fancy-free, Jack, an ex-war hero bomber pilot, promptly asked me to effect an introduction. I tried to explain that 'Pacey', as she was fondly known, was regarded as more like one of the boys than a sex bomb, for her ability to drink most of us under the table. What I neglected to tell Jack, however, was that Pacey swiftly informed me that she did not fancy him one little bit. Undeterred, he proceeded to get pissed, so did Pacey and so did I. At the end of the night, flamboyant Jack ordered a crate of champagne – how he could afford it on his wages I never discovered – and the three of us wound up in a cab for a trip to his cottage in Guildford. Out came the Frank Sinatra records, on came Jack's line of chat and up to bed I went to leave the pair of them to it.

I was awakened in the early hours by the sight and sound of Pacey being pursued round the bedroom by a naked Jack. It happened to be a king-sized bed I was in, so Pacey leapt into one side of it beside me, beseeching me to protect her from Jack's unwelcome advances, and Jack jumped in the other side trying to fight his way past me into the arms of his 'beloved'. It took a while for the rumpus to die down and for Jack to surrender gracefully, so that the three of us could all get some kip. Unfortunately for Pacey, Jack had remembered her telling him the night before that she needed to be up early to go to a morning press film showing in the West End. He cruelly failed to set the alarm clock, with the result that poor old Annie woke up well and truly late. After taking a few lumps out of Jack's face with her long fingernails, she then insisted that I accompany her back to London post haste.

In the buffet on the train back to London, she slaughtered half a dozen miniature vodkas and then made her way to the film premiere all of two hours late. Fortunately for her, the film just happened to be a biblical epic which ran for some four hours and was entitled *The Greatest Story Ever Told*. Less fortunately for her, however, after she had slagged the film off something rotten in the paper next day, the cinema management complained to the editor that she had been seen arriving for the show hopelessly late and that this was not the first time recently that Miss Pacey had written bad notices of films she had been late arriving for. Then they politely suggested that she should be dismissed from her position forthwith.

When I asked Pacey later how she had managed to save her job, she gave me one of her cheekiest grins and said: 'Let's just say I came up with the greatest story ever told.'

Sadly, her own life story turned out to be one of the saddest ever told when she wound up as a desperately sick alcoholic and had the Last Rites said over her on more than one occasion. In happier times, she had married the night news editor Mick Rhind, whom I mentioned earlier. And Mick used to tell us how he would have to play what was a role reversal in those days, that of the husband waiting at home for his wife to come in late from the pub while the dinner burned in the oven.

Another lady journalist of that era who could match any man drink for drink was Annie Lloyd Williams of the *Daily Mirror*. And I relate the following anecdote to emphasise that despite the dog-eat-dog approach when it came to pulling off an exclusive scoop, there was a wonderful cameraderie between the men and women of Fleet Street if ever one of the opposition was in trouble.

And trouble was exactly what I expected when I awoke late one night lying on a bench in the Mirror office pub, 'The Stab'. It was officially named the 'White Hart' but earned its nickname 'The Stab In the Back' for obvious reasons. However, no knife came within miles of my spine that night – the very reverse, in fact.

Annie and I had been among a group of reporters who had gone to Heathrow airport early that morning to welcome home Britain's victorious team from the 1964 Tokyo Olympics, where Mary Rand, Ann Packer, Lyn Davies and Ken Matthews had all won gold medals. Inevitably, there was a champagne breakfast celebration, the highlight of which for this randy young reporter was the sight of golden girl Mary Rand having her hair blow-dried in her hotel room, clad in only the briefest of underwear. But the press pack concentrated most of its efforts on 15-year-old swimming water babe Linda Ludgrove, who had won no fewer than five medals. She lived in south London and after the story was done and dusted we retired in time-honoured fashion to the nearest local hostelry. Such a jolly, impromptu piss-up transpired that the whole crowd of us newspaper nutters – reporters and photographers – were soon joined by the *Daily Mirror* night news editor Dan Ferrari, who lived locally and invited us home to his house for a meal.

When I came to in The Stab that night, it was with the sudden, icy-cold fear that I had no recollection whatever of phoning over my story. My voice must have been trembling when I rang Mick Rhind at the *Herald* night desk from the pub to inquire if there were any queries on my story. Taken aback, Mick said: 'What's come over you? The new conscientious Batty, all of a sudden. You've never, ever contacted us about a story you filed hours ago.'

When I read my piece the next day, it was given a big spread with a by-line on top and I could not recall having written one word of it. No wonder! For I later discovered that Annie Lloyd Williams, who had matched me drink for drink and then some, had written not only her own piece but mine too, when she realised I was never going to come to the line on this occasion.

It was the first time I had ever missed a deadline and I was mortified. Because, like the rest of my colleagues, I took great pride in my professionalism. 'It doesn't matter what you give them, whether it's the Lord's Prayer or Egyptian hieroglyphics,' I had been told by one old veteran, 'just so long as you give them something.'

It still had not remotely occurred to me that drink was becoming a problem. The only problem with drink, as far as I was concerned, was that I could not get enough of it. Yet by now I really was burning the proverbial candle at both ends. I had quit the Covent Garden flat, where the early morning din of the market kept me awake even on the few occasions I did manage to try to snatch some shut eye, and moved into a luxury house in Horton Street, off Kensington High Street, which was owned by a refined Indian gentleman. Those were heavenly days and nights for young single people. London was a bedsitters' paradise in those days, with rents so affordable that half a dozen of us were able to share this beautifully furnished house at the knockdown rate of £26 a month each in rent. And for this we each got our own bedroom and the share of a marvellous lounge and a luxury kitchen. All journalists, we managed to last about nine months before the landlord understandably kicked us out because of the noise from the uproarious parties we held almost every night.

Our 'rat pack' lifestyle coincided with the opening of a club called the Rheingold. It belonged to Henry Zeisel, who had been a famous Austrian violinist and who, incidentally, later owned the fabulous racehorse which he named after his club. Visiting the Rheingold was enough to make even a gambling addict like me swear off the dogs and the poker. The place was literally packed with beautiful girls of almost every nationality under the sun. And in its early days there were never more than a dozen or so men in the place. Shrewd old Henry had made it free admission for the many hundreds of girls who had come to England to work as au pairs in the early sixties, and practically every one of them was the pick of her home town or village in the beauty stakes. As press men, me and my house mates were given the run of the place for a while until, of course, it eventually became as packed with males as Wembley Stadium when word of it eventually got out to the rest of the city.

I was to meet Heidi, the beautiful German girl who became my wife, there. But this was after I had been forced to move again – this time to an equally luxurious pad in a very upmarket block near Baker Street station. My flatmates here were the late Neville Hunter of the *Daily Sketch*, a piss artist par excellence with whom I had lived in Kensington and who became my best man and best friend until he died prematurely, and a solicitor named Rick, who like Neville hailed from Middlesbrough. We also had a singer-songwriter pal Johnny Stevens, who was down on his luck at the time and became our unofficial butler.

Of all the unbelievably riotous nights Neville and I enjoyed together, I suppose the most memorable was when we got nicked after the Snow Drop Ball at the Royal Albert Hall. This particular saga had started at lunchtime when I was whistling on the way up the steps to the *Daily Herald* building as the editor, Dick Dinsdale, happened to be walking in front of me. He suddenly stopped, turned round and demanded of me, 'Where's that bloody music coming from, cock?'

Startled, I replied: 'It's only me whistling, guv'nor.'

'Well, pack it in,' said Dick, 'I thought it was a bloody jukebox coming up the stairs.'

Dinsdale was a rough old diamond who always wore his trilby hat at a jaunty angle but whose bark was worse than his bite. Part of his notorious 'barking' image came from the fact that if he did not particularly like a story you submitted, he would simply scrawl 'All Balls' in big capital letters all over it, and then order you to write it again. But the soft side of him was that whenever Doug Long or his successor Ken James sent him a letter suggesting that I be sacked, he would simply take me to one side and growl: 'You'd better watch your drinking, cock.'

On the evening of the jukebox incident, our proprietors Odhams Press were holding the aforementioned Snow Drop Ball for charity and a dinner-suited Dinsdale was in attendance with editor-in-chief Lord Jacobson. Our sister paper the *Mirror* was organising the event and their showbusiness writer Don Short had invited my mate Neville and me, free of charge. He told us to turn up at the artistes' entrance to the Royal Albert Hall. What he had neglected to tell us, though, was to turn up sober.

Don let us in as arranged and then went off to attend to his business. Neville and I found ourselves in the corridor next to the dressing rooms. Imagine our delight when we opened one and found ourselves slap bang in the middle of that glamorous dancing troupe, the Tiller Girls. As I was chatting one of them up, they all began running and, still talking, I found myself in the wings of the stage as Frank Ifield was singing 'I Remember You'. A pub singer of some repute myself,

I naturally joined in and I was reliably informed later that Dinsdale went ape shit at the sight of 'that walking bloody jukebox' again.

I was soon ushered back to the safety of the dressing rooms where Neville and I somehow persuaded two of the Tiller Girls to allow us to escort them home, which they informed us was in the vicinity of St John's Wood. On the way, the taxi driver must have been eavesdropping and discovered that Neville and I were both financially embarrassed. Presumably fearing his fare would be unpaid, he drove straight up the rank of a nearby police station and deposited the pair of us there. Whereupon Neville, who sported horn-rimmed spectacles, wore pinstripe suits and therefore could look extremely respectable when sober, decided to straighten out this little misunderstanding. But he must have been slurring his speech pretty badly when he informed the policeman who had come out to greet us: 'Good evening, officer. I am Neville Hunter of the *Daily Sketch*, this is my colleague Peter Batt of the *Daily Herald* and these young ladies are the Tiller Girls.'

'Yes, and I'm bleedin' Napoleon,' replied the constable as he led us inside to meet the desk sergeant.

Believe it or not, a couple of nights later I was singing with the old flower girls in the 'Radio Arms' when Bill McLelland came over to me and said that Dick Dinsdale and Sidney Jacobson were at the other end of the bar and had told him to tell me that if I did not stop singing immediately, I would be fired on the spot, as they could not hear themselves speak. 'Mum', the landlady, heard this and promptly barred Dinsdale and Jacobson for upsetting her favourite customer. How I talked my way out of that tight corner God only knows, but I surely must have sensed then that the day or night would inevitably come when, as my old man would have said, 'Dolly would be done dancing.'

That day should have come when both men first caught sight of the outrageous expenses bill I presented the paper with for my coverage of the death of Sir Winston Churchill. The *Daily Herald*, whose circulation had been dwindling for years, had become the 'old' *Sun* by now as Odhams revamped it in a desperate bid to keep their famous paper alive. News came over on the agency tapes one bitterly cold evening that Churchill, the great statesman, the giant of history, the indestructible Winnie, was mortally ill at his London home in Hyde Park Gate, Kensington. I was immediately dispatched by Mick Rhind to do a doorstepping job in the middle of a freezing blizzard.

Although Sir Winston was just into his nineties, my gambling instincts told me that an old warrior like him would not depart this mortal coil in a hurry. In my first phone call from outside the great man's home, I managed to persuade Mick of this too, and suggested that I should book into the nearest hotel for the duration of my vigil. No sooner had I managed to clinch a hotel room than all my rivals on the other daily papers did the same. Fleet Street was soon ensconced in the plushest hotel in fashionable Kensington and it was not long before we were joined by the world's press and television.

It so happened that I had a date with Heidi that night, so I telephoned her to meet me at the hotel and when I signed the register, she happened to be standng beside me. Now Heidi never actually slept there, but the desk clerks must have assumed she was about to because unknown to me, he had marked the reservation down as Mr and Mrs Batt.

As I had anticipated, it took the old British bulldog

Winnie nine days and nights to die. And by then, practically everyone on my paper had visited the hotel for either a slap-up meal or a card school and drinks on the bill. It was not that we were disrespectful towards Churchill. In fact, because we were all of the wartime generation, it was the very reverse. But in Fleet Street boys had always been boys and the same went for the girls, too. However momentous this slice of history we were covering happened to be, it was still all in a day's work for us and that applied to all the 'visiting firemen' from the news room, the features department, the art department and whoever else had the slightest excuse for dropping in on us throughout these seemingly endless Kensington days and nights.

It was while covering this story that I earned another mention in the 'legends of Fleet Street' annals. Hyde Park Gate was bursting at the seams with journalists and television crews, but with Sir Winston's condition remaining critical but unchanged, there was very little in the daily bulletins for the press to get their teeth into in the way of copy.

Every evening, a Rolls-Royce driven by a lady in uniform pulled up outside the house and Sir Winston's physician Lord Moran disembarked. I say 'disembarked' but that is probably too virile a word to use. For Lord Moran, who seemed to me to be every bit as old as his patient, was, to say the least, not in the best physical shape himself. So much so that to me it looked as if it was going to be a photo-finish as to who went first, Sir Winston or his doctor.

'Tottered', then, would be a more accurate description of his Lordship's departure from the car. And when he had finished his examination, a policeman would help him to get back into the rear seat of the automobile, whereupon his legs would be covered with a rug and he would be driven away without a word being exchanged. We would then have to wait for a spokesman to appear later with a bulletin which said absolutely nothing except 'condition unchanged'. So, in desperation one night, I pushed myself to the front of the police cordon just before the car pulled away and through the still-open car door mouthed the words: 'Sinking fast is he, sir?' I had previously noticed that dear old Lord Moran was in the habit of nodding all the time in the back of the car, anyway. So when everyone behind me started screaming, 'What did he say, Batty? What did he say?' I took advantage of that old adage, 'A nod is as good as a wink,' and informed them that his Lordship had said that Sir Winston was 'sinking fast'. And that two-word headline appeared on the front of practically every newspaper around the world next morning.

In the event, it took the tough old so-and-so another four days to die and I was told on the grapevine much later that his widow, Lady Churchill, had not been too pleased to read that prognosis from his Lordship. It turned out that Lord Moran died not long after this, so the whole episode was thankfully laid to rest.

The whole episode, that is, except the little matter of my hotel bill. When it arrived at the *Sun* office some weeks later, I am told that messrs Jacobson and Dinsdale were so taken aback with the total amount that they instructed their hatchet man of a managing editor, Mr Andrew Mellor, to come down on me like the proverbial ton of bricks.

When I was called in to see Mr Mellor, he came up with an opening line I shall never forget: 'Taken to holidaying at home, have we, Mr Batt?' And when he threw the bill at me, it was as thick as a telephone book and had Mr and

Mrs Batt written in unmistakeable letters at the top of it. Now, like any self-respecting Stepney boy, I am definitely not a 'grass' by nature or intent, but there was nothing left in these dire circumstances but to plead not guilty and mistaken identity, and to point out that anyone who was anybody on the paper had availed themselves of the hotel's hospitality.

Mr Mellor then ordered me to go and rattle a begging bowl around the building and return to his office with considerable contributions from all these people that I had, naturally, refused to name. It was a week or more before I reported back to him with the princely sum of seventeen shillings and sixpence. But by then, even Sir Winston was history and it was simply a case of another day, another dollar and another written warning for yours truly.

My news desk pal Colin Hart, who, incidentally, is Jewish, was so knocked out by this story that when I married Heidi a few months later, he immediately invited us round to his house for dinner and to listen to a brand new LP record of Churchill's famous wartime speeches which had been brought out to commemorate the great man's demise. It completely slipped his mind that Heidi was German and she, poor girl, had to endure one of the most uncomfortable evenings of her life as she listened interminably to Winnie 'fighting them on the beaches', etc., etc.

CHAPTER ELEVEN
HEIDI

Heidi Maria Petmeki was born in 1943 in Berlin. Of Hungarian descent, her first days in war-torn Germany made my own brief experiences of the London Blitz seem like a vicarage tea party by comparison. After fleeing that ravaged capital city as an infant, she was brought up by nuns in early childhood in Bavaria and later lived in a children's home until the age of 12, when she was eventually reunited with her mother, elder twin brothers Reinhard and Gerhard, and her younger brother Hans Jurgen.

I became her 'knight in shining armour' – my fanciful words, not hers – when I rescued her from the clutches of a touchy, feely slob who was giving her a bad time on the dance floor of the aforementioned Rheingold Club. She was only 20 years old at that time, and had the beautiful face and figure of a graceful fawn at bay as she attempted to wriggle free of the unwanted attention she was receiving from this dancing bear. Her plaintive eyes happened to catch mine at my regular place at the bar and

I was smitten. Being a lifelong masochist, I made the snap decision to move in, tap her tormentor on the shoulder, say 'excuse me' and steel myself for a right-hander to the jaw. Thankfully, the guy departed without protest and I managed to shuffle Heidi around the floor until the music stopped.

We have been partners ever since and that was way back in 1964. She told me later that her friends warned her to have nothing whatever to do with me, and God only knows how many times she must have wished she had taken that advice during the 35 stormy years that have passed since our meeting. In May 1965, we were married at Tottenham Register Office when I was so skint that my brother Jim had to bung me the seven shillings and sixpence for the licence. He was in the process of moving into a new house at the time, so he decided to hold the piss-up there as a combined wedding reception and housewarming do. Everyone present agreed that there had never been a wedding knees-up quite like this one, which was attended by some of the hardest men in London and a host of Fleet Street reprobates. I remember overhearing one conversation in which a tipsy Anne Pacey asked a well-known ticket tout the way to the toilet and he replied: 'Dunno, darlin'. But when you find it, just mention my name and they'll give you the best seat in the house.'

In the time-honoured 'chauvinist pig' traditions of my upbringing, the blokes stayed in one group and the women had no choice but to congregate in another. I passed out and slept on the sofa with the best man, and poor Heidi walked the streets with her Austrian bridesmaid half the night wondering what sort of a crazy country this was. But having that teutonic tendency for attention to detail, she put matters right the following

July by insisting that I married her again in church in Germany, with all the trimmings.

We started married life in a one-bedroom top-floor flat in the seedier regions of Ladbroke Grove, which came as a terrible culture shock to Heidi, who had been an au pair girl in upmarket Hampstead. Our first child, Jenny, was born in 1966. That historic year, England won the World Cup, of course, and I remember thinking that with her touch of jaundice, Jenny was a dead ringer for Jimmy Greaves, who was, unforgivably, dropped by Sir Alf Ramsey while he was suffering from hepatitis.

It was a big year, in a footballing sense, for the fledgling Batt family, too. As Spurs were going through an indifferent spell after those heady days of the Double-winning team, I managed to break the White Hart Lane habit and started reporting Saturday football matches for the *Sunday People* as a freelance. It was not long before the *People* sports editor, Neville Holtham, offered me a job as his staff sportswriter in the Midlands, but there was a slight catch in that I had to own a car. As I did not possess the proverbial pot to piss in, this looked like being out of the question until I marched into the Covent Garden branch of the Westminister Bank and told the manager that although I had never yet had a bank account, I would now like to open one and borrow the money for a car. His first question was why did I not have my wages paid into a bank? Whereupon, in what I thought was all sincerity, I confessed that I was a compulsive gambler and drinker, but I was about to turn over a new leaf now that I was a husband and a father. Then out popped my white rabbit, when the manager casually asked me about the girl I was married to and when I said she was German, he said he was married to a German lady, too, and he agreed to lend me £600 to buy a brand new motor.

But such was the defective sense of direction in practically every area of my life that when we set off for Birmingham, Heidi, baby Jenny and me wound up in Nottingham instead. Worse was to come, though, when after eventually installing us in a tiny flat in Brum, I set out to make my first call at a football club in the area by introducing myself to Jimmy Hagan, the manager of nearby West Bromwich Albion. I had not reckoned with the mind-boggling mysteries of Spaghetti Junction, that jumble of flyovers and underpasses which, even for seasoned drivers, make Britain's second city such a nightmare to negotiate. Me? After about two dozen failed attempts to find the turn-off to West Bromwich, I let frustration get the better of me, pulled up next to a pub and got pissed instead. This was to set an unforgivably weak pattern of occasional criminal drunk-driving and not so infrequent bouts of totally reckless behaviour which was to lead me eventually into madness and near death. The only consolation was that I never killed anyone in the process, but this was due to God's grace and not mine.

For the immediate future, however, life was to be a laugh a minute and a thrill a minute in the mindless pursuit of instant gratification. The biggest thrill of those first few weeks in the Midlands was that I was to cover all the World Cup group matches in that area. The first of these happened to be the one and only time Heidi was ever to accompany me to a football match. It was between her own Germany and Argentina.

The Midlands area for which I was to be responsible was huge. It took in Aston Villa, Birmingham City, West Bromwich Albion, Wolverhampton Wanderers and Walsall in the west, Nottingham Forest, Notts County, Derby County, Leicester City and Peterborough in the east and Coventry City and Northampton Town in the south. And when it came to claiming the generous petrol allowance for mileage expenses, it was a licence to print money. Even a lorry driver would have been hard pressed to cover the ground my travels were scheduled to encompass each week.

My task was to analyse each hard news item and gobble up every crumb of gossip to come out of all or any of these famous old clubs. The main emphasis was on transfer news, which was a very big deal newspaper-wise in those days. I was also expected to write a Midlands column every week and, of course, do a Saturday match report, as well as attend midweek matches in a purely watching brief. In summer, I was also instructed to do likewise to cover Warwickshire, Worcestershire, Leicestershire, Derbyshire, Nottinghamshire and Northamptonshire county cricket clubs.

If I had not had such a predilection for visiting the Hall Green, Perry Barr, Kings Heath and Monmore dog racing stadiums, too, that new car would have been paid for in no time at all. As it was, I was soon forced to sell my gleaming Austin because of my gambling debts and to run around in a clapped-out old Triumph Herald, whose windows I kicked in on many a night when it would not start and eventually abandoned forever in a flooded car park.

Fortunately for Heidi and Jenny, my salary was enough to keep us in reasonable comfort in our rented flat, but she saw much less of me than she would have liked. She had the consolation of the other Midlands newspapermen's wives for company when it came to a bit of social life, but she was less than thrilled on one occasion when I had a rare night in and had to pop out in my carpet slippers to the pub over the road for a packet of cigarettes – only to get waylaid into an all-night poker school and not return until next morning.

How this beautiful guardian angel of a soulmate has continued to love me for as long as she has is one of life's deeper mysteries, and one for which I am truly grateful. But she had to give me some hard lessons along the way.

CHAPTER TWELVE
MIDLANDS

If moving from London to Birmingham came as something of a culture shock, it was as nothing compared to the astonishment which awaited me on my switch from news reporting to full-time sportswriting.

Until then, I had suffered from most fans' innocent misconception that, in their social lives, professional footballers would be, if not exactly choirboy types, then at the very least health-conscious fitness freaks. Imagine my amazement, then, when I discovered that most of them loved a drink, or two or three, and that a high percentage were out-and-out piss artists between matches. The advantage they enjoyed over the rest of us, of course, was that they could sweat out their hangovers in training. Theirs was the kind of lifestyle which would have suited me down to the ground – except for the training bit, of course. And I was even happier to learn that the hospitality at Midlands clubs was so warm and lavish that after midweek evening matches most of us reporters were not expected to crawl out of the various boardrooms and secretaries' and managers' offices until well into the wee small hours.

This free drinking became such a major part of our lives that on match days and nights the press corps would, more often than not, share a couple of cars and appoint one of our number as the non-drinking driver of each vehicle for the night. I sometimes wondered why I never drew the short straw for this tiresome chore. On sober reflection, I can see that the other lads could not trust me to lay off the sauce. Mind you, most of my press mates enjoyed the socialising every bit as much as me and, sadly, unlike me, some of them did not live to tell the tale. Of our little band of brothers, Alan Williams of the *Daily Express*, Peter Ingall of the *Daily Mirror*, Mervyn Thomas of the *Daily Mail* and John Moxley, the top Birmingham freelance all died young, although I must hasten to add, for fear of distressing their families, that booze probably never got a mention on the death certificates. Some did survive and prosper, of course, and among them were Jeff Farmer of the *Daily Sketch* and Bob Driscoll of the *Sun*, who are now Head of Football for Central Television and Sports News Editor of the *Daily Mail* respectively.

I make this point about football's drinking culture not to blow the whistle on my old sparring partners, but to underline the fact of how astonished we all were when I managed to get the *Sunday People* barred from all 92 English Football League clubs over a 'booze' story. Well, in fairness to the top brass who introduced the ban, it was not just a story but a series, running over three weeks, which featured the life and times of a hell-raising Birmingham City inside-forward named Bobby Thompson – not to be confused with a Wolves full-back of that name and of a slightly later era. Red-haired Scot Bobby told of drunken nights in pubs and clubs and even drunken performances on the pitch. He named names and teams and the Football League was so furious that the *Sunday People* was declared *persona non grata* – not just me, the by-lined ghostwriter of those pieces, but every man jack of the *People*'s reporting staff.

Today, similar revelations would scarcely raise an eyebrow, but in that so-called age of innocence it supposedly sent shockwaves down to the very toenails of all those high-minded officials.

It meant that *Sunday People* reporters, countrywide, had to buy a ticket to their matches and cover them from the stands and not the more convenient press boxes, which had all-important telephone facilities in those pre-mobile phone days. But they all suffered the inconvenience of the ban with such good grace that the *People* had neckties made especially to commemorate these unusual events, which had an inscription of a skull and crossbones and carried the slogan 'Banned by all 92'.

The ban was lifted after a season or so, but this series, along with a few other scoops which I came up with, earned me the nickname of 'naughty boy' among some of the more toffee-nosed League and club officials. I still enjoyed a wonderful cameraderie with most of the players, however. In those days there were no such animals as agents, so paying players simply to exchange opinions and personal details was not even dreamed of. Nor was the idea that footballers would become the millionaire pop star icons they are now.

As a sportswriter for a specific district, I was often with some players on an almost daily basis and we regarded each other as much more than mere 'contacts'. We enjoyed genuine friendships together and matched each other pint for pint. And these social get-togethers were not strictly confined to just press men, either. In the Spurs local, 'The Bell and Hare' in Tottenham High Road, for instance, such local heroes as Jimmy Greaves and Alan Gilzean could often be found drinking with the fans after matches. Today's stars strut their stuff in fashionable restaurants, nightclubs and catwalks, with paparazzi waiting on the pavements outside, and good luck to them. But I should imagine those ivory towers they inhabit with only a few, often ill-chosen, sycophants for company can be very lonely places at times.

The golden rule in the old days was that a sportswriter never broke a confidence. If we had revealed everything we had been told, we could have basked in glory for a day or two but it would have meant not only losing a personal friend but breaking a trust, which would have spread round all the dressing rooms in no time and left you out in the cold. Our bosses were often less than happy about this arrangement, of course, but they recognised the need for continuity and were selective about how much pressure they put on us to get stories. For most sports editors, it all depended on the worth of the story as opposed to the value of the contact. Some stories you just could not sit on, no matter what. I have a phrase for this kind of story and, for me, there is no other way to describe it. I call them 'Well, I'll be fucked' stories – the kind of revelations which have the reader choking on his toast and marmalade.

One such story which the *People* splashed exclusively all over its front page concerned the then captain of England's cricket team, Brian Close. In its own way, this tale was as sensational as the Eric Cantona scandal just a few years back. Cantona, you will remember, attacked a fan during a match at Selhurst Park by aiming a kung-fu kick at him and was banned from the game for several months.

In the 1960s, Close was skippering his native Yorkshire against Warwickshire at Edgbaston when he was barracked by the crowd for using deliberate go-slow tactics in the field. Beset by personal problems off the field at the time, Brian suddenly lost it and jumped into the members' enclosure, grabbed an elderly Warwickshire member by the throat and shook him like a rag doll. This sensational incident had gone mysteriously unreported in the newspapers – no doubt under the cricket writers' unofficial old pals' act. When I received a tip-off about it the day afterwards, I followed it up and found it was indeed true.

What I did not foresee was that it would cost Close the captaincy of the England cricket team, when the MCC stripped him of that title in the middle of a Test series. I am not and have never been a sadist and if I had known what the consequences would be, I would have agonised over filing the story. Proud Close was every inch a man's man and a particular hero of mine for the way he had stood up to the fearsome West Indies pace attack of Wes Hall and Charlie Griffith, stripping off for the newspapers to take pictures of his bruised and battered body to prove it. And from the point of view of personal safety, I can distinctly remember wincing in anticipation of what he could do to me when, soon afterwards, I saw him fielding, without a helmet, a few yards from the bat, at silly mid-on and being struck on the forehead by a full-blooded hook shot from the batsman. Not only did he not go down, this teak-tough Yorkshireman simply shook his head and moved forward two paces.

That story summed up the downside of being a newspaperman, the part which meant you were never going to win a popularity contest for doing your job. And it also explains the memorable off-the-record quote which

Noel Cantwell once gave me. Cantwell, the former West Ham full-back, was manager of Coventry at the time of our conversation, and he recalled that while he was starring for Manchester United towards the end of his playing career, he was being groomed by Sir Matt Busby to take over the managerial reins at Old Trafford one day. According to Noel, in the list of 'dos and don'ts' which Sir Matt had drawn up for him, the great man advised: 'Treat the press the way you would treat a policeman.'

Well, if I was a policeman, men like Stan Cullis, Johnny Carey and Matt Gillies, who were the managers of Wolves, Nottingham Forest and Leicester City respectively during my stint on their patch, were definitely my chief inspectors. In contrast to the 'in your face' attitudes of many young people nowadays, thirty-somethings, as I then was, were expected to respect middle-aged men like those three esteemed managers. Cullis, once a legendary England centre-half and manager of the fabulous long-passing Wolves team of the late 1950s, even took it so far as to have me standing to attention with my thumbs down the seams of my trousers whenever he was giving me a 'rollicking' – Stan's own choice of word, incidentally, because I never heard him swear.

But he came up with plenty of 'flippings' and 'floppings' during his frequent admonishments. I'm sure Stan, who revelled in his newspaper nickname of the 'Master of Molineux' before he left Wolves to take over Birmingham City, regarded us young press men as members of his team. And I thought that, in addition to bursting a blood vessel, he was sure to place me on the transfer list the day I published what he thought was his 'top secret' list naming the players he intended to sell that coming close season.

One young manager who was to go on and earn a

similarly abrasive reputation for himself was Brian Clough. 'Old big 'ead', as Clough later became so famously known, was the fledgling young boss of Derby County at that time when they were still in the lower divisions. A publicity conscious young man, Brian got me into plenty of trouble one day when he rang my boss, Neville Holtham, in London to complain: 'I bet Batty puts Derby on his mileage exes on a regular basis,' and when Neville confirmed that indeed I did, Brian rasped: 'Well, that big bugger hasn't been near nor by here in weeks.' It was ironic, then, that obtaining an interview with Cloughie, some 20 years on, without paying for it, was almost as difficult as gaining an audience with the Queen.

Another manager who felt he had grounds to gripe about me in those days was Jimmy Hill, who was in charge of Coventry City. The first time he agreed to see me, shortly after my arrival in the area, he chose the strange venue of his local hairdresser's shop. As I fired off my questions, Jimmy was having his beard trimmed with his back to me in the manner of a Hollywood mafia don. Some months later, he telephoned me at home to complain about something I had written about his team in my weekly column. When I tried to persuade him that newspaper comments were all just part of the general football entertainment industry, he published my remarks in Coventry's next match programme and held them up to ridicule. Another irony, that, from someone who was to go on to get his living from television.

Little slings and arrows like these were nowhere near upsetting enough to spoil my overall enjoyment of this wonderful new way of life, however. Especially when I began making regular trips to different European countries with some of the Midlands teams. On one such trip, I came into contact with the real-life mafia, rather than the Jimmy Hill version of it, when the West Brom team and their accompanying press mates got a little too raucous in an after-match nightclub celebration in Bologna and the local don had to answer an SOS to send a couple of minders to cast a watchful eye over us. But the thing I remember most about that trip is sipping onion soup in a cafe at Bologna railway station with the West Brom and England winger Clive 'Chippy' Clarke, and him telling me all about the five babies he and his wife had lost prematurely, while tears streamed down our cheeks.

As you get older, it is the emotional moments in life which stick most in your mind. I can't remember a single detail about the match itself except that Helmut Haller of the West German 1966 World Cup team was playing for Bologna, but I shall never forget poor Chippy's personal despair. If he happens to read these lines, I can only hope and pray that he and his wife were eventually blessed with children.

It was around this time that my second child, Danny, was born. Despite my wife's mild protests, I named the boy after the skipper of the 1961 Spurs Double team. Danny Blanchflower was the only footballer I ever met who could talk and write about the game as imaginatively as he played it, although Charlie Cooke, that great Chelsea and Scotland ball artist, was also an intellectual conversationalist on any subject he cared to discuss. I was to become quite pally with Danny in later life when he wrote for the *Sunday Express* and managed Chelsea for a brief spell. He and I even appeared in a film together which was called *Those Glory Glory Days* and was written by the first woman football writer, Julie Welch, who then worked for the *Observer*. Rather appropriately, I was seen in the film taking a leak in the men's toilet at White Hart Lane.

When my son was born in hospital in Solihull, I remember thinking – no disrespect to my Brummie mates – that 'Birmingham-born Danny Batt' in the programme notes would take a bit of explaining away by his cockney old man when he made his England debut. But it was nearly a lot more complicated as he was only a day or two away from being born in Germany.

Daniel's birth and the circumstances surrounding it bring back some very shamefaced memories for me. He was born in August 1967, just after the Arab–Israeli Six-Day War. I remember that dramatic conflict took place that summer because I happened to be on a tour of Scandinavia with Aston Villa at the time and the papers were, understandably, full of it. It had been pre-arranged with Heidi that as soon as Villa's tour was over, I should proceed by boat and train to Berlin, where she was on holiday with her family and our 18-month-old daughter, Jenny. Having been cleaned out by some very shrewd Villa card sharps, I found myself in the not unusual state of suffering from a hangover and being virtually skint when I waved my football pals goodbye in Copenhagen. Fortunately, the boat and train tickets had already been purchased and I had only to survive one night in a hotel before setting out next evening for Berlin. Unfortunately, I had a few too many that night and could only pay the hotel bill via a 'useless' National Westminster Bank cheque, because at that time there was no such thing as a Euro cheque and there was a strict limit on the amount of money you could take from England into Europe. I was already well and truly over the top of my allowance. I can still see the hotel manager's angry countenance as he threw me out into the street the next morning and, worse, the look of anguish on the poor old night porter's walrus-moustachioed face as the manager sacked him on the spot for accepting my well-intentioned but worthless cheque in advance.

That next day, a Saturday, I wandered around Copenhagen potless, peering enviously into the windows of delightful looking bars and restaurants and wondering how I would possibly survive this day and the following two days of the journey without food and, worse, without a drink. As the day wore on, however, I noticed that the pavements were becoming packed with people and as I looked for somewhere to park my bags, there on the steps of one of the best hotels in the city stood a whole line of white rabbits in the shape of a group of British press men and women who happened to be covering that day's royal wedding between a Spanish prince and a Danish princess. Naturally, I made myself busy borrowing money from them left, right and centre, choosing to ignore a few feeble protestations that they were all on this ridiculous overseas limited-expenses deal. So it was one very happy, well fed and watered bunny who joined his wife, daughter and in-laws in Berlin 48 hours later. It shames me to say this now, but I soon gambled away what was left of the money I had borrowed at the horse-trotting meeting at Mariendorf race track, so I decided to set off for home early and leave Heidi there for a few more days. Stony broke when I arrived back at our flat in Stratford Road, Birmingham, my gambler's antennae picked up the scent of money as soon as I walked through the front door. It was lying on the doormat in a brown envelope and was a cheque for £25 from the government to purchase a pram. Down to the post office I went to cash this princely sum, which was about a week's wages then. I was met with arguments from the counter clerk that only the mother could cash this State handout. Using all my powers of persuasion, I eventually left the premises with five crisp £5 notes and promptly lost them all at Hall Green dog track.

I am afraid that these confessions do not get any better. For when Heidi arrived a few days later and Danny was born almost immediately, I was up in Manchester having an after-match drink-up with Malcolm Allison, Noel Cantwell and a few other footballing mates. Still, at least Heidi had brought her mother with her this time, who, although she could not speak a word of English and I could not understand German, managed to give me a bigger bollocking than ever Stan Cullis did. But such was my weird alcoholic personality that I was happy to be getting told off for my sins, because that seemed to ease my guilty conscience. Perversely, getting away with it always made me feel worse.

However, I must admit that I met my match and more the day I foolishly agreed to a drinking contest with 'Slim Jim' Baxter, one of the greatest wing-halves Scotland ever produced, and that includes Dave Mackay and Billy Bremner. Baxter, who was in decline by then, had just signed for Nottingham Forest for £100,000 – big money in those days – and I had got the story exclusively for the *People*. On his arrival in the Midlands, Jim had soon got to hear about my drinking exploits but when he and I agreed to meet at his new home only two days before he was due to play in an an FA Cup tie, I assumed I would be in reasonably sober company.

Not a bit of it. For no sooner had his beautiful wife cleared the lunch dishes than this ultra-competitive football genius saw me to the door and, out of her earshot, suggested that he and I go for a few bevvies.

The choice and the measure of his tipple first astonished and then shipwrecked me. It was medium sherry and it came in schooners. After a pub and club crawl which went on through the rest of that day and most of the night, I was ill for 48 hours and was still suffering from a throbbing head and heaving stomach when I marked him a top eight out of ten and man of the match two days later.

At the time of the Baxter transfer, the Nottingham Forest committee was chaired by Tony Wood, a hatchet-faced dictator who later joined the board of Arsenal. He despised the press, especially me, because of the stories I kept getting from Forest without his consent or knowledge. So when Forest travelled to play a European match in Germany, he banned me from the team coach – for we used to travel on the same coach as the players in those days, as well as staying at the same hotels.

But such was the 'million-dollar' back-up I got from my boss Neville Holtham that I was instructed by my paper to hire a chauffeur-driven Cadillac and stay right behind the coach at all times, to show that the *People* were no poor relations to anyone. To top that all off, it turned out that my room in the hotel, which was booked separately from the main party's, was the only one with a mini-bar in it. You can imagine how popular that made me with the Forest players and, of course, my press mates.

The biggest surprise I got, from the football point of view, during my two-year stint in the Midlands came when I covered an FA Cup semi-final between Nottingham Forest and Spurs at Hillsborough in 1967. Most of the Forest players had become great friends of mine, but I still found the old allegiance to Spurs too difficult to break free of and it was the Lilywhites I was secretly rooting for from the neutrality of the press box. It was to stay like that with Spurs throughout my career, despite the close links I was to form with many of the other London clubs. Spurs went on to beat Chelsea 2–1 in the final that year, which

I was lucky enough to cover as a leg man for the *People*'s number one writer Maurice Smith. And the run-up to this match was to bring me my first encounter with Tommy Docherty. The Doc and I were to become bosom pals, but on the first occasion I ever spoke to him, he pretended to be his father, who was long since dead. I rang him at his home to arrange a pre-Cup final interview at the team's hotel and, as he did not know me from Adam at that time and had no great desire to speak to me, he put on a false, faltering voice and told me it was Mr Docherty senior speaking and that he had no idea where his son Tommy was or when he would next be home. That was a typical Docherty stroke and we had a giggle or two about it in the years to come when I always found that his irrepressible nature and black sense of humour made him one of the most entertaining drinking companions the game had to offer.

I was to be at the Wembley final again the following year, too, this time with West Brom when they beat Everton 1–0 with a goal from Jeff Astle. Going to Wembley with one of the teams as their local district man was a great experience, as it meant attending your club's Cup final banquet and sharing either the celebration or the wake with the players, which invariably made great copy for your newspaper. For the press boys, the big day itself was always preceded by a monstrous 72-hour annual piss-up, the highlight of which was the Football Writers' Dinner which included the Footballer of the Year presentation. Our Midlands mob always stayed *en masse* at the Kenilworth Hotel near the British Museum in Bloomsbury and close to the Great Russell Hotel which was favoured by Sir Matt Busby and his chairman, Louis Edwards, whenever Manchester United were in London.

That West Brom–Everton post-match piss-up provided

me with more than a few anxious moments. After the banquet, most of us wound up in the swanky Astor Club in Berkeley Square, Mayfair, courtesy of my brother Jim, who did a bit of unofficial minding there in those days. 'Sulky', the club's famous master of ceremonies, had helped the players dispose of their surplus tickets on the black market and then had the nerve to turn some of them away at the door when they arrived in the wee small hours because he said he was full up.

After we had managed to straighten out this little misunderstanding, the first editions of the *People* turned up and I had to buy up the lot of them and stick them under my arse on my seat for the entire celebration, so that the WBA manager, a very nice man named Alan Ashman, did not get a peek at it. For all over the back page was scrawled the headline: 'I'll Never Kick Another Ball for Albion' by Bobby Hope. Hope, a tiny ball-playing Scotsman, was the team's playmaker and there were he and I coming out with this exclusive bombshell of a transfer request on the very morning after his team had won the FA Cup.

Needless to say, I did not share the train back to Birmingham with either the team or the officials next day and, thankfully, I had the entire close season in which to lie low. But as it happened, I did not have to face them again because Neville Holtham decided to offer me a job in the *People*'s London office.

CHAPTER THIRTEEN
PEOPLE

When I returned to London, I was a 35-year-old married man with two young children. The spoilt, immature side of my typically Gemini split-personality was excited by the prospect of an existence which stretched out before me like an adventure playground. I would not have changed lifestyles with anyone.

Yet, paradoxically, discontented thoughts of mortality, failure and decay kept seeping up from my subconscious. On sharing these thoughts and feelings with some of my contemporaries, we reached the conclusion that these strange emotions were commonplace for men who had reached the halfway mark in the generally accepted lifespan of three score years and ten. I was to learn much later, though, that these were also the typical thoughts and feelings of a practising alcoholic.

This temporary preoccupation with death and despondency obviously had its roots in the fact that I had recently lost my beloved sister Vi, who had died from breast cancer at the age of 39. I remember feeling desperately cheated that during Vi's last, almost unendurable days in hospital, my mother and my brothers and me had been prevented from holding her in our arms and telling her how much we loved her and that she, poor girl, had been unable to do the same to us. It does not seem possible now that only 30 years ago conventional attitudes towards cancer and death were so unenlightened that so many of us were afraid to even speak either of those dreaded words to each other when they applied to us or our loved ones. On our visits to the hospital, we played out this painful charade of pretending – us to her and she to us – that she would be coming home soon and then going off on holiday somewhere, when she was only days away from leaving us forever.

After my sister died, my mother was never the same woman. She seemed to shrivel up and harden inside. Her life turned full circle when she went to live in a flat with an outside loo, where she survived for almost another three decades, but her home was no longer the spiritual haven to which the Batt family all migrated from far and near in times of joy and sadness. As for me, I was selfishly sad that my children had been deprived of what would have been a wonderfully loving aunt.

On a more pragmatic level, I had to solve the problem of finding a home for my family. And after a couple of experiments in rented accommodation, Heidi and I settled for a £6,000 town house in Ewell, near Epsom, which appealed to me because I had heard that the Epsom stable lads frequented the pubs in the area and passed on information – most of it dud, as I later found out at considerable cost.

One man from whom I was definitely not going to get any information – for neither love nor money – was Alf Ramsey, the England manager, whose shadow hung over every young football reporter's life like some dark angel of Nemesis. Although Alf had a few trusted pals among the senior football reporters, guys who had enjoyed a working relationship with him during his playing days such as Reg Drury, Laurie Pignon and Desmond Hackett, young upstarts like myself were looked down upon by him as nothing more than out-and-out pests to be swatted accordingly. Once, I was summoned to the great man's presence to receive a bollocking over something which I had written and as his rage subsided, I decided to press my luck by trying to get a little bit of exclusive news out of him.

I began my counter-attack by saying: 'I'm not trying to get round you, Alf, but . . .'

At that, he spluttered: 'You will never get round me young man – never in a month of fucking Sundays.'

Another young colleague received an even more withering put-down once when, in front of a gathering of us young hacks, he began his post-match questioning of the great man with what turned out to be this aborted preface:

'I play football every Sunday, Alf, and . . .'

Alf fixed my little mate with a stare which suggested he was something the cat had just brought in, and then said: 'Is that wise?'

Obviously, none of us could be anything other than respectful of Alf's unique achievements. But whenever he came on high and mighty, I consoled myself by visualising this description of him which was relayed to me by his old Spurs and England team-mate Eddie Baily, who said: 'When Spurs won the league in 1951, the thing I remember most about our celebration party was the sight of Alf sitting on the loo, scoffing a sausage roll.'

Fortunately for the likes of me, most of the players of

that era did not take their images as seriously as Alf, and many of them made great drinking companions, which was just as well because one of my specific jobs on the *People* was to keep their glasses filled as I pumped them for info for my 'Soccer Chatter' column. This column was dedicated to every last dot and comma of transfer market news, in which our readers were assumed to be intensely interested, and which I was expected to discover.

I did this by accompanying that old ex-Charlton folk hero of a goalkeeper, red-haired Geordie Sam Bartram on the rounds of the London clubs' training grounds, where we invariably had a few drinks with some of the players.

This kind of behaviour made Sam and me very unpopular with managers, who guarded their transfer secrets as zealously as some latterday Government ministers guarded their own sleazy ones, but it endeared us to the players because, like most human beings and certainly like most newspapermen, many of them enjoyed nothing more than to gossip about the comings and goings of the other people in their little world. But this was the aspect of my new job that I utterly detested, especially when it led to men like West Ham manager Ron Greenwood, whom I had first known in my *Stratford Express* days, telling me that his main ambition was to keep his name and his team out of my newspaper. Millwall manager Benny Fenton, a player whom I had hero-worshipped as a boy, once regaled me in a corridor in front of several of my colleagues, telling me that I crawled under doors and listened at keyholes. I still don't know how I kept my hands off the little sod, but if I had whacked him it would have meant not just an early bath but a premature end to my career.

On the plus side, however, some of the players who befriended me back then became managers themselves, a situation which led to much valued long-term friendships for me. Among them were Terry Venables, George Graham and Joe Kinnear. I can think of no other job in the world which could have opened the door to this kind of privilege for a one-time East End tearaway. Nevertheless, I constantly begged Neville Holtham to get rid of this embarrassing gossip stuff and to let me write a more modern, idiosyncratic column in its place. The main reason for this, although I did not admit it to Neville, was that to do this kind of work which required a revelation one week and a reconciliation the next, a man needed a skin as thick as a rhinoceros. I had him on the verge of agreeing with me until the paper commissioned some market research and found that the most widely read feature in our entire publication was, would you believe, 'Soccer Chatter'. I was summoned to the office of Bob Edwards, the editor, where I was congratulated and given a pay rise. When, little more than a year later, I told Bob I was leaving to join a daily paper, despite the offer of a car to persuade me to stay, I puzzled him by insisting that 'Soccer Chatter' was my main reason for leaving. It was the one and only time an editor was ever to ask me not to leave him!

As it turned out, letting me go was probably the best day's work Bob Edwards ever did for the *People*. For in addition to all my other character defects, there was something in my make-up which made me flip the moment I went up the stairs of an aeroplane – not an entirely desirable trait for an occupation which demanded an inordinate amount of travel. The sense of anticipation, the unrealistic expectations of adventure and the thought of entering into the unknown filled me with the unrestrained excitement of a kid at Christmas. With the benefit of hindsight, I now realise that I really needed the in-flight booze to bring me down and steady my nerves rather than to lift me to greater heights of exhilaration, as I thought it would do. For travelling with a group of people when you were about to become the unelected judge and jury of their performances and behaviour would have tested the nerves of the most thick-skinned individual, which, when sober, I most definitely was not. Only a fool could imagine that you could criticise sportsmen and women in print and not strain your friendship with them as a result. The price I and my sportswriting colleagues had to pay for this good life – and presumably our younger successors still do – was that as the go-betweens of our bosses' insatiable appetite for newspaper-selling controversy, to maintain the cameraderie we enjoyed with people whom we sometimes hero-worshipped required the balancing skills of a tightrope walker.

Possibly the greatest hero of them all, as far as I was concerned, was the late, great Bobby Moore. I had known Bobby since my *Stratford Express* days when, as a teenager, he replaced another wing-half who died young, John Smith, who had just been transferred to Spurs. On my first ever full England trip, to Belgium in February 1970, skipper Bobby took me by the arm and introduced me to every one of the northern players whom, at that stage of my career, I did not yet know on a personal level, and told them: 'This is my mate, Batty. He's one of the best. Look after him and give him any help he needs.' And this was a man whom many people, who did not know better, wrongly imagined had the same cool, calculating personality in his day-to-day life that he displayed on the pitch.

But if the England trips, lorded over by the disciplinarian Sir Alf, were understandably serious affairs, the annual close season England Under-23 tours were altogether more relaxed and offered ideal opportunities for ravers like me to have a right old jolly-up. Readers were not biting their fingernails over the results of these matches, but our sports editors knew they were ideal for making contacts with the younger stars which would come in more than useful for the paper in years to come, and were therefore willing to foot the bill for us. And indeed, it was on tours like this that I first struck up friendships with the likes of Kevin Keegan and Mick Channon who, along with Alan Ball, Peter Osgood and Peter Shilton, became horse racing buddies of mine. Mick Channon and his England team-mate Frannie Lee both became successful trainers of racehorses, of course, and provided me with some winning information on occasions.

As most of us press men were at least one generation older than the Under-23 stars, we never looked to lead them astray at the drinking game. But there was plenty of opportunity for that in each other's company. One Under-23 tour which sticks in my memory for the strange variety of the venues as well as the variety of off-field mischief was one I made for the *People* to Belgium, Holland and Madeira. England played Belgium in Ostend, which was almost home from home but whenever I travelled anywhere, I still had that wide-eyed wonderment of the cockney kid who had never expected to wander further north than the Watford Pump in his entire life. Not so for the man from *The Times*, David Miller. David was always impeccably dressed, except that he neglected to wear socks and always reminded me of the 'Great White Hunter'. The match against Belgium was due to kick off on Sunday evening; but on Saturday night I heard David casually ordering a taxi to take him from our hotel to the airport. When I asked him why, he astonished me by replying: 'Oh, I'm popping home for Sunday lunch tomorrow, I've got some guests coming.' For all my so-called devil-may-care reputation, I would not have had the bottle to be that laid-back in a million years. But David caught the Silver Arrow flight from Ostend to Southend and was back next afternoon in plenty of time for the kick-off. He earned my wide-eyed admiration for that piece of cool.

David was even cooler than this when we moved on to Holland and I set our wooden hotel on fire through smoking in bed. This was a careless, dangerous and, I now realise, unforgivable habit of mine when I retired for the night in an inebriated state, and I usually compounded this little crime by lighting up the moment I woke up as well. On this particular occasion, I crawled out of bed in the morning with my customary hangover for company, splashed some water on my face, slipped on a pullover, a pair of trousers, shoes and socks and left the room without looking behind me. It was only when I returned from my head-clearing walk that I saw Miller in earnest conversation with the irate hotel manager. It seemed that I had set light to the sheets, blankets and carpet before the room maid discovered the flames and raised the alarm. In my absence, David, who was the unofficial leader of our press party, had sweet-talked the manager out of having me arrested, but had agreed that my paper would meet the damages. The result was that for months letters were being sent from Holland to the *People* and to the Football Association calling for my blood and Dutch money. I can't remember how this little problem was resolved except that I did not get the sack for it. But I was soon going to be claiming my expenses from a different Father Christmas, in the shape of that most famous of all media moguls, Rupert Murdoch. He was about to start a new newspaper – and I was to be asked to join.

CHAPTER FOURTEEN
SUN

For every journalist who was in any way professionally responsible for the birth of the *Sun* on a November night in 1969, it was like first having to endure the pains of labour and then experiencing the exhilaration of being born again.

I cannot speak for the printers, or the advertising and circulation departments, but journalistically we were a bunch of mavericks and misfits. No one who was holding down a top job on any other newspaper was likely to throw in his or her lot with the Australian pirate Murdoch who had pillaged the title for peanuts. And all those level-headed Fleet Street people who had resisted his blandishments to join in the adventure appeared to have had their judgements well and truly vindicated when this much-heralded, 'bold, brash' newcomer hit the breakfast tables next morning with all the exuberance of a lead balloon. If our infant publication was not exactly still-born, it was certainly malformed, but that did not stop us from loving it.

Not that any of us was surprised at its less than triumphant entry into the world. For while the paper was still in the preparation stage, the cynical prediction already rampaging around the office was that you would be able to spot a *Sun* punter on sight because his lips would be moving while he was reading it. The reality turned out to be worse than that: no one on the staff could read it without moving their lips either.

That first edition was such a mish-mash of misprints, hopelessly inadequate edition times and ill-prepared stories and features that most of us would have offered odds of at least 100–1 that we would survive for much longer than a month. Typical of this slapdash approach was that I investigated and then wrote up the historic front page splash about a horse-doping scandal while I was still serving my notice on and being paid by the *People*.

But the incredible story of the rise and rise of the soaraway *Sun* has been told elsewhere, so I shall restrict myself to a spot of hubristic musing along the lines of who would have believed that within a few years of its conception, proprietor Rupert was to become the most powerful media tycoon on the planet, editor Larry Lamb was to be knighted and I was to win the Sportswriter of the Year award?

That first night will live in my memory for ever. Murdoch himself created the perfect egalitarian atmosphere by turning up on the editorial floor in shirtsleeves and providing us with barrels of free beer which we guzzled as we worked. There was a cameraderie and comradeship which humankind's herd instincts seem to find so comforting, be it in belonging to a nation or a neighbourhood, a political party or a football team, and there was that feeling which, for me, always surpassed any other of being in at the beginning. It had been this existentialist prospect of living your working life a day at a time which attracted me to newspapers in the first place. But, sadly, it was not long before the uglier, power-driven side of all such organisations prevailed.

A strange paradox about essentially creative industries like the newspaper business is that they are run on despotic lines whereby the editor and his cohorts are given the power to indulge their egos and exercise their personal whims and fancies in much the same way as the dictator of a banana republic. And within months of taking over the *Sun*, editor Larry Lamb had decided that this was his baby and no one else's. He was to go on to claim much of the credit for turning it into the publishing phenomenon it eventually became, and on the rare occasions he addressed any of us on a personal level, he was in the habit of using archaic, insulting words like 'insolent' to describe our behaviour if he thought we were being less than respectful to him. Still, I am told I had Larry to thank when I was made number one football writer 'on merit' after being number two to an older, well-respected colleague and friend, Steve Richards, who quit just a few weeks into the new enterprise. And this appointment was to provide me with the happiest two years of my life to date.

I find it hard to credit how I could be so excited and fulfilled by being in a job which kept me from sleeping in my own bed for at least three or four nights of any given week. It was not as if I had some dragon of a missus to contend with at home. Almost everyone who came into contact with Heidi remarked on her beauty and her caring personality. And absolutely everyone who met her and also knew me well would say they could not imagine why she put up with me and my unpredictable antics.

But, supremely selfishly, I thought I had it all. We had

moved upmarket by a couple of thousand pounds into a new town house in Sydenham, south London, which, as was to be the case with all our many house moves, Heidi chose without the knowledge that the reason I was so keen on the location was because it was very near Catford dog track – as if I was not already away from home enough in the evenings! We had two of the prettiest, sweetest-natured children any man could wish for, and we had made friends with quite a few of the neighbours. I was convinced I truly loved my wife and kids, but, to my subsequent shame, I obviously did not yet know how to love or even to give. For whenever I was home, I would sit on the edge of a chair yearning to be out and about again. If I was not suffering from some kind of soul sickness, I was definitely addicted to excitement and must have had a desperate need for recognition and fame and fortune of some kind or another. Maybe I was a 'wannabe' celebrity without ever admitting it to myself.

If life could get any better than this it was only in my dreams, when I sometimes scored a hat-trick for England against Scotland at Hampden Park, or had the world heavyweight champion helpless at my feet in Madison Square Gardens. And, come the buds of May 1970, I was beside myself with excitement at the prospect of what the night porters of South America would make of me and the more unruly of my newspaper mates when I set out on a seven-week journey through Colombia, Ecuador and on to Mexico for the World Cup finals. In the supremely well enunciated words of Frank Sinatra, that guv'nor to top all guv'nors, this kid from Stepney was about to 'beat the birds down to Acapulco Bay' on the coat tails of Sir Alf Ramsey and his all-conquering English robots – although, in glorious defeat, they were to turn out to be far from the automatons we believed them to be and became, without doubt, the best team England have ever had.

To give younger readers an idea of how magical this kind of travelling was then, I must point out that when I first started flying in the 1950s it was still such a novelty that we got suited and booted in our Sunday best to flirt with the beautiful, hand-picked air hostesses. By 1970 the garb had changed to casual shirts, flared trousers and platform-heeled shoes. But the package holiday boom was still a few years away, so those of us lucky enough to be embarking on this exotic sporting adventure must have been envied by almost every young man in England.

In those days we were expected to write mini travelogues as well as sports reports. But none of us could have topped the great Desmond Hackett when, a decade earlier, he had written in the *Daily Express*: 'Dateline: somewhere over the equator – Monday, Tuesday or Wednesday. I know where I am, but because of the time differences, I don't know what day it is.' Des neglected to mention that the in-flight booze might have had something to do with his feeling of disorientation. But even this piece of journalistic flamboyance could not compare with the style and panache which earlier cricket scribes and boxing writers must have oozed as they circumvented the globe by ship, travelling to cover fights in America on the *Queen Elizabeth*, no less.

Many of the sportswriters I travelled the world with then became bosom pals of mine, which was very understandable when you consider that we spent as much, if not more of our time together than we did with our own families. But in Bogotá, the capital of Colombia, we nearly met our collective Waterloos. More than one of us, yours truly included, were to receive cables telling us that we were about to be fired. We had run slap bang into one of the biggest news stories of the decade when Bobby Moore was arrested and jailed on a charge of stealing a bracelet from a jewellery shop. Or, more accurately, we should have run into it, but Fleet Street's finest were nowhere to be seen during the whole fantastic episode.

With the exception of my old cockney mate Vic Railton of the London *Evening News* who had gone down with a stomach bug at the time of Bobby's arrest and incarceration we were guzzling free beer on a coach which was taking us on a courtesy trip to some ancient caves to see the actual concrete slab on which the Aztecs or Incas (I was too pissed to remember which) once carried out their gruesome human sacrifices. The bracelet incident happened on the day after England had beaten Colombia 4–0 in a friendly and we had all been frisked for guns as we entered the stadium. We had already cabled our follow-up stories on the match and were about to embark on a plane that evening for Mexico City.

The first hint I had that anything was amiss was just after take-off when Vic, who was sitting behind me on the plane, tapped me on the shoulder and said: 'Don't get too excited, Batty, but if you start counting the heads on this flight, you will discover that one very famous blond one is missing.'

I could not believe what Railton was telling me when he recounted the details of what had happened to Bobby back there. But knowing him as well as I did, I could believe dear old Vic's explanation that he had swallowed doing the story exclusively because his bottle had gone when it came to being stuck in Bogotá on his own. As a newsgetter, dear old Vic had no peer – he had more reliable contacts and pals in the game than the rest of us put together. But turning himself into a foreign correspondent was not his game. He dreaded going out of town, never mind out of the country, and fish and chips were much more his cup of tea than chilli con carne.

But his tip-off sent a chill down my spine when I heard it. We were five hours' flying time from Mexico City and I knew that, by now, the news would have got back to London via the agencies and that we would not get a sniff of it for six more hours at least. When I passed on these terrible tidings to the other press men, some of us held a little wake on the aeroplane knowing that our jobs were almost certainly doomed. Worse, when we arrived in Mexico City local stringers were awaiting the plane's arrival to get reaction from Ramsey and the rest of the team and, to our collective chagrin, filling the rest of us in on the story, which was already appearing in the English newspapers by now.

Also waiting for me in my hotel room was a lengthy cable from my sports editor Frank Nicklin telling me that Larry Lamb was demanding my instant dismissal and that he, Lamb, was also accusing the football writers of sitting on the story to protect their pal Bobby. I could not help thinking how I had once broken a front page story that the nation's cricket writers must have agreed to suppress when I got poor old Brian Close the sack. And I considered the truth of that old maxim, live by the sword, die by the sword.

But it was the next part of the cable which bothered me even more, as Nicklin insisted that the only way I could redeem myself was to get on the next plane back to Bogotá and interview Moore while he was under arrest.

'This is just typical of desk men,' I stormed back at him over the phone. 'Bogotá happens to be a day's journey away, not round the bloody corner.' And I added that I was convinced Bobby was innocent and would be back with the team in a matter of hours.

Wrong again! It was a week before Bobby rejoined us and the trumped-up charge was dropped and revealed for what it was – a publicity stunt by the jewellery shop owner.

This tale has a humorous little sting in it, however, in a wickedly funny crack Bobby's fun-loving first wife, Tina, made to me at a party on the eve of England's homecoming. I happened to show Tina the ring I had bought for my wife and she asked me how much I had paid for it. Then when I told her, she quipped: 'You shouldn't have spent all that on it – Bobby could have flogged it to you for half the price. That's his game, jewellery, innit?'

My drinking playmates in Mexico, in addition to my press colleagues, included such great footballers as Tommy Docherty, Billy Bremner, Johnny Giles, Charlie Cooke and Terry Hennessey, who were all there as spectators, and David Sadler, who had been one of the six players Ramsey had been forced to 'send home' from his original squad of 28. Brian Kidd, the current Blackburn manager, had also failed to make that cruel cut, along with none other than the fanatically dedicated goalkeeper Peter Shilton, whom I used to phone when he was a teenager at Leicester only for his mum, invariably to quip: 'You'll have to hold on a minute, he's hanging up by the bannister stretching his arms.' And she wasn't joking, either.

The sickest of all the jokes the sporting gods had ever laid at the feet of England's football followers was when Shilton's former Leicester goalkeeping mentor, Gordon Banks, was laid low by a stomach bug on the eve of the England v West Germany quarter-final. Having been beaten only 1–0 by Brazil thanks to that most famous of all Banks's saves from Pelé, England were favourites to dispose of the Germans and to go on to meet the Brazilians again in the final. That they did not was largely due to the fact that Banks's deputy Peter Bonetti, the Chelsea 'Cat', had an uncharacteristic stinker of a game as Gordon's eleventh-hour replacement between the sticks.

I have never been more upset by the result of a football match than I was by Germany's 3–2 win after extra time in the scorching heat of Leon. I had broken one of the few good habits of a lifetime by having my one and only bet on a football match. Lunatic gambler that I was, it was nevertheless a superstition of mine never to bet on a match involving my favourite football teams. But I had been so confident of an England victory here that I had put the entire expenses allowance for the rest of my stay in Mexico – 400 dollars in travellers cheques – on England to win. And at half-time I was so confident of collecting that I even began to feel a little sorry for the Germans, who were being so comprehensively outplayed. Little did I know then that this was the one footballing nation which was to frustrate England again and again in the years to come. From a personal point of view, this was the second time Germany had kicked me in the bollocks – first they bomb me out and then they clean me out.

That night after the match we had the wake to end all wakes – the England players and their press mates. In the course of it, I managed to emulate my big brother Jim by turning minder and knocking out a Mexican pest of a fan who was giving our boys a bad time. This little bit of bravado seemed to endear me to most of the players for a long time to come. But one crazy evening before I eventually went home, I was in real danger of never living long enough to tell the rest of this tale.

A crowd of us pressmen, together with most of those football star drinking pals I mentioned earlier, visited a well-known English pub/restaurant, the only one of its kind in Mexico City. What started out as a reasonably sophisticated night's drinking degenerated into a noisy sing-song from us Brits. Now for some reason, the English team had never been very popular in Mexico throughout the tournament, so our songs did not go down too well with the locals, who retaliated with their own more tuneful renderings in a South American beat. But it was all good-natured teasing until some loud-mouthed Yank who had attached himself to our party, and whom none of us had ever clapped eyes on before, told the Mexicans to 'shut the hell up'. In an instant, this macho Mexican mob were telling us that our mothers were all whores, and it looked like being 'off at all meetings', as they used to say whenever a rumble broke out round my way back in the old days. As the rest of the customers cleared out a bit sharpish, we found ourselves facing the Mexicans in what must have resembled a clenched-fisted battle line. Their spokesman assured us that they were 'all brave Mexican boys' – and having seen some of their excellent boxers in action, I had no doubt about that – but I retorted: 'And we are all brave English boys, mate,' only to be reminded by Tommy Docherty and Hugh McIlvanney that there were brave Scottish boys, too.

My hope that I could keep their spokesman talking and so avert a major punch-up was soon dashed when he suggested that we all stepped outside to settle our differences. And on the way down the stairs, my blood turned to water as I saw a dozen white-coated chefs emerging from the kitchen carrying a selection of weapons ranging from meat cleavers to knives.

By the time we had all spilled out on to the pavement, I could practically read the headlines in tomorrow's papers back home already, when suddenly half a dozen taxis screeched up to the kerb with their doors already open. Thank God, one of our more sensible and senior colleagues had nipped downstairs to phone the cab company as the trouble first flared up and his foresight saved us. We got into the cabs in as dignified and defiant a fashion as we could manage, mouthing a few empty threats but all of us very relieved to surrender to that old saying that discretion can sometimes be the better part of valour – especially when faced with the prospect of having a kitchen knife plunged into your guts.

Before we bid farewell to Mexico, there is one other little anecdote which went down in the 'Batty' archives, and it involved Billy Bremner and I sleeping together and me missing a deadline over it. I hasten to add that we were both well pissed at the time and that Frank Clough was occupying the other bed in our room in a similarly comatose state. Because of those early *Sun* edition times I mentioned, Frank and I had to be on the phone at the crack of dawn with a story every day in Mexico, hours before our rivals needed to stir themselves. On this occasion, though, when the telephone rang beside my bed, Billy's hand suddenly flew out and grabbed it before I was properly awake. Obviously mistaking the call for room service, his fierce Scottish voice bellowed down the line: 'Another two cuba libres please, chief!' and he hung up. Back in those days there were often lengthy delays with long-distance telephone calls and this proved to be the case when I tried to get back to the *Sun* office with no luck and no chance of catching the early editions. Frank Nicklin must have been so pleased with our coverage so far that he let the incident pass, because he did not refer to it again until I got back to London, when, in the office pub the next day, he moaned: 'I spent hours trying to reach you one day and when I eventually got through they must have connected me to the wrong room, because all I got was some bloody Scotsman ordering rum and cokes.'

A couple of decades on from this heady period of my life, when I reached such a low point that I was in danger of dying from alcoholism, I spent many agonising hours trying to analyse why drink and sport were such unlikely bedmates.

It seems to me that, in my case, alcoholism may simply have been brought on by an excess of energy and that it was adrenalin that I was hooked on as much as drink. It is easy to understand how a footballer who has just scored the winning goal in a European Cup tie would still be so full of adrenalin hours afterwards that he would have less chance of going to bed sober than he would of sleeping with Madonna. In the same way, it would be impossible for a reporter to remove the images and emotions from the same evening from his mind without the aid of a soothing sedative or two. And we were under more stress than other mere spectators because we were expected to compose lively, readable sentences and paragraphs about the action, as well as having to suffer the more prosaic duty of having to let the facts interfere with the flow of a good story.

The consequences of all this were that if you did attempt to go to bed with a good book and a cup of cocoa immediately after covering a pulsating sporting event, sleep would never come because the perfectionist inside you would be forever punishing itself about a clumsy phrase here and a wrong fact there. I know about this from bitter experience because when I later tried to do this wonderful job in a state of permanent sobriety, I found it almost impossible.

For now, however, my life was too full of constant movement and excitement to worry about anything more than living up to that oldest of all footballing clichés about taking it one match at a time.

In foreign parts, once our previews had been sent to the office, it was a ritual on the eve of the next day's match for every man jack to congregate in one of the hotel rooms, each clutching his bottle of duty-free booze, to engage in what was euphemistically termed a 'pre-dinner cocktail party'. It was never very long before the whole bunch of us was swaying like a field of Wordsworth's golden daffodils to form a vision of heart-warming cameraderie which I shall always treasure in my memories.

Arguably, the most unforgettable soccer scribe of them all was the incomparable Geoffrey Green of *The Times* and the BBC's *Sports Report*. An Oxford soccer blue in his youth, Geoffrey, by the time most of us knew and loved him, was a silver-maned, stick-thin figure who spent the soccer season in a tent-like fur overcoat with a piece of string as a belt, carried a mouth organ in his pocket, which he frequently played, drank like a fish, wrote like an angel and had the most marvellously mellifluous dark brown voice which would have made even Richard Burton slightly envious. An incurable romantic in every sense of the word, he had a paternalistic affection for Bobby Charlton which knew no bounds and brooked no argument, a passion for jazz which was almost as intense as his love of the old glory game and, late in life, he fathered a daughter whom he absolutely adored. During the course of his globe-trotting odyssey of an existence, Geoffrey acquired more friends and acquaintances of more different nationalities than any other man I ever knew, and he made it a rule to sample vast quantities of the local brew of whichever country he happened to find himself in, with, more often than not, the most amusing or bizarre, but never disastrous consequences.

There are so many Geoffrey Green anecdotes that only the very best of them can fit into this limited space. The one which captures his extraordinary personality most accurately for me concerns a trip to report on Red Star Belgrade versus Spurs in 1972. One of Geoffrey's most mysterious gifts was his capacity to appear to be sleeeping it off peacefully in the press box one moment and then, when the telephone from his office rang at his elbow, to launch, wide awake, into a stream of purple prose as effortlessly as if he had not missed a kick during his slumbers. Being the old pro he was, of course, he would pause occasionally, cover the receiver with his hand for a moment and politely ask his nearest neighbour to fill him in on what had been going on during his reverie.

On arrival in Belgrade, he was whisked away from the airport, playing his mouth organ, which was always a sign that he had enjoyed plenty of liquid refreshment on the flight, by a crowd of what looked like local partisans and were obviously old comrades – never to be seen again until the customary pre-match banquet which had been laid on by our hosts. These were occasions when the directors and dignitaries of the two clubs exchanged gifts. For some reason, which I never did fathom, our Yugoslav host who gave the welcoming speech made an inordinate fuss of the visiting press, describing us all as 'poets in the glorious English tradition', and we were inundated with an embarrassing mountain of gifts. Suitably touched, the British press men around the table convened an emergency meeting and agreed that one of our number should reply on our behalf. It was with some trepidation that we were just about to accede to Bernard Joy's request that he should do the honours, because it was not for nothing that we all called him 'Bernard Gloom'.

But at our precise moment of need, a 'rat-arsed' Geoffrey made his entrance. And what an entrance it was. He staggered through the doors of the banqueting hall, being supported at each elbow by the Yugoslav compatriots who had greeted him at the airport. I knew how far gone he was when he kept shouting, 'Over the rainbow, babies!' which he invariably did when well and truly sozzled. But in desperation, I whispered in his ear that we needed a speech from him. We found him a seat at the table, into which he slumped with his two minders still standing guard over him, and he surveyed the scene, sobered up on the spot, rose to his feet and began talking in the unique fashion in which only he could about the white table cloth and the red roses on the table. He told our hosts that the white tablecloth reminded him of the snow in Munich airport when Manchester United were returning from a match against Red Star in 1958 and that the red roses evoked memories of the innocent blood which the beloved Busby Babes shed on that tragic occasion. Soon, every person at that table was in floods of tears and the British press corps was festooned with another mountain of gifts.

A trip to a remote region of Romania with Arsenal also sticks in my mind mainly because of Geoffrey and his other eccentric comrade-in-arms, Desmond Hackett. This town of Bacau was so isolated that old ladies with brooms like witches swept the roads there. When Hackett and Geoffrey strode along what passed as the pavements together, the locals would run out of their houses and applaud. Hackett always wore a brown bowler, which he frequently made reference to in his pieces in the *Daily Express*, and Geoffrey in his strange garb resembled a Bohemian of the long gone days before Communism. And this pair of ageing Brits made such a colourful spectacle for the locals that they could not resist the impulse to applaud them on sight. So that when messrs Green and Hackett arrived at the open-air stadium with the rest of the English press corps in tow, we were given a standing ovation by the huge crowd every step of the way as, for some obscure reason, we were requested to skirt the pitch before taking our seats.

Another occasion I can recall Geoffrey being roundly applauded behind the Iron Curtain was in Sofia, Bulgaria. He and Hackett partook of a few too many over lunch one day and Geoffrey mounted the plinth of a statue to deliver a rallying cry to the citizens. With so little alternative entertainment on offer in those parts at that time, a sizeable crowd soon gathered to listen. But the oration was delivered in English, of course, and predictably the natives soon became a bit restless.

When one of them dared to interrupt Geoffrey by commenting loudly in his native tongue, Geoffrey mistook him for a heckler, but when he retaliated by calling the man Groucho Marx, he was surprisingly met with a round of applause and was at the centre of so much enthusiastic back-slapping that the police had to be called. Whereupon Hackett mistook them for a guard of honour and began lining them up for inspection!

One fine day in Malta, I was never more glad to see anyone than I was to clap eyes on messrs Green, Hackett and McIlvanney – in reverse order. It was the morning after an undistinguished international between Malta and England in which England had scraped a 1–0 victory on a pitch which was as pockmarked and sandy as a building site back home. This trip had been a bizarre one from the start. A couple of days before the match, Ian Greaves, the blunt-speaking manager of a northern Football League club, had commented in the *Sun* that the Maltese were just a bunch of Spanish waiters and that England should run up a big score. So when we arrived at the airport there, it was besieged by thousands of fans baying for English blood and carrying placards proclaiming: 'We are the waiters – you are the bastards.' Mr Greaves, presumably, was safely back home watching all this on the television news.

Because of traffic congestion in the narrow streets of the island, we were requested to arrive at the ramshackle ground no less than three hours before the afternoon kick-off. And when we got there it was already full to capacity. The English journalists were shepherded into an elevated press box which appeared to be on stilts and resembled a cross between an old Francis Drake-type galleon and the ramparts of a medieval castle. Whatever, with nothing to amuse them for the next three hours, the Maltese spectators laid siege to it. They even tried to get at us on ladders and planks and rocked our wretched box so much that we were convinced it would collapse. In the course of my travels with English football teams, I have frequently been spat at, ducked bottles and stones and stood toe to toe with the 'enemy', but that was the scariest experience of them all.

This had nothing to do with my relief at the unexpected meeting I had with my three colleagues the following morning. That nightmare had begun the moment I awoke in my hotel room, fully clothed and flat out on the carpet. We had enjoyed the mother of all booze-ups the night before, but it had been spoiled by the knowledge nagging at the back of our minds that Sir Alf Ramsey had insisted the England party take a flight at the crack of dawn to return his players to their clubs as soon as possible. I vaguely recalled leaving the party to go upstairs to pack at about 4.30am ready for the 5am departure. I knew nothing else until I was disturbed by the familiar sound of the maid hoovering around my prostrate body.

Normally, my cockney mate Reg Drury mothered me and made sure I was 'on parade' with the rest of them for departure, but on this occasion everyone left in a fleet of different taxis instead of a coach and it transpired there had been a mix-up about who was present and who was not. The fear I now felt was even more intense than when we were being besieged the day before. I rushed out onto the verandah of my room and looked down into the marble well of the luxury hotel to see that it was empty and stone cold silent, where just a few hours previously it had been so lively. I felt like crying for my mum. We often used to chide the footballers for being a bunch of spoiled babies who had everything laid on for them by their clubs but, seasoned world traveller that I was, I realised then that I had always relied on my mates to shepherd me in and out of airports, hotels and football grounds because I was as often as not half cut.

I searched my pockets and discovered that I had just a little bit of loose change left. This sent me into a blind panic and I flew downstairs to inquire if every last one of my mates had left. As I took those stairs, three at a time, I could not believe that my 'blood brother', Hugh McIlvanney, had left me behind. Thankfully, the man at reception said try room 355 and the blood surged back into my veins. When I arrived at room 355, the door was wide open and Hugh was lying fully clothed on his back on the bed with his eyes open. When he saw me, he simply said: 'I thought you'd left me here and I was just trying to work out which one of your legs I was going to break first when I got home.'

Thankfully, Hugh still had some money and downstairs at the bar our situation started to look a lot more cheerful, especially when Desmond Hackett joined us, to be closely followed by Geoffrey Green. All four of us had failed to respond to reveille, so, naturally, a long haul piss-up began as we plotted our next moves. The first problem I had to confront was to file a follow-up piece to my paper, which still had those ridiculously early first editions to fill. For a bit of fun, the other three decided to dictate a paragraph each in rotation for me and dispatched me to the cable office, like a messenger, to send it, assuring me that I would undoubtedly win a Sportswriters of the Year award for this classic piece of *Observer* cum *Times* cum *Daily Express* prose. Predictably, the four of us missed many more planes before we finally fell into a first-class carriage at Gatwick airport station which was occupied by what looked like an Oriental bureaucrat in rimless glasses and a pinstriped suit. As he surveyed this unlikely foursome – Hackett in his brown bowler and carrying a bunch of flowers for 'dear heart', Green playing his mouth organ, McIlvanney singing Irish rebel songs and me in my East End gangster's three-piece suit, I could have sworn I saw his lips move and that he was silently mouthing to himself: 'English is vellee funny people!'

Another incident I am equally ashamed of was when Hugh McIlvanney and I stupidly got involved in a drunken scuffle with each other in a tavern in the shadows of the Acropolis on the eve of Chelsea's European Cup-Winners' Cup final in Athens. Bernard Joy, fearing the worst, went and knocked on Chelsea manager Dave Sexton's hotel door in the middle of the night to inform him of the fracas – as if Dave did not have enough to worry about.

Incidentally, Sexton, whose boxer father Archie was a famous knock-out specialist, could have sorted the pair of us out with one hand tied behind his back. Dave was a difficult man to get to know and had the reputation of being a prickly character in his early days as Chelsea boss. But once he was satisfied that he could like and trust you, there was no more generous-spirited man in football than him. When he was manager of Manchester United, I happened to mention that my son played rugby and he gave Danny an All Blacks shirt that had been presented to him on a close season tour of New Zealand. He also threw in Joe Jordan's number nine Manchester United shirt as a bonus. Dave has had tragedy and illness to cope with in his later years, but it is wonderful to catch a glimpse of him on the touchline on TV occasionally, still coaching the England Under-21s.

The only other football character I knew with a right hook to compare with Dave's was Scottish international Paddy Crerand of Manchester United. An extremely cultured passer of the ball on the field, he was a loveable but tough-as-teak character off it. Paddy got lumbered with the self-appointed job of George Best's minder both on and off the field, and he looked after the wayward Irish genius like a Dutch uncle whenever any Jack the Lad wanted to have a go at George, which was often.

For the benefit of younger readers, I can testify that Best was every inch the icon that time has turned him into. I never, ever clapped eyes on a footballer with more all-round talent than him anywhere in the world, nor one with more natural grace and charm off the field. And if his insatiable thirst for living went on to warp that personality occasionally and cost him so dearly, his survival instincts are also to be truly admired. I remember travelling with him to one of his big 'comeback' matches in Lisbon's Stadium of Light to play for Tommy Docherty's Manchester United in a testimonial match for that legendary Portuguese hero, Eusebio. Unfortunately, George succumbed to a late night in the casino on the eve of the match and did not recapture the youthful form which had got him christened 'El Beatle' in that part of the world. But his name put so many bums on seats that Eusebio had many thousands of reasons for being grateful to his fellow footballing genius.

When George was still very young, I was invited to tea by his mother and father in their Belfast home one day and was greeted with old-world courtesy from both of them. It is amazing how much George has grown to resemble his father, Dick, facially in his own middle age. What is also amazing, to my mind, is the astrological link between George and other wayward sporting idols such as Paul Gascoigne, John Conteh and Eric Cantona. All of them are split-personality Geminis. As a Gemini myself, while I am definitely no genius, I am certainly wayward enough to have made something of a study of the Gemini characteristics – if only to find a cop-out for my own defects.

Two major plusses in my life happened in 1972 which temporarily chased away the personal demons. First and foremost was the birth of my youngest daughter Caroline, who turned out to be a real daddy's girl. And then I was promoted to sports columnist by the *Sun*. I did not know whether to laugh or cry about this appointment, because although I wanted to write about other sports too, by now I knew there was so much I was going to miss as a day in, day out football writer. That privileged job had opened the door to friendships with some of the most idolised players of their day and many of them have helped me out under the old pals' act since. Many of the top managers of the 1980s and 1990s, who could command big fees for interviews, always went out of their way to talk to me free of charge when I was down on my luck and visited them rattling my freelance begging bowl. Indeed, during one of my subsequent periods of unemployment, Kevin Keegan even tipped me off exclusively about his transfer to Germany because he knew I was in dire need of the money his story would earn me.

One group of people which I was certainly happy to be saying goodbye to, however, were the football hooligans – a social phenomenon which had evolved around that time. Travelling all over the country on trains with them on board was like being a war correspondent, and we press men were often regarded by them as the enemy. Their wanton war of attrition, which regularly involved smashing up carriages, delaying trains for hours with regular tugs at the communication cord and wrecking buffet cars, soon resulted in nightmarish journeys with no buffet facilities, no lights, ripped seats, broken windows and with not a railway employee or a policeman to be seen. It was only later when they took to trying to lay waste to towns and populations that the trains were guarded and properly policed.

My own personal tactic in dealing with them was to give as good as I got with the guttersnipe verbals – it takes one to know one – and I matched them 'fuck' for 'fuck' and eyeball to eyeball. The most uncomfortable moment I endured from the hooligans was when hundreds of young Manchester United fans recognised my face from my regular picture in the *Sun* and trailed me from the station to the Old Trafford ground, singing: 'If you hate Peter Batt, clap your hands.' I turned round from time to time to growl at them, but that only made them worse. But this embarrassing episode was to fade into insignificance in my memory compared to the thought of a slice of hooliganism which was to be much closer to home and was perpetrated by people who should have known better.

In the early 1970s when rugby league team Leeds played in their Challenge Cup final at Wembley, a few of them chose the Astor Club in which to wind down later that night. It so happened that I was in the club in the company of Arsenal and England hard man Peter Storey and his sportswriter pal Jeff Powell. We were guests of my brother Jim and his minder mate Les Burman. On the way out, Storey found his way barred by one of the huge rugby league players, who was seemingly sleeping it off on a chair in the foyer. When Peter politely asked this man monster if he would mind moving his legs so that he could get to the door, the Leeds man called him a piece of shit and informed Storey that he would have to crawl under his legs first. Les, who was a fanatical Arsenal supporter, moved in to restore order and the next thing I heard was the crack of his fist on the rugby player's jaw. Within minutes, the place was full of brawling Leeds players doing battle with Jim and Les. As Storey, Jeff Powell and I stood there wide-eyed, the foyer of the posh Astor club was soon full of prostate, semi-conscious rugby league players. Even though I had seen Jim in action a few times before, it was a truly astonishing sight to see him go to work on those rugby league men. Ironically, when Arsenal lost to Leeds in the soccer Cup final that year I had predicted in my preview that 'Storey would smash Leeds', but I think that must have been to curry favour with my Arsenal pals such as Frank McLintock, George Graham, Pat Rice, Bob McNab, Ray Kennedy and Geordie Armstrong, who, incidentally, had themselves been forced to indulge in a spectacular street brawl with

Lazio players after an unseemly European match in that city. I had to chuckle some time later, however, when Peter and Jeff had a tiff and Storey snarled at him: 'I just wish there was a ball between us.'

Personally, all I wished for years afterwards was that I would not be spotted by any of those rugby league men when I visited their city in future, because I was informed by a northern rugby league journalist that my name had been noted as a participant in this unsavoury incident, even if it was only as a non-combatant.

But my lifestyle was beginning to give me a battering anyway. Nearly everyone I knew drank to make themselves sociable, even if they did not stay that way in the course of a session. But there were exceptions – towering exceptions, at that. The men I should have taken my cue from were giants such as Bill Shankly and Jock Stein, who were living proof that you could hold everyone in your company spellbound without needing to take so much as a drop of the hard stuff. For all I know, Bill and Jock may have drunk themselves into a stupor behind the lace curtains of their homes, but I and everyone else I knew in the game never saw alcohol pass their lips. Yet on match nights, they would hold us all entranced with their word-spinning magic, while sipping cup after cup of tea.

Admittedly they had plenty to talk about, which meant that they had a captive audience, but both of them were blessed with that famous Celtic talent for story telling. I remember once asking Jock why Scots like himself and Bill and the incomparable Sir Matt Busby made such good soccer managers and he replied: 'Because we Scots are like dogs with a bone. When we get our teeth into something, we never let it go. There will always be good Scottish man managers.' Alex Ferguson and George Graham later proved his point emphatically.

As for Shanks, so many of his quotations have already been printed that he is in danger of rivalling Robbie Burns in Scottish folklore. The one that tickles me most is: 'If brains were gunpowder, he wouldna have enough to blow his cap off.'

I fell into that category, myself, of course.

But just to prove that old point that life is never fair, what a bitter irony it is that both these wonderful physical specimens died young of heart attacks and I am still here to tell the tale. The same could be said, too, about the England football team doctor who was so alarmed at my drinking and smoking habits that he warned me I would die if I did not stop soon – and then fell dead himself a few months later while out jogging.

CHAPTER FIFTEEN
COLUMNIST

When Frank Nicklin offered me the job of being *Sun Sport*'s first ever columnist, he said he regarded it as a 'very big deal' appointment. Unlike these modern times, when columnists seem to occupy more column inches than news and features, your very own column then was still a rarity.

Frank conducted this piece of business in the traditional setting where he and his contemporaries hatched all their plots: the office pub. In this case it was the bar on the corner of Fleet Street and Bouverie Street which we had christened the Peanut Parlour, for no better reason than the counters were always full of bowls of peanuts. On this occasion, our side of the bar was full of buckets of Frank's bullshit, too. Knowing full well that his budget would not run to it, he promised me – and followed up his promise in print in the paper – that I would be given a free rein to roam the world of sport, commenting on all the big events, despite the fact that he already employed a boxing writer, an athletics writer, a tennis writer, a golf writer and several racing writers, and was just about to replace me as chief football writer with my Manchester mate, Frank Clough. Very few newspapers could afford to send two men globetrotting to the same event, least of all *the Sun*, which was only just starting to break even. So Nicklin, who was a wizard when it came to psychology and kidology, more or less conned me into the job by issuing a challenge, because he knew I could not resist them.

'You'll never be able to cope with it,' he goaded. 'You will always want to be one of the boys, you will never be able to to walk the corridors of power like me.'

'You're bleedin' right, I won't,' I replied. But then I surpised him by saying: 'I'll take the extra money, though, if there's any on offer.'

Frank was surprised by my reaction because his cynical philosophy, which he claimed had been proved correct time and again, was: 'Just give' em a bigger picture in the paper and they'll work for nothing.' He assumed I would go for glory and was so surprised when I asked for money instead that he agreed to negotiate a big rise for me. And that was to be the only time in my career that I ever got the right rate for the job again. Because when you are down and out, as I was to be on so many occasions later, newspapers, like any other business, will take full advantage of you financially.

Still, I must confess that old 'Nick' was definitely half right, because my hat size grew another several inches when the *Sun* began splashing my picture all over the front and back of London buses.

The real reason for my rapid rise to this ephemeral slice of fame was that he and Larry Lamb were using me as window dressing. Our *Daily Mirror* rivals had just appointed Frank McGhee to replace the legendary columnist Peter

Wilson, who was retiring, and the *Mirror* was making such a song and dance about it that Nicklin decided he had better have one too, just to 'keep up with the Joneses'. What, in fact, he was really offering me was an old man's job of sitting in the office every day and pontificating about sporting events by reading the flow of copy which came into the office via the *Sun*'s other sportswriters and the agencies.

Within days of falling for Nicklin's blandishments, I was gutted to have given up my lively life as a football writer for this sedentary office job. And as was my wont, I never stopped moaning about it. Again, it was not until many years later that I realised why I had hated it so much. At Alcoholics Anonymous, one of their many wise sayings is: 'Opinions are not worth a pinch of dog shit. But experience is gold dust.'

The *Sun* kept giving their readers the impression that I had five rows of teeth and that I would put everyone's house in order from the Football Association to Forfar Athletic. But I was not the slightest bit interested in sporting politics – all I wanted to do was to write about what I saw and felt. Foolishly, then, I found myself drinking even more than I had done when I was still on the road – partly from frustration and partly to fuel my batteries to keep up this daily grind of opinionated tosh.

Another big lesson I would learn later in AA was that I was not special and different and that, like almost every other alcoholic, when I had manipulated or nagged my way to the point that I wanted to reach in any situation, that was usually the precise moment when I blew it. So it was to prove on this occasion. I had no sooner talked Nicklin into letting me write features instead of opinions than I was briefed to go to Holland to write about the soccer sensation of the time, Johan Cruyff.

The big difference in my working pattern now was that I was going to be travelling alone, without the pack to protect me. I was soon to discover that I should not have been allowed outside the door on my own, let alone go hopping on boats, trains and planes.

Memories of that little trip to Holland were as blurred as so many others were to become when I was functioning in a state of alcoholic blackout. I was to learn that I would be capable of committing murder while under the influence of drink and not remember a thing about it next day. I can vaguely recall, or think I can, playing what I thought were several frames of snooker in a bar in Amsterdam and losing a nice few quid of my exes to the locals, but what puzzled me most was that in my weird recollection the snooker tables had no pockets. That little mystery turned out to be the least of my troubles on this particular assignment. I wrote what I considered to be one of my best ever pieces on Johan Cruyff and phoned it over to the office. On arrival back at Heathrow, I bought a copy of the *Sun* and then another morning-after livener and settled down to reading what I thought would be a massive double spread, even though I could not remember a single sentence of what I had written. Turning the pages more and more frantically, I discovered to my dismay that there was not a word on Cruyff and no Batt by-line. So I stormed back to the office and, in Frank Nicklin's absence, began playing hell with his deputy, Alan Sleaman. Alan politely informed me that my piece was tucked away in his drawer and suggested that I should read it at my leisure before continuing my tirade.

To my horror, the introduction read: 'Hi diddle, diddle, Cruyff's in the middle and Batt's run away with the spoon . . .'

Booted and suited, modelling for the *Scotsman* in 1959 during my wonderful time working north of the border. (The Scotsman)

One of too many drinks in the Cross Keys. (Chris Smith)

(From left to right) Mother Louisa, brother John, me and Heidi, and brothers Jim and George at our wedding on 15 May 1965. I was so skint at the time, Jim had to lend me the money for the licence. (Chris Smith)

The glamorous wedding reception at Jim's new pad. It was attended by a combination of Fleet Street reprobates and some of the hardest men in London. (Chris Smith)

Scoring the winning goal in an Over 30s v Under 30s football match in Regents Park. (The Sun – Jay)

Perhaps I got carried away, because here I am (standing fifth from the right) taking on the England World Cup squad in Mexico in 1970. (Daily Mirror)

The new John Wayne. Visiting a cowboy town near Reno ahead of the McCrory v Jones fight in the mid 1980s.

Working hard at the *Daily Star*, with photographer Roy Chaplin (centre) and Bob Driscoll (right). (Roy Chaplin)

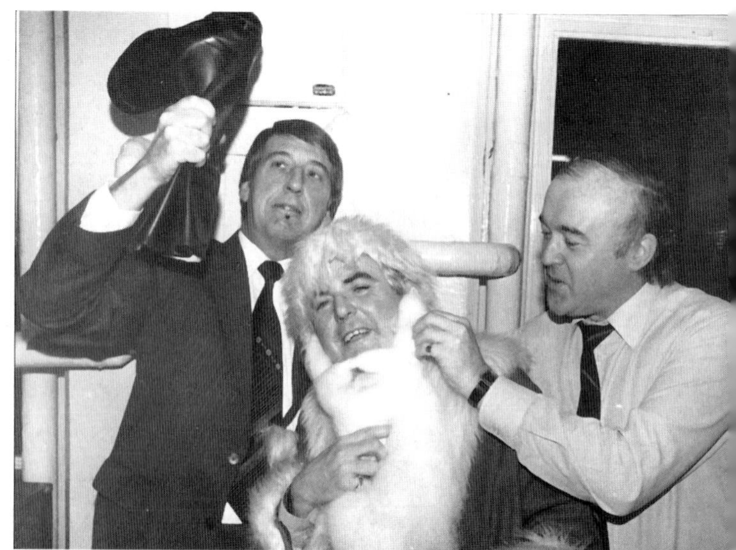

Sharing a cigarette with Brooke Sanders, the champion amateur jockey. She helped me to go through the card in Malta – but sadly could not help me get my winnings through customs. (Daily Star)

Muhammad Ali in 1983, 'The Saddest Story Ever Told'. When I mistook his onset of Parkinson's Disease for a drug problem, it nearly became my last story, too. (Daily Star – John Dawes)

With Star birds to help me, I invaded France to save our sausages in 1981. What the locals made of it I have no idea. (Daily Star)

As one of the early script writers for *EastEnders* I suddenly had a new role – one that paid very well. (Sunday People)

KICKING G!*!!* CORONATION ST.

LONDON BOROUGH OF WALFORD
ALBERT SQUARE
E20

With Michael Elphick in 1995, another who had his problems with drink. (Daily Express – John Paul)

The Seven Ages of Man.

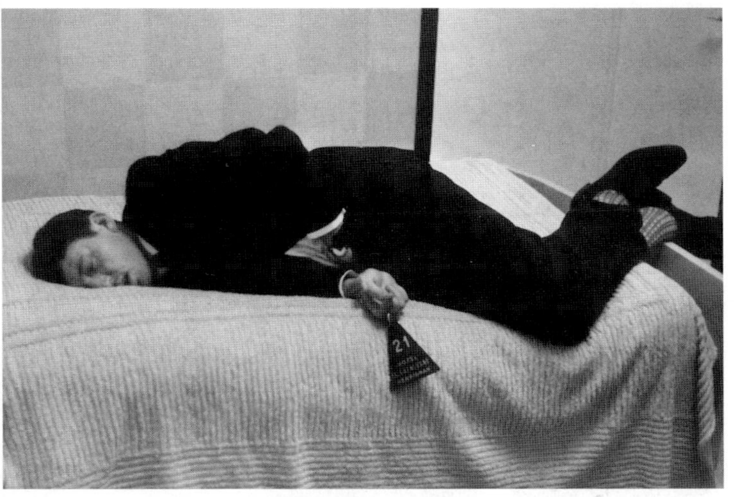

At my daughter Jenny's wedding in 1994. (Left to right) Me, Heidi, Jenny, Peter Reynolds, son Danny and daughter Caroline.

With my grandson Alexander. Only now, after so many years of battling with alcoholism, have I finally found a new sense of calm and tranquillity.

So, far from trying to frustrate me, Sleaman had done me a massive, career-saving favour. At this early stage of my addictive behaviour, it seemed that I still had enough charm going for me for Alan and everyone else to laugh it off. But although I solemnly swore that I would never drink on the job from here on in, I did not learn from my mistake and was soon at the sauce again. I was still unaware then, of course, that one of the definitions of a chronic alcoholic is that he or she keeps making the same mistakes expecting a different result.

Poetically, it was the man that Nicklin called the 'Avon Lady' who did a a successful makeover job on me. He was the *Sun*'s new editor, Bernard Shrimsley. Larry Lamb had just been appointed editor-in-chief of the *Sun* and its sister paper the *News Of the World* and Bernard, who earned his nickname from Nicklin because 'he was always changing my bloody make-up on the back page,' turned out to be a kind and courteous guv'nor. He was considerate enough to suggest that the paper and I should solve our dilemma by breaking new ground. Bernard's idea was that I should do 'fly on the wall' pieces from inside the dressing rooms and behind the scenes. The surprising result of his brainwave was that a succession of these kind of articles on football, boxing, racing, snooker, tennis and golf won me the Sportswriter of the Year award for 1973 and made me flavour of the month again as the first ever award-winning writer or reporter in the *Sun*'s short history.

Within a couple of years of tasting that little morsel of glory, I was to lose my job and a big new house in the country, but it was not until years later that I discovered that I was, in fact, crossing the line from problem drinking into full-blown alcoholism. It would have been entirely accurate but too simplistic to put my demise down to pride before the fall.

I started going on frequent boozy 'walkabouts', a habit which Frank Nicklin ingeniously countered by regularly putting a blurb on the back page of his paper, asking: 'What is Batt Up To?' He had no idea, of course, but it was enough to get me to make contact and await further instructions.

In addition to that blurb, the only other thing that was guaranteed to get me back to the office like a homing pigeon was the chance to draw a 'yeller' – these were the yellow chits we used to sign at the cashiers as advances against expenses. One night I found myself at a party in a lock-up pub down in London's dockland, immediately after an England football international at Wembley. It was run by a great mate of the players and of mine who, incidentally, was the landlord of the Blind Beggar pub when Ronnie Kray shot George Cornell's brains out there. The beauty of this little boozer was that the players and their mates could unwind far from the gaze of the madding crowd.

I woke up next morning stretched out on a bench in the bar, dead to the world and as drunk as a skunk. Finding myself locked in, I poured a quick livener from behind the bar and began shouting through the window at passers-by to rescue me. After about half an hour a man did manage to prise the ground floor window open just enough for me to be able to climb through it. At first, I had no idea where I was until I saw a number 6 bus approaching and there on the front of it was a poster of my face, with its fashionable Mexican-style moustache, staring down on me. Knowing the number 6 stopped in Fleet Street, I staggered aboard with the intention of getting to the office, grabbing a 'yeller', cleaning myself up and making my way to Wentworth for the golf which I had been told to cover.

I sat on the back seat and went through my pockets, only to find them empty, so I asked the conductor when he came round if I could leave my name and address with him and pay later. He took one look at my dishevelled appearance and ordered me off his vehicle. This sent me into a panic and, in desperation, I went into a grandiose routine which I hated having to stoop to, but was along the lines of 'Don't you know who I am?' Obviously, he did not know and did not remotely care who or what I was, but when I played my trump card and informed him that my picture was all over the front of his bus, he reluctantly agreed to ring the bell, stop for a moment and accompany me to investigate my claim.

The conductor, a West Indian, was suitably amazed and impressed, and exclaimed: 'Man, I shall dine out on this for years.' Then he graciously gave me a free ride.

Around this time this self-will of mine was running into riot after riot. One such occasion was a testimonial dinner for Geoff Hurst at the Hilton Hotel in London. At the press table were a crowd of my mates including Hugh McIlvanney, Ken Jones, Norman Giller, Harry Miller, Reg Drury, Peter Corrigan and Gordon Williams, who co-wrote the popular *Hazell* detective books and TV series with Terry Venables. On the West Ham table were insomniac Bobby Moore and my fellow alcoholic Jimmy Greaves, who had both recently been sent home from Blackpool on the eve of an FA Cup tie by manager Ron Greenwood for nipping out for a few drinks at ex-boxer Brian London's club, because they thought their match had been snowed off.

The press table grew more and more riotous until it was by far the noisiest in the place. Apparently, I went up to sing 'My Way' and just as I reached the line 'Regrets, I've had a few' fell backwards off the stage, splitting my head open and spilling blood all over my dinner suit. I regained consciousness just in time to see Gordon Williams rising gamely to his feet after being caught by a hook off the jab from Norman Giller, who had been a useful amateur boxer, and to watch Hugh McIlvanney stripping down to his waist in a bid to get his slice of the action.

When I arrived home in the early hours, I was told by Heidi that I opened the front door by smashing my fist through the glass window and unlocking it from the inside. She said that the astonished taxi driver, who had accompanied me up the garden path, exclaimed: 'Does he always come in this way, luv?' Then he promptly legged it.

Getting home was always something of a problem and my *Sun* mate Bob Driscoll and I managed to outdo every other dinner-in-the-dustbin story by a distance once when, in an attempt to get back in our wives' good books, we arrived at Victoria station at around 6pm to make our way to our respective homes. We must have decided to celebrate our superhuman effort of dragging ourselves away from the office pub by having a quickie before boarding. The next morning we awoke bleary-eyed, both wondering where the hell we were, only to gaze out of the window of the bedroom we were sharing and down onto platform 14 at that same Victoria station. It seems that we had overdone it yet again and booked into the Grosvenor Hotel, which seasoned boozy travellers will know adjoins the station.

Given this form line of ours, it was somewhat optimistic and foolish of Bob Driscoll and I to join, just a few weeks later, *Sun Sport*'s newly formed luncheon club. The idea was that once a month, half a dozen of us would forgo the routine liquid lunch to eat a proper slap-up meal together – one month fish, the next Chinese, the next Italian and so on and so on through the card.

Sadly, it all went predictably pear-shaped at our very first attempt when after lunching in Sheeky's famous fish restaurant in Soho, the next thing I remembered was Heidi, clad in her night clothes and dressing gown, picking me up in the family car as I decamped from the milk train at Haywards Heath station at four o'clock the next morning. Her only words to me on the drive home were: 'I trust you enjoyed your lunch.' Needless to say, the lunch club was rapidly disbanded.

Another memorable train journey was when a crowd of us sportswriters held a wake for dear old Bert Barham, football writer on *The Guardian* and an ex-prisoner of war of the Japanese, who had just died. One of Bert's favourite football grounds was Ipswich, where the Cobbold brothers on the board of directors were renowned for their generous hospitality.

We decided to have the wake in the buffet bar on the long train ride home. Inevitably, the gathering got a bit raucous and I must have been doing my fair share of cussing and swearing when a fellow traveller, not one of our party, stuck his ruddy face close up to mine and said in a broad Suffolk accent: 'You can't be Peter Batt – I recognise you from your photo, but you can't be he.'

When I sheepishly confessed that, indeed, I was Peter Batt, this fellow traveller replied: 'But he don't speak like thee. Surely, he speaks posh, don't he?'

I may not have spoken posh, but I definitely travelled posh. Another perk of this job was a first-class ticket wherever you went, and I became increasingly hooked on travelling by train. Inter-city was bliss itself as far as I was concerned, especially when I was sitting in the warmth of a luxurious seat with half a dozen miniature whiskies lined up on the table in front of me and the rain was drizzling down the carriage window. It felt like being back in the womb. There were no mobile phones then so a train or a plane was the only place where you were in limbo and the office could not reach you.

I know that I always felt better about myself if I was on the move, especially on the rare occasions when one particular drink – whether it was the third, the sixth, the thirteenth, whichever – hit just the right spot and for a few wondrous minutes I felt omnipotent. I not only believed in God, I was God, I knew every last secret of the universe and there was nothing on this piddling little planet that I could not do if I felt like doing it. But when the spiritual blind came down again moments later, I was, as often as not, fearful and paranoid.

Some heavy drinkers will wonder how I can remember so much about my life when I was sloshed so often. The answer is that I can remember the consequences of my boozy actions, but the bits in between come only in flashbacks which penetrate the blackouts. Bout drinkers, such as I was, are not permanently pissed or 'topped up', as some functioning alcoholics are.

And when it comes to damaging yourself, it is not how much you drink, it is what drink does to you. When drink starts costing you more than money, then you are in serious trouble. I have plenty of pals who can drink me under the table, but are not alcoholics – such are the genetic, chemical and emotional vagaries of the human condition. The great Carl Jung once wrote: 'All alcoholics are in search of spiritual wholeness.' I knew what he meant, but had no idea how to envision that state except through a glass darkly.

By now, I was suffering from a threefold illness which

was mental, physical and spiritual. But it was an illness which told me I had not got it. I was allergic to alcohol and, at the same time, had a crippling compulsion to drink it. Like most practising alcoholics who are still in denial of the disease, I was turning into a typically Jekyll and Hyde personality. My family, friends, colleagues and employers were slowly getting thoroughly sick of my Mr Hyde persona, but were, out of affection and kindness, still hoping that the more acceptable Dr Jekyll side of me would eventually win the struggle which they could see was going on inside me. I, however, was still blind to the reality of it all.

As a result, I was still getting away with blue murder both at home, in the office and at my local pubs and dog tracks. And I was still mistakenly convinced that I was Mr Nice Guy. At the *Sun*, I could do pretty much as I liked, including dancing on the tables and tossing the odd typewriter across the room. I even slung a whole series of telephone books, one at a time, at Frank Nicklin once, but like the good footballer and cricketer he had once been, he took them all in his stride, gathering one on his chest, trapping another under his foot and knocking a couple of others through slips and past silly mid-on. Of course, I was always full of what I thought was genuine remorse after my every misdemeanour, and Frank, like everyone else on the paper, would shrug off my antics and say, 'It's only Batty,' as if every office in the country had a head-banger like me to put up with.

The first real hint that the head men might just be getting well and truly pissed off with me being a pest which managed to pierce my alcoholic's armour came on Derby Day 1973, when I was sent to write the traditional 'Hogarthian' Epsom Downs column on the day's events. My attention to minor details of the day's events was seriously diverted, however, when Morston romped in at 25–1 in the big one. It so happened that, without him being aware of it. I was following *The Guardian* tipster Richard Baerlein's advice around that time, and Richard had gone out on a limb for Morston even though this colt was still only a maiden. So I waded into the bookies with one of my biggest bets ever. The late Richard was a silver-haired Old Etonian of somewhat regal bearing and manner. But even an unflappable old racing stager like him must have been mildly astonished when a large, bellowing cockney oaf standing behind him in the press stand suddenly leaped on his back, knocking him almost to his knees as his fancy passed the winning post in front.

I had stationed myself in Richard's vicinity so that I could eavesdrop on his comments as he watched the race through his binoculars. I was never that good at gauging a horse's chances during a race, but I knew Baerlein was a past master at it. I was holding my breath, crossing my fingers and offering up a silent prayer as jockey Eddie Hide guided Morston into the lead in the final furlong. But I nearly died of fright when Lester Piggott's mount drew almost upsides him. Hoping for the best, but now fearing the worst, I was desperately waiting for a sign from Baerlein that I was going to be a winner and, by God, it came when Richard suddenly shouted confidently: 'Come along Edward, take him home!'

With that, I let out a great roar of triumph and engulfed this man whom I had not even been introduced to in an unseemly bear hug, which was decidedly non-U behaviour as far as the rest of the seen it all, done it all racing scribes were concerned.

Inevitably, I proceeded to get well pissed, putting my column deeper into jeopardy with every passing minute to deadline time. When panic about this eventually set in shortly after the last race and I phoned the paper to give them my piece, knowing that I was short of facts and quotes and technical information I ad-libbed a personalised piece about the Old Etonian and the cockney. Bernard Shrimsley stuck my story on the spike of unwanted copy and was forced to fill the space allotted to me with whatever other Derby titbits he could lay his hands on.

So I was hauled into the office for a bollocking next morning, which I took manfully because the performer in me always appreciated some kind of reaction to my work – good or bad – just so long as it was not apathy. In fairness to myself, I read the offending article later and reckoned that even if it was a little off-beat, it was entertaining enough to have been used – and I promised myself that if they ever did this to me again I would kick up fuck.

In the early summer of 1974, I was sent to Germany to write columns about the finals of the World Cup, for which England had failed to qualify. This was the competition in which an excellent Scottish side, captained by my old mate Billy Bremner, failed to make the quarter-final stage on goal difference, even though they were undefeated in their group. Thousands upon thousands of their tartan-clad fans had been camped in hillside tents, evoking memories of the ancient clans.

But even the Scots' 'sick as parrots' homecoming was not quite as disastrous as mine. For, after a day-long wake on schnapps in Deutschland, Hugh McIlvanney and I arrived home at London airport, according to *Private Eye* magazine, 'tired and emotional'. We had a rumpus with some of the porters at the baggage collection point and I landed flat on my back on the luggage carousel, pinned there by a posse of porters while one of their number, a beefy guy answering to the name of Fred, slung numerous ponderous punches at me to the accompaniment of McIlvanney's voice loudly laying the odds on the outcome of the fracas and inviting bets from the crowd of people who had gathered to watch this unseemly spectacle. *Private Eye* featured me in several of their piss-taking snippets around that time, in which they labelled me as the 'Dirty Digger's (Rupert Murdoch's) favourite hack'.

This was another roller-coaster of a year for me. The lowest point of it came earlier in that World Cup stint in Germany when the undiagnosed gall stones from which I had been suffering for years crippled me to such an extent that I had to miss a game in Berlin to be nursed by Heidi's brother Reinhard and his wife Barbara. The highest was when I was given another chance to visit relatives, this time in South Africa when I covered the last part of the British Lions' triumphant undefeated tour of that country.

Frank Nicklin had made a rare professional error by underestimating the impact the Lions would have on our rapidly expanding readership. Dismissing rugby union as an upper-crust game which would not interest our working-class readers, he was shocked to receive shoals of letters from Welsh coal miners and other sections of the working-class sporting public demanding that he get someone out to South Africa for the finale of the tour. I turned out to be that someone and to help me to negotiate what, for me, was virgin territory, I asked Philippa Kennedy, a very attractive young lady reporter on the paper, to give me a letter of introduction to her brother, Dr Ken Kennedy, the Irish hooker, who was a member of this particular pride of Lions. I was clutching this missive when I first made contact with the Lions' legendary Irish captain, Willie John McBride. And it would have served me well had I not been recognised by another Irish ace, Mike Gibson.

Gibson, a soccer fan, had remembered seeing my picture in the *Sun* the morning after I was presented with the Sportswriter of the Year award. And the caption contained this mischievous paragraph from Nicklin which I am convinced the sadistic old devil had written specifically to get me into trouble at some time in the future.

It read: 'Peter Batt revels in catching the God-almighty, money-daft, jumped-up sporting star with his pants down. And you can take my word for it, this award won't change Big Batt!'

Nicklin's ploy worked a treat for him. And you, too, can take it as read that this little revelation did not go down too well with this fearsome group of warriors I was hoping to become pally with. At an after-match celebration the following night, I was knocked off my feet and splattered against the wall by the jet of water from a fire extinguisher brandished by one of the Lions, and the new suede jacket which I had recently treated myself to became a complete write-off. Still, once this off-beat initiation ceremony was out of the way, the generous-spirited Lions treated me as one of their own – until I bowled at them in a Lions versus British Press cricket match and they knocked me to all parts of the boundary.

But it was immediately after the Lions had returned home that I was to cross a personal boundary of a very different kind. This one was a spiritual boundary and it was to have profound effects – good and bad – on the rest of my life.

My oldest sister, Louise, had settled in South Africa many years earlier. Her husband Jack Weatherston, the parish priest with whom I had lived in my childhood, had been a vociferous anti-apartheid spokesman and before his untimely death in a road crash in the early 1960s had become the Dean of Pretoria. Louise and her two children, Susan Jane and Martin, had endured more than their share of emotional suffering, for in addition to Jack's unexpected death, Susan Jane had contracted multiple sclerosis and Martin had lost his six-year-old son, Luke, to a brain tumour.

I had arranged to spend a few days with them at their idyllic home in Kenton-on-Sea, which was a little settlement of white colonial-style bungalows, looking for all the world like a postcard featuring the houses of the New England Bible Belt in America. Religion had been the last thing on my mind when I set out on that Lions trip, and it still was when I first put my feet up on the verandah of Louise's delightful home, which overlooked first a river and then the sea. It truly was God's own country, in terms of scenery, even if it was Hell on Earth as far as racial discrimination was concerned. But after a couple of days, I was able to overcome my disgust with my big sister for staying put under such a Godless regime and 'enjoying' the good life with a black maid and a black gardener. For it seemed to my then arrogantly judgemental mind that they had already been punished enough.

Yet, as we sipped our sundowners in the cool of the evening and caught up with the past 20 years, I found much of the suppressed guilt and shame of my alcoholic treatment of my job, my wife and my children suddenly flooding to the surface and needing to be confessed. I was mildly astonished to hear myself admitting to my sister and my niece and nephew that I was always seeking instant gratification and that I was constantly putting my family's future in jeopardy by my reckless behaviour. In my deepest conscience was locked away the knowledge that I was a terrible show-off and that one of my masks was the carefree, last-of-the-cowboys persona which insisted that I was not going to be a mortgage slave like the rest of my colleagues. I was not going to eat shit for the bosses like them, I was going to be a free spirit.

Confronted by such immaturity, my sister and her kids suggested that I was sorely in need of some humility and, as newly converted Pentecostals, suggested that they laid hands on me and speak in tongues on my behalf. I felt as if I was in something of a trance when I agreed to let them do this, almost casually deciding that I had nothing to lose and that I might as well humour them. But the effect upon me of this little ritual was incredible. No other word could describe the feeling of blissfull well-being which filled my senses. In an instant, I was at peace and genuinely loved the world and everything in it.

When I made the long journey back home, I found myself actually loving anyone and everyone that I came into contact with. At the airport, on the plane and in the taxi to my house – all places and situations when I would normally behave like a bear with a sore head – I experienced a peace which passed all understanding. And this astonishing feeling persisted for at least a fortnight after I had settled back into our big new house in Cuckfield, Sussex. So much so that I found myself telling my pals in the local about it, a confession which predictably brought much head-shaking and some out-and-out piss-taking by way of a response. I did not pluck up the courage to tell anyone in Fleet Street about my weird experience because I knew I couldn't risk the blow their ridicule would bring to my reputation – this was long before the wave of New Age literature swept over from California, making many people a lot less sceptical about strange spiritual experiences.

Heidi was very impressed by the sincerity of my new-found feelings of salvation, but knowing my volatile all-or-nothing personality she was understandably afraid that I might go right over the top by jacking in my job, losing the house and attempting to convert passers-by to the Holy Spirit on street corners. She was right about the job and the house, but wrong about the street corners. Faced with an ever-increasing inner urge to abandon everything to follow Jesus – I now know that this was either divine intervention in my life or an alcoholic cop-out – I eventually took a conscious decision to reject Him and became an even heavier drinker and gambler, and within a year had boozed and betted my way into unemployment and a period of misery for us and our children.

For cursed now with a conscience as well as this twin addiction, I started doing crazy things in my cups like smashing up hotel bars and heaving inanimate objects through shop windows. Twice I spent nights in police cells and three times I made appearances at magistrates' courts on two separate charges of criminal damage and one of drunk-driving. One of my cases at Marlborough Street magistrates' court was even reported in the local paper under the heading, 'Writer tries to rid world of aliens.' Still half-pissed when I appeared in court, I decided to play to the gallery when I was charged with throwing a few traffic cones with bleeping lights through a shop window in Oxford Street in the wee small hours of yet another drunken morning. So I told the judge I was merely trying to rid the world of these bleeping alien pests, and was very heavily fined for my crass stupidy. And just to compound my insanity, having had my finger prints taken the night before, I now congratulated myself for having joined big brother Jim as a bona fide member of the criminal fraternity.

On another occasion, I was having a 'quiet' drink in the bar of the Charing Cross Hotel – with Bob Driscoll again – when I suddenly went berserk, tore the mock statue of Queen Eleanor off the wall and flung it into tables full of drinkers. I knew all about Queen Eleanor, the widow of King Edward, the hammer of the Scots, who placed a statue at every place his courtiers stopped when they were returning her body to London after she had died during the Scottish wars, and that Charing Cross commemorated the last stopping place. I tried to explain to the judge that this was an insult to the Scottish race, and was again heavily fined and told to seek psychiatric help.

But when I was breathalysed for drunken driving and judged to be way over the top, I had the luckiest break imaginable when the prosecuting officer failed to put in an appearance to give evidence before the Greenwich stipendiary magistrate and my case was dismissed. Most of my mates were convinced that brother Jim and his associates had 'nobbled' the copper concerned, but my escape must have been down to Heidi's guardian angel. This time, though, she forced me never to drive drunk again and this was one of the few sensible rules I was ever able to adhere to.

It was not long after this that I well and truly nobbled myself on the *Sun*. The inevitable end, when it came, arrived with all the impact of a damp squib. There was no hell-raising and there were no histrionics involved in my departure, just an inflated ego, irresponsibility and perhaps more than a hint of fear in my decision to quit the paper in the summer of 1975.

The Australian cricketers were touring this country at the time, spearheaded by that frightening fast bowling team of Dennis Lillee and Jeff Thomson. I wrote a piece about 'gelding the Lillee', suggesting that the only possible way we English had of combatting this fiery character was having him gelded. Bernard Shrimsley, in addition to being polite and friendly, was also decidedly prim and proper in his approach to journalism and he spiked my column on the grounds that the reference to 'gelding' was too crude and insulting to appear in a 'family' newspaper like the *Sun*. Keeping the arrogant vow that I had made to myself a couple of years earlier when my Derby column was spiked, I wrote a letter of resignation, which was accepted with such alacrity by Bernard that I could almost hear his sigh of relief when it was handed to him. And I must confess that I felt the same way as he did. I read somewhere, I think it was in a book by the Russian dissident Alexander Solzhenitsyn, that the moment an arresting officer touches your collar, you are flooded by a feeling of relief that the struggle and tension are over, if only for a fleeting moment.

The struggle and tension of holding down my job on the *Sun* had been getting me down for some time, so perhaps my resignation was merely a way of throwing in the towel. I deluded myself that the job was beneath my talents and that I was being punished for turning my back on Jesus. In retrospect, I now know that I was suffering from the paranoid symptoms which so many other suffering alcoholics feel when they are victims of the illness.

Within days of jacking it in, I was consumed with fear for the future of my wife and my three children, and even went so far as to humiliate myself by asking for my job back. When this request was met by a point-blank refusal, I went back to what I knew best – kicking up fuck – and kept demanding that I be released from serving my three months' notice.

I topped it all off with an unforgettable 'performance' when I lurched back from the pub one night and began singing an old First World War song which was all the rage at the time because of a televised beer advertisement. The words went: 'Goodbye-ee, goodbye-ee, wipe the tear, baby dear, from your eye-ee. Though it's hard to part I know, I'll be tickled to death to go . . .' In the ad, rank after rank of soldiers take up this refrain, beginning in a whisper and rising to a crescendo.

Well, in the big open-floor office of the *Sun* that night, this song was sung, first by the sports staff, then the sub-editors' table, then the news reporters, and so on and so on until the whole building was ringing with chorus after chorus of it, while I waved my handkerchief and stared at Bernard Shrimsley and Larry Lamb, who stood there sheepishly before beating a shame-faced retreat while I laughed like a clown. It turned out to be the last time I laughed in months. For unemployment, at the age of 42 and as the father of three young children, was no bowl of cherries as it had once been in my youth.

CHAPTER SIXTEEN
EVENINGS

The only glimmer of consolation Heidi could take from me plunging my family into the horrors of life on the dole – except that I was far too proud to sign on for unemployment benefit, anyway – was that she would not have to wait on Haywards Heath station anymore in the early hours of the morning to guess whether I was going to get off the train she was meeting, or if I was going to be sleeping off a skinful of booze and go snoring on to the end of the line in Hastings.

With my usual impeccably bad timing, I had chosen the worst moment in some 20 years to throw myself out of work. Frank Nicklin had warned me that a recession was on its way, and he was not joking. The result of this was that our lovely new house began to drop in value week by week. And worse, no matter how much I fancied myself as one of the best sportswriting operators in the business, a new job was almost impossible to come by. Newspapers then did not really use freelances as they do now, and the only way a reporter could get work was by filling dead men's shoes or taking over from someone else – and no one else was about to commit professional hara-kiri like me. The only thing to do was to wait and pray for a lucky break. As I sought refuge in the bottle, my desperate mental meanderings even had me killing off the mates whose jobs would have suited me best by having them drop dead suddenly.

Neville Holtham, my sports editor on the *People* and a genuine family friend, gave me a reprieve from my melancholy ramblings by arranging for me to cover a soccer match for him every Saturday. So my sportswriting career had come full cycle: I was back where I had started 10 years earlier. This time, though, I did not stay the course. Within a few weeks, I had pressed the self-destruct button again.

It was after reporting a match at Ipswich, a place which has cropped up before in this story. I don't know what was so dangerous about Ipswich, except that it was one of the longest rail journeys of all and, as such, meant too many hours were spent in the buffet polishing off the miniature whiskies. All I can remember about that disastrous Saturday was that after filing my match report and boarding the homeward-bound train, I awoke at station called Robertsbridge, in deepest Sussex, in the early hours of Sunday morning.

I had never heard of Robertsbridge, let alone visited the place, and obviously this was not the best time to break that particular duck. Startled, I jumped out of the train like a scalded cat and knew instinctively that I had made a mistake. But it was too late. Before I could take my disorientated thoughts into protective custody, the train was already on its way to the comfortable civilisation of Hastings and its numerous bed and breakfast establishments. In this remote spot, I was going to be lucky to see a cow, let alone a person. And as for civilisation, all I could make out in the darkness was the dull light coming from the nearby railway signal box.

I climbed the steps of this box with the intention of asking the signalman inside it what time I could catch a train to Haywards Heath. Perfectly naturally, or so my addled brain reasoned it, I picked up a nearby housebrick with which to knock on the railwayman's door, figuring that the noise of the brick hitting the wood would enable him to hear it above the creaking din of his old-fashioned signal handles.

The next thing I remember is being arrested by the local policeman in his Panda car and being driven to his home to await further developments. I then remember him telephoning a minicab for me and sending me on my way without pressing criminal charges.

When I was eventually able to reckon up the charge of the minicab journey, which was £30, plus the £90 price of a new pair of bifocal spectacles to replace the ones I had presumably lost on the journey from Ipswich to Liverpool Street or in one or other of the station buffets en route, I decided that it would be a lot cheaper to stay at home on Saturdays and try to earn my living in the betting shop instead. Needless to say, it was only a matter of months before we were forced to put the house up for sale and resume our lives with next to nothing in material terms.

After five months in limbo, my luck finally changed when Michael Herd, the sports editor of the London *Evening Standard*, decided to employ me as a 'commentator'. This was a new-fangled word he had to come up with for columnist because it was a job which brought his staff up to one over budget on his payroll. I could have kissed Michael's feet in gratitude, even though I assumed this job was going to stretch me, as it required a more upmarket writing style than that which I had employed on the *Sun*. It did, indeed, demand more from me, but I need not have worried for I was told, in confidence, just a few months later, that I had won the Sportswriter of the Year award again.

My work prompted a request from the *Standard* editor Charles Wintour which Michael Herd later told me he had been dreading. Mr Wintour, who was an intellectual of a cold, academic and somewhat haughty disposition, had informed Michael that he would like to meet his new sports commentator and instructed him to arrange a lunch date for the three of us. As we were perusing the menus in a plush London restaurant, Mr Wintour poured me some wine and politely asked me if I would like eels as a starter.

To Michael Herd's horror, this, I was informed by him later, was my reply: 'Do I like eels? I was brought up on 'em. My old man was a Billingsgate fish porter and he used to bring 'ome live ones, still wriggling. And do you know how he used to kill 'em? 'E used to bash their 'eads on our tin bath.'

I was never asked to meet Mr Wintour in person again. But then I was never able to settle on the *Standard* long enough to want to.

Changing from evening work back to crack-of-dawn endeavours was such a shock to my system that I was never really able to adjust to it. The atmosphere on the *Sun* had lived up to all my expectations of the newspaper offices that I had seen in old black and white Hollywood films. We all worked in one huge room to the constant clatter of typewriters and the cries of 'copy boy' as messengers were sent scurrying away to the subs' desk with our written offerings. I have never experienced such a stimulating environment. Practically everyone swore like a sailor, smoked like a chimney and guzzled down pints of beer on their frequent breaks between edition times. A few of us even managed to find time to sip whisky from our desk-drawer supply in the deluded conviction that it helped us to compose our sentences and paragraphs properly.

It was no different on the *Standard* except that it was all carried out in the cold light of day, with your eyes still full of sleep, and not in the invigorating boozy glow of eventide. And even worse, as far as I was concerned, was that my pieces often had to be written at home in the middle of the night in time to catch the first edition.

Still, I managed never to put a foot wrong at the *Standard* and that must have been why I was approached by its main rival, the London *Evening News*. The *News* sports editor, Peter Watson, had obviously heard that I had turned over a new leaf and he offered me a job which would take me all over the world again, unlike the deskbound one I was currently holding down. His main carrot was an offer I could not refuse, the promise that I could cover the upcoming 1976 Olympic Games in Montreal. So I thanked Michael Herd profusely and told him I was moving on again. And there were no hard feelings on either side except my own twinge of disappointment when I learned that I was to miss out on the Sportswriter of the Year award because I was changing papers the very week it was due to be announced in March.

In my new life on the *Standard*, I had been pitched against the most famous sports columnists in the game, such as Ian Wooldridge, Frank Keating and Michael Parkinson. Not a lot of people knew that Parky was a distinguished sportswriter as well as a television star and that he had once covered football matches in some decidedly humble press boxes. As for Ian Wooldridge, he was to become as big a hero for me as Hugh McIlvanney already was. Not only could the man write like an angel, he could drink me under the table and still have the steely self-discipline to carry himself as if he was stone cold sober. The only way I could ever tell Wooldridge how much I admired, respected and even envied him without blushing is through these pages. I admired and respected him, as did every other sportswriter in the world, because of his professional brilliance, and I sorely envied the way he was able to hold his liquor. It was Ian who first introduced me to the delights of the dry Martini cocktail, which I always drank – often with disastrous effects – whenever I was in America.

Mind you, they did not make a bad job of shaking and stirring a dry Martini in Montreal, either, and that was where I found myself in July when, true to his word, Peter Watson sent me to cover the Olympics as the *Evening News* columnist. Athletics had never been one of my great sporting loves although, as a gambling man, track events held the fascination that any kind of race would have done for me.

I soon showed my ignorance, however, when attending the swimming, which always comes first in the Olympic programme. I turned to my nearest companion and suggested that if only they had a betting shop hereabouts we could clean up on traps three, four and five, because they seemed to be the only ones which got in the frame. As my only previous swimming experiences had consisted of accompanying the water rats in the polluted River Lea in my boyhood and the odd dip in a hotel pool, I should have kept my big mouth shut. My companion, a veritable water babe by comparison, quickly pointed out that the reason lanes three, four and five kept doing so well was because that was where the fastest heat winners were always drawn in the semi-finals and finals we had just been witnessing. Still, all this personal navel-gazing was soon overshadowed by a handsome, moustachioed Scotsman, David Wilkie, who won gold and silver medals for Britain in the pool and gave us some lovely copy to whet our whistles as we moved on to the more glamorous track and field events.

Montreal was not my first stab at covering athletics. I had accompanied the *Sun* athletics correspondent, my old mate Colin Hart, to Rome in 1974 to write features about the European Championships. As he came out of the concrete jungle of the East End just the same as I did, I often wondered what his form lines were when it came to pole vaulting or throwing the javelin. I felt sure that in his boyhood he must have seen the odd geezer chucking a hammer at another bloke's head outside a boozer at closing time on a Saturday night.

Anyway, in Rome, Colin fixed me up with an interview with the celebrated long-distance runner Brendan Foster, who happened to be sharing a room in the athletics village with a future star miler, Steve Ovett. When I encountered Brendan, he was lying on his bed, with Ovett looking on in sympathy from across the room. Brendan tried to inform me that he had a stomach bug and could not go through with the interview.

This is what he told Colin later. 'Batty then bullied the life out of me by saying: "If you think you're in trouble now, that's nothing to the trouble you will be in if I I don't get a few nanny goats [quotes] from you for the Currant Bun [*Sun*] so that I can cop me green gages [wages]."'

And from that moment on, the good ship *Sun* was

always known as the Currant Bun by all who sailed in her.

Brendan, an educated Geordie, insisted that he had not understood a word I said and had been forced to get Brighton boy Ovett to interpret for him. As both are now television commentators all these years on, I just like to think I was giving them elocution lessons at the time.

If memory serves me, Great Britain had such a disastrous time at the 1976 Olympics that Foster was our only athletics medal winner, and that only a bronze when everyone had forecast a gold. I struck gold for the *Evening News*, though, with my usual 'golden bollocks' luck. I was telephoned at the break of dawn, London time, one day by Peter Watson, informing me that Great Britain had won the gold medal for the Pentathlon and demanding copy immediately, if not sooner. As this event had been taking place over several days at a venue God knows how many miles away from Montreal, and as what I knew about shooting, running, fencing, swimming and horse riding could have been written on the back of a postage stamp, I feared I was a dead man as far as this story and with it my future was concerned. But sitting opposite me in the press centre at the very moment I took that call was Bob Harris, who was then a track and field expert and is now head honcho at the new Sunday paper *Sport First*. An old running mate from way back in my Birmingham days, Bob saved my life by nonchalantly passing across the desk a little black diary in which the captain of our victorious Pentathletes had recorded every minute detail of the four-day event – most of which were splashed all over the *Evening News* in London later that day.

I shared a room in Montreal with an even older mate, Hugh McIlvanney. He did not have to compose his massive *Observer* pieces until Friday nights and, like so many of us, he could not settle down to write until his deadline was literally upon him. And he was not exactly into Ovaltine and a book at bedtime the rest of the week. Some nights, I knew how our wives must have felt when I lay in bed awaiting his gladiatorial entry into the room. It was not as if I had suddenly turned into Goody Two Shoes, but I was working round the clock and snatched a few hours' kip whenever I could, usually when Hughie was still full of running.

One Tuesday morning, tired of my mate tipping me out of bed and demanding that I either join him in a sing-song or fight him, I begged him to go out and do his work at the beginning of the week so that we could have some relatively peaceful nights. He agreed to try and made elaborate arrangements to interview the Cuban superstars, runner Alberto Juantorena and boxer Teofilo Stevenson, in their training camp. This was no easy task because it meant spending a day tugging at Red tape to get past the Communist bureaucracy. I presumed Hugh had succeeded because I never clapped eyes on him again until the early hours of the following Friday when he came in and gave my bed a good kicking. When I asked him what he had been up to all the week, he muttered something about the Scandinavians having stolen his notes. He had obviously been on the mother and father of a binge with some of the crazy Scandinavian journalists, but as for them stealing his notes – well, I looked him full in the eyes and said: 'Scandinavian, bollocks! You've put those notes down a lavatory somewhere and pulled the chain on them, because you can never write a word until the hounds of hell are up your arse, can you?'

Hughie's guilty grin told me I was not far off the mark. And neither was he when he sobered up and got round to writing his copy throughout that night. It was his customary masterpiece – with or without notes.

I was never around to hear him telephoning it over to his office, though, because Fridays happened to be my big play nights as our roles were reversed and he would throw me out into the corridor for interrupting his train of thought. So I would hump my mattress onto my shoulder and go and knock on Reg Gutteridge's door.

In Reggie's own words: 'Batty would lie down on his mattress on the floor at the foot of my bed like a pet pussy cat. And then, after growling a few rambling words, he would finish with an imitation trumpet blast, through his fingers, of the Last Post.'

Reg, the famous boxing writer and television commentator, had been like a cuddly uncle to me for more years than I care to remember. I first knew him when I was taking his copy at the *Evening News* in the mid 1950s, and then I ran into him regularly at boxing shows down the years. Now he was lumbered with taking me under his wing all over again. He was covering the boxing for the *News* in Montreal and had been instructed by Peter Watson to 'mind me' for the duration of these Games, a task he accomplished magnificently because I had the rare distinction of not receiving one written warning, or even a bollocking, from the office throughout my entire stint in Canada.

A few months after Montreal, Reg and I were together again to cover the third Muhammad Ali v Ken Norton fight in New York. A D-Day veteran, Reg lost a leg during that campaign and has an artificial limb which gives him a slight limp. At that time, September 1976, the film *Midnight Cowboy* was all the rage. It starred John Voight as a fun-loving cowboy making his first trip to New York and Dustin Hoffman as Rizzo, a crippled little down-and-out who chaperones the cowboy around the Big Apple.

On the way to the weigh-in, the pair of us were larking about like a couple of kids, imitating the Cowboy and Rizzo. And when we nearly got run over, Reg stole a famous scene from the movie by kicking the yellow cab which had almost hit us and screaming: 'I'm walking here . . .' just like Hoffman did in the film.

This bit of nonsense had a weird little postscript when we arrived at the weigh-in, for who should we find standing almost next to us in the crowd of VIPs but Dustin Hoffman himself, who was being managed at that time by the British boxing bigwig, Jarvis Astaire.

Reg and I have used these nicknames for each other ever since and whenever I was out of work and out of luck, he used to send me postcards from his trips to America addressed to 'Cowboy Batt', and which always featured a cowboy on the front. The one I liked best was of a poor old thirsty cowboy lying face down in the desert with vultures circling over him. Reg may have a black sense of humour but he has a very kind heart, which he has demonstrated by always being there for me during the bad times as well as the good. And I was honoured to be asked to assist him to write his own autobiography *Uppercuts and Dazes* when he reached his early seventies.

This particular Ali–Norton fight was being staged at the old Yankee Stadium baseball field, and it was the only time in my sporting life that I thought I was about to be crushed to death by the mass of fellow spectators. For what was probably the one and only time in history, the Bronx police force was on strike and all hell broke loose as a result. The signs had been ominous when it was announced that the world's media would be transported through Harlem in locked vehicles and that no one was to leave en route under any circumstances. With only a skeleton strike-breaking police protection and security staff on duty, muggings were taking place inside and outside this famous old venue. After the fight, a nightmare engulfed the press pack when the tunnel housing the dressing rooms became a mass of trapped humanity. We were lifted off our collective feet, gasping for air and most of us were convinced we were going to suffocate or, at the very least, have our ribs broken. At my right shoulder, a man wearing spectacles was hitting a policeman one, two, three, four, five, six blows to the face. I braced myself expecting retaliatory truncheons and prayed that the ridiculous baseball cap I was wearing would protect me. The man distributing this fancy millinery to the press earlier had promised: 'These are so that the cops know which heads to crack.' Thank God he was right.

A disaster was only averted when a posse of huge black men in vivid suits appeared at one end of the corridor, hoisting a woman above their heads and shouting: 'Make way for Ali's Ma!' And somehow this group of muscular minders, with their regal cargo still held aloft, managed to cut a swathe through what appeared to be an impenetrable mass of humanity into the great man's dressing room. I squeezed in behind them and, to emphasise just how near the point of collapse I was, my semi-delirious mind had me remembering, at that precise moment, one of the first pieces of advice that was given to me in my reporting days. This was: 'Always take advantage of confusion.' It was passed on by an old soak of a reporter who, whenever a big story broke and diverted the attention of his superiors on the news desk, would dash across the road to the pub for a quick one. The old reprobate used to leave his jacket draped across his chair and a cigarette burning in his ashtray. But he fooled no one except himself.

Anyway, when I finally arrived at Ali's feet, I was the first press man to make it this far. The king, himself, looked on the point of death, too. He had been judged to have won the fight on points, but only after taking a fearful battering from Norton, the same man who had broken Ali's jaw on a previous bout. Tired, bruised, bleeding, aching, Ali was stretched out on the rubbing table with his arms folded across his chest, looking like a mountain lying in state.

He confessed: 'I am good and hurt tonight. I am getting tired and old.' But he shrugged off retirement, saying: 'As a black man, I must go out good. I must retire on a night when I am at my best.'

The world now knows that The Greatest left this decision far too long and made it far too late, as I was to find out for myself when I got an amazing world exclusive interview with him at his Los Angeles home in 1983 – of which more later.

From New York, I went straight on to Toronto to interview British racing driver James Hunt at the Canadian Grand Prix. I remember having to send my piece back to London in the middle of the night and was struggling to stay awake, awaiting the office's telephone call, when, whisky in hand, I noticed that the hotel television set in my room was showing a soft porn movie entitled *Emmanuelle.* Believe it or not, I had never seen a blue movie before and I certainly had never noticed that they were available in hotel rooms, as I spent most of my off-duty time on trips in hotel bars. Anyway, Emmanuelle's antics on screen succeeded in keeping me awake for my deadline. But she cost me a big bollocking a couple of weeks later when the managing editor noticed that she had been itemised on my hotel bill and had got on my expenses claim without me noticing it.

This reminds me of another lovely little 'exes' anecdote from a few years earlier on the *Sun*. I had taken Heidi and the kids out to Sunday lunch at a very nice country restaurant, which happened to be only a few miles from where my boss Frank Nicklin lived and one he knew well. Carelessly, I submitted the bill on my expenses claim without twigging that it said on it two lunches and two halves. Now Nicklin and I had always enjoyed a love-hate relationship, and this little incident happened during one of the 'hate' periods. Triumphantly he strode out of his office into the big room, waving my exes form and thrusting it under my nose. In front of all my mates, he roared: 'Gotcha this time. This has to be worth the sack.'

I looked up to see his forefinger pointing at that restaurant receipt as he said: 'Try talking your way out of that.'

But instantly another trusty white rabbit hopped into my mind in the nick of time and I found myself ad-libbing: 'I took two jockeys to lunch with the photographer. And you know what those poor little sods are like when it comes to weight watching.'

It has to be emphasised here that none of us reporters and writers on the road ever regarded manipulating our expenses as cheating. The problem was that we could spend half our salaries entertaining contacts with booze but you could only claim money back if you had receipts, and as very few barmen would entertain that sort of nonsense for round after round, we used to make it a case of swings and roundabouts where getting back what we actually spent was concerned.

But expenses were the least of my worries by now.

Deadlines were the nightmare. I sometimes still wake up with the night sweats, having had terrifying dreams about missing deadlines by getting on the wrong train, turning up at the wrong stadium or not being able to get near a telephone. As much as I was enjoying my life as a roving columnist, it meant that I had to do most of my writing from hotel rooms in the middle of the night after I had attended some evening event, then stayed around to get the necessary quotes, never getting back until after midnight. And I did not have to write a mere report, I had to fill half a tabloid page at least three times a week. For someone like me, this meant relying on the whisky bottle more and more in the mistaken belief that it would keep the adrenalin flowing and help to stimulate me.

For the first few months on the *News*, in my alcoholic arrogance, I used to tease Peter Watson when he rang up at 7am by pretending that I had gone out on the piss all night and gone missing. Many of the hotel night porters in England, and even some in Europe, got to know me and my antics very well, and aided and abetted me in this game by telling Peter that Batty's bed had not been slept in, causing him grievous anxiety before I rang back to let him in on the so-called joke.

But the 'joke' misfired badly one morning when the man at the other end of the line happened to be Vic Wakeling. Vic, who is now the head honcho of Sky Sports, had just joined the *News* from Birmingham and had been appointed as Peter Watson's deputy.

He was standing in for Peter, who was on a day off, and I remember thinking, through my splitting hangover headache, that it was a shame that I had to do what I was about to do to a new boy. For when he chirpily asked me what gems I had for him that morning, all I could think to tell him was: 'Fuck all!' And this time I was not lying.

I was told later by a sub-editor, who was in the *News* office at the time, that Vic had put his hand over the receiver and said: 'I think Batty is having a laugh with me. He reckons he's got nothing for his column.'

But when Vic checked with me again, all I could do was to admit that, although I was extremely sorry, I did, in fact, have 'fuck all' To Vic's eternal credit, he did not blow the whistle on me. But by then it was not so much a question of if I would get the sack, but simply when.

Peter had taken to always addressing me as 'poet' and I responded by nicknaming him 'patron', but I was told by colleagues in the office that he used to turn the air black and blue by calling me every swear word he could lay his tongue to when I played these stupid games. He took to trying to explain to me time and again that if I failed to come to the line with my copy, he would be left with half a page to fill at a moment's notice and no one to comment on the main event of the previous night. I used to nod seriously and sympathetically at such times and assure him that I would bear his words in mind next time I filed. But I was to learn that alcoholism made me oblivious to other people's needs. Oh, I would sincerely apologise and even rack myself with guilt over my self-centred behaviour, but I was incapable of stopping it – at least until I learned to put the cork permanently in the bottle.

What I did not have the courage to confess to him, or anyone else, was that feeling of dread as I sat in a lonely hotel room with nothing but virgin sheets of paper in front of me, which often looked as cold and forbidding as an ice-bound river or as daunting as a desert.

Ironically, Peter was almost as responsible as I was for getting me my first 'yellow card'. In October 1977,

Scotland were playing Wales at Anfield in a make-or-break qualifying match for the 1978 World Cup finals in Argentina. The paper had forgotten to book a hotel room for me and by one of those strange quirks of fate, the *Sun* had also neglected to book a room for my travelling companion and mate, Alex Montgomery. Undeterred, Alex and I settled down to a slap-up liquid lunch on British Rail in which we happened to share a table with a rich Liverpool nightclub owner and his glamour 'baby doll' wife, neither of whom we had ever clapped eyes on before. The nightclub owner told us that we had as much chance of getting a room in Liverpool, which would be bursting at the seams with Scotsmen and Welshmen, as we had of 'screwing his missus'.

After the match, which kicked off in the evening and which Scotland won courtesy of a hotly disputed penalty decision for a 'phantom' handball, we discovered that our lunch companion had not been exaggerating. The Adelphi, where we usually stayed because it housed the Liverpool Press Club in its basement, looked like a war zone, with prostrate drunken bodies everywhere. And it was the same all over the city, with not a bed to be had for love or money. As the Press Club did not shut until the early hours of the morning, we were not too bothered about finding somewhere to kip – until the night air hit our boozy heads and I suddenly remembered that I had to be on the phone in a few hours with a column and that I had better damn well find somewhere to sit down and write it. It was then that Alex remembered that, as the nightclub owner had toasted us over that British Rail lunch earlier, he had generously given us his address and told us to knock him up if we could not find a bed for the night.

We managed to get a taxi to take us to the address we

showed the driver, but it turned out to be a seemingly never-ending journey through the Mersey Tunnel to the other end of Liverpool. When we finally arrived at the big, imposing house, situated in its own grounds, the taxi driver scarpered as soon as we had paid him. We crunched our way up the gravel path, peeped through the living-room window, which had all its lights blazing, and saw 'baby doll' stretched out on the sofa in a flimsy night gown, looking for all the world as if she was rat-arsed pissed.

And indeed she was. But on hearing me bash on her window, she came to the door, game as a pebble, and let us in. We had just settled down for a drink or two when hubby arrived home in a huge Rolls-Royce and announced that he was none too pleased with this situation in which we all found ourselves. Good as gold, though, he told the pair of us to jump in the back of his 'Roller' and drove us on another marathon journey to what he said was his son's flat, gave us the key and told us to leave it under the mat when we left. The flat did not possess a phone, or an alarm clock, but I crashed out convinced that light sleeper Alex would call me in an hour or so. Unfortunately, we both overslept and when I saw the time, 6.45am, I grabbed a pair of trousers and a shirt and legged it barefoot in the freezing cold to the nearest phone box, which happened to be in a local shopping area.

Now, it takes a long while to put a column over on the phone, especially when you are ad-libbing every word of it as I was with this one. So by the time I was finished, an irate queue of would-be public telephone users had formed and then were on the point of calling the police as this barefoot geezer with his shirt hanging out kept telling them all to stop banging on the telephone box window and to 'fuck off out of it'. Tragically, I missed the first edition, leaving a hole in the paper until the second edition, and for my pains received a written warning informing me that if this kind of thing happened again, I, too, would be invited by the *Evening News* to 'fuck off out of it', or words to that effect.

I was in trouble again a few months later when I got into a silly argument with a picture desk mate in the office pub, 'The Harrow'. This particular guy had the reputation of being a mouth almighty when he was in drink, and he went over the top and insulted me. I asked him outside and he followed me, somewhat reluctantly, into the street. It was in the dead of winter and I was wearing a sheepskin coat which restricted my movements. At least, that is my excuse for the debacle which ensued. Well pissed, I took a swing at my opponent, he ducked and the force of my haymaker pitched me head first on to the stone steps of the Harrow, which were razor sharp. I was carted off to hospital, where I was detained for a couple of nights because my forehead had split open like a melon. When I returned to work sporting two lovely black eyes, my second yellow card was waiting – and this one had been authorised by the editor himself, Lou Kirby.

It was not long before I was to be detained in hospital again after a drinking bout, this time when I severed the ligaments in my big toe. Vic Railton, the *Evening News* football correspondent, had died suddenly of a heart attack. Vic was such a much-loved personality that West Ham, his local club, held a testimonial match for him in which every member of the first team played against a showbiz XI and there was a crowd of 12,000. And the wake after his funeral, which was attended by half the footballing celebrities in London, turned out to be so fierce and so sad that I kicked the glass front door in when I got home and Heidi had to rush me to casualty because I was bleeding like a pig. Just what it was with my wife and glass front doors, I never did find out.

Heidi soon had much more than carting me off to hospital to occupy her mind, however, when early in 1978 the inevitable eventually happened and I got my third 'yellow', which, of course, meant a 'red' and a sacking. On this occasion, for some reason which has long since disappeared into the mists of time, a crowd of us wound up in a Greek restaurant in Goodge Street after an evening match and indulged in a riotous bit of customary plate throwing. Somewhere in the fog of that distant blackout, a mental picture still comes to mind of that Irish goalkeeping genius Pat Jennings stretching out his huge hand to prevent one of the flying pieces of crockery from hitting his face. The next thing I remember is being stretched out, face down in bed in the famous Waldorf Hotel, when I felt someone frantically shaking my shoulders. When I looked up, I was staring into the face of my red-haired mate Peter Watson. I must confess that it makes me blush now to think that I used to have the cheek to get the office to book me into hotels for midweek events so that I did not disturb my wife and kids at night.

It transpired that I had left the phone off the hook, put a 'do not disturb' sign on the door and missed the first edition by a mile.

This time, Peter could not save me from the editor's wrath and he had arrived to have a cup of coffee with me and to tell me so. He told me later he was in a 'right old nervous lather' about having to tell me my fate, but that I made it easy for him by simply shrugging my shoulders and saying: 'I suppose this means the tin tack, patron?'

'Watto' rushed back to his busy office relieved that I

was going to go quietly, but he was horrified a few hours later when, refuelled with whisky, I lurched through the back door of the big room and advanced on the editor and his cohorts on the back bench to regale them. I later learned from Steve Stammers, now a football writer on the *Standard* but at that time one of my colleagues on the *News*, that I told the assembled executives, among other things, that none of them could 'write a bleedin' postcard' and that all the messenger boys in the office lined up and applauded my outrageous performance.

There was nothing left for poor old Peter to do but get my minder Reg Gutteridge to escort me off the premises.

The only consolation I can take from my departures from the *News* and the *Sun* was that, in both cases, it took a very good man to replace me. John Sadler, who was promoted to replace me on the 'Current Bun', is one of the most talented and respected sportswriters in the business and a thoroughly nice guy, too. And Patrick Collins, another long-time close friend, who took over my *Evening News* column, went on to win a string of awards on the *Mail On Sunday*. Although in Patrick's case, it forced me to face up to the uncomfortable fact that I was now getting much too old in the tooth for this juvenile delinquent behaviour – I mean, Patrick's dad, Pat, had once been a football reporting colleague of mine, for God's sake!

But even this disastrous sacking was put into perspective by the news that my oldest brother John had just died of a heart attack at the age of 57.

CHAPTER SEVENTEEN
EXILED

The poor man from the management staff of the *Evening News* who came to my home to confiscate my office car a day or two after I was sacked had such a pitiful expression on his face that I felt obliged to put my arm around his shoulder and comfort him with a few soothing words, such as 'It's not your fault, mate,' and 'Please don't blame yourself.' He seemed so racked with guilt, so crestfallen and so desperately embarrassed by the unenviable task he was being asked to carry out that I felt more sorry for him than I did for myself.

It did not take long for my mood to change, however. Unlike all the previous times I had been sacked, that exhilarating, new-found feeling of freedom from responsibilities which I described earlier was on this occasion as brief and fleeting as the sweet bird of youth.

I had to face the fact that at 44 I was no longer a spring chicken and that as much of my life was behind me as in front of me, and that to misquote dear old Oliver Hardy, 'This was another fine mess I had gotten myself into.'

The trouble with my messes by now, though, was that they did not affect just me anymore. The piles of shit I was still pulling over my head were spilling out all over my family, too. We had only just about got on our feet again after the last bout of unemployment only a couple of years earlier. We had lost our big house in Cuckfield and moved to a smaller one in Sevenoaks in Kent. But extravagant as ever, I was sending my son Danny to the fee-paying Sevenoaks private school.

So far I had managed to 'live well' because, like most alcoholic personalities, I was a genius at borrowing money from bank managers and loan companies and the like. But with no salary coming in, this 'lifestyle' was obviously going to come apart at the seams again sooner rather than later.

Usually the last one to know anything about myself, even I could sense by now that my head was becoming a dangerous place to inhabit. For in addition to worrying about the welfare of my wife and three children, I was full of that much more poisonous bile, self-pity. Once again I had put myself out of work with no redundancy pay, no pension, no nothing – except the few weeks' wages and expenses that were still owed to me. I used up most of this with cheap-day train trips to Fleet Street and back.

But these turned into daily nightmares when I was made to face the unthinkable fact that no one, but no one, wanted me to work for them anymore. This was not strictly true in that they were prepared to accept freelance pieces from me, but such an 'untouchable' had I become that no editor would allow me to darken the door of his office again.

I could wander from pub to Fleet Street pub and club to Fleet Street club, but when it came to trying to gain entry into a house in my own village, I could only press my face against their windows and then turn away to howl at the moon. To a gregarious animal like me, this exile felt like Hell on earth. In truth, this was just my journalistic penchant for exaggeration working overtime again. Years later, I was to find out what real exile into a real wilderness felt like.

So, finding myself stuck out 'in the sticks' with no wheels, the only place in which I could drown my sorrows was in the Bullfinch pub just yards across the road from where I lived. And this was when I first crossed that deadly line from what I kidded myself was social drinking with groups of other people to solitary guzzling with the specific intention of 'getting out of my head'. The only things which stopped me from sinking into the oblivion of round-the-clock drinking were the licensing hours – the pubs still closed at 2.30 in the afternoon in those days – and shortage of money, which restricted me to pints of lager rather than my preferred slugs of whisky.

Facing the day became more and more difficult. It took a huge effort to get out of my dressing gown and into the bathroom. And I even turned the simplistic chore of shaving and showering into a morning-long, time-killing ritual, pausing to smoke cigarettes between every separate little task.

Our financial plight meant that Heidi was forced to take a job, which was a blessing for me in that I did not have to face what I imagined would be recriminatory looks from her and the kids, who were in school. But in fact, far from being hostile towards me, they were still loving and sympathetic.

When the pub turned out in the afternoons, I would lock myself away in the study and make imaginary telephone calls in my head in which I had long phantom conversations with colleagues as if I was still working.

I was eventually saved by the bell when my old boxing mate Reg Gutteridge, who had by now become something of a fairy godmother by keeping in regular touch and looking out for my interests whenever he could, made a real-live telephone call to tell me that I had been invited to lunch at a posh West End restaurant by his pal George Walker.

George, a contemporary of my brothers George and Jim, grew up in the East End and became an extremely tough light-heavyweight boxer. He had been involved in arguably the bloodiest fight ever seen in a British ring when he clashed with Dennis Powell in Liverpool back in the fifties. Later, he successfully managed his 'golden boy' brother, the crowd-pulling heavyweight Billy, and went on to make and lose a fortune as the head of the multi-million pound Brent Walker organisation. He is now making a comeback in Russia, of all places, even though he is touching 70.

At the time of Reg's phone call, George was at the height of his fame and power as one of this country's leading financial giants. He was already into films as a producer and distributor, but over lunch he told me that his big ambition was to make the definitive English gangster film – a subject that, because of our backgrounds, he and I both knew plenty about. He suggested that Reg should be my unofficial, unpaid manager and keep me on the straight and narrow by cracking the whip over me while I wrote a screenplay for him, for which he paid me £1,500 cash in advance. This unexpected windfall not only kept the financial wolves away from my door but, more importantly, the project fired me with enthusiasm for life again and in my usual all-or-nothing fashion, I was soon buying books on screenwriting and burning the midnight oil fashioning fictional gangsters and storylines from the real memories of my misspent youth. And me being me, my unrealistic expectations soon had me dreaming of off-shore tax havens in Jersey and the Cayman Islands.

Meanwhile, George was making a film called *The Stud,* which relaunched the career of Joan Collins. He invited Reg and me to view rushes of it in the private film studio which was housed in his Mayfair offices. Reg and I told him it was the worst load of old pornographic cobblers we had ever seen in our lives. George just told us to behave ourselves and pray that it was a winner so that he and his company could invest the money *The Stud* made in the film that I was writing. So when *The Stud* was shown in the local cinema at Sevenoaks, I was standing outside gloating over the queues and cheering the punters through the doors.

Sadly for me, *The Stud* was such a box-office smash that, just as I was putting the final touches to my script, George was forced to inform me that his board had out-voted him and that my film would have to be put on hold while they made a similar, money-spinning follow-up called *The Bitch.* But George consoled me by inviting Heidi and me to spend a weekend at his gaming club in Westcliffe-on-Sea and then go off and write an opening episode for a series called *The Gaming House,* which he hoped to sell to television. Again, he bunged me an advance of £1,500 to 'keep me off the streets', but in reality it was to keep me out of the boozers and betting shops for Heidi's sake.

Still, although none of those sweat-stained words of mine were ever transferred to celluloid, the effort of composing them had given me back my self-esteem. For it is amazing how soon you lose confidence in yourself if you are out of work for any length of time, and I suspect that applies to any profession or trade. Somehow, I now found the courage to stand in wait for the *Daily Express* sports editor Ken Lawrence, when I knew he would be due in his office pub, and I found the necessary mixture of arrogance, aggression and downright humility, to bully, cajole and finally beg him to put me to work in some capacity or other. Thank God, Ken weakened and offered me casual work on a daily basis. Then, within weeks, the Good Lord Himself intervened personally on my behalf when he decided to create another new newspaper to get me out of trouble yet again! And this time I did not even have to move out of my seat to acquire the new job, because Express Newspapers announced they were starting a new tabloid called the *Daily Star* and within minutes of that announcement I was being summoned to the new editor's office to be told that I was to be his very first appointment – his 'star turn' for *Star Sport*.

The *Star* was born in November 1978 and I was reborn at least a couple of months prematurely, in September that year. The new editor was Peter Grimsditch, the best one I ever worked for by a distance in that he seemed knocked out by my wild man image and indulged my every whim. I loved him for several reasons, not least because although he was editing a tits-and-bum tabloid, he had won a double first at Oxford for Greek Classics and as a self-taught slob myself, I have always been in awe of educated men. Secondly, I loved him because he was lively, boyish and tiny and I felt protective towards him and wanted to tuck his red head under my arm and 'mind' him.

Within days I was being whisked up to Manchester, where the *Star* was to be produced and printed, and I was ensconced in a room at the Midland Hotel, where I languished in luxury, leaving my plush new living quarters only to venture forth on dummy runs to places like Greece, Dublin and – would you believe? – Palm Springs and San Francisco. All this when the new paper was still on the drawing board – talk about beyond my wildest dreams! I went to Palm Springs to do mock coverage of a Davis Cup tennis match between the USA and Great Britain, and there I palled up with old running mates like Ken Montgomery of the *Sunday Mirror*, Nigel Clarke of the *Daily Mirror* and Ron Atkin of the *Observer*. Sadly, they told me later I used to get so pissed in that playground of the Hollywood stars that I would bully the night porter in the early hours of every morning demanding that he fix me up with a minicab to Sydenham – an address I had abandoned years ago.

Back in England I discovered that 'Grimbles', as everyone on the new paper affectionately called him, had at last appointed a sports editor in Arthur Lamb, a sports desk sub on the *Express* in Manchester. Arthur immediately asked me to 'mark his card' when it came to staffing the sports side of the paper, and I was soon able to procure jobs for several of my old mates.

'Grimbles' and Arthur plied me with an embarrassment of riches in that they wanted me to cover every sport from tennis to tiddlywinks and as soon as the paper hit the streets in the north of England, where it first came out, my picture was plastered all over the place again, on railway stations and city hoardings. Then when it hit London a few months later, my mug shot stared back at me from underground escalators.

While the paper was still appearing only in the north, I was summoned to the same pub in which I had waylaid Ken Lawrence a few months earlier and offered the top sports job on the *Daily Express*. I declined that offer out of loyalty to 'Grimbles' and because I did not want to miss out on a trip to Australia with Mike Brearley's England cricket team. When I returned, the paper was being printed in London and I was able to leave my luxury pad in the Manchester Midland and rejoin Heidi and the kids in Sevenoaks. But from there I was off around the world again for football with Brian Clough and Peter Taylor and their twice European Cup-winning team, Nottingham Forest. I flew to Tokyo and back in the space of three days with Forest for their match against the South American champions.

In South Africa, for a world heavyweight championship fight between Gerrie Coetzee and John Tate, 'Grimbles' diverted me to Soweto to do a news feature on apartheid and then confessed that he was cooking up a plot to make me his roving news man – shades of my earlier dreams of following in the footsteps of heroes like James Cameron, Vincent Mulchrone, Rene McColl, Don Iddon and Noel Barber.

But the most memorable trip of that period – for all the wrong reasons – was when photographer Frank Barrett and I went to Malta in the depths of a snowbound, fixture-wrecking British winter to seek out some sporting action somewhere on the globe. Brooke Sanders, our champion lady jockey at that time, was off to Malta to take part in the European lady jockey championships and as she was an old mate of mine from my racing days, she invited Frank and me to accompany her.

Bubbling Brooke left the lady champions of Germany, Italy, France and the like in her slipstream as she cruised to the title. In all, I think she won three of the races on the six-race card and managed to tip me the other three winners, too. Because my booze-befuddled brain had no idea what the local money was worth, I steamed into the bookies with my gloves off, piling each winning bet straight back at them. It was the one and only time I have been through the card in my life. Soon, I had this wallpaper lolly hanging out of every pocket and a crowd of local punters cheering me on.

Typical of every mug punter, though, there was a hard luck ending to the story. I was too pissed to try to change the money back into English that night and Frank and I were booked on a crack of dawn flight home next day. Tragically, when I attempted to leave the country with my still uncounted 'fortune', it was confiscated at the airport. Don Mintoff's socialist government was in power on the island at the time and I was informed that no one was allowed to leave there with local currency in their sky rocket. When I protested loudly and vehemently, I was ushered into a tiny room and body searched. I was convinced that my interrogators were just about to stick red-hot needles up my fingernails when I eventually 'swallowed' it and settled for going home skint, as usual.

Back home, I seemed to be more popular than ever in the office and, as was my alcoholic wont, I began to take more and more liberties. The London sports editor of the *Star* at the time was the late John Morgan, who had run the *Express* sports department when that paper was in its prime. John could drink Bell's whisky faster and more furiously than any other drinking man I ever met – and I met a few in my time. Consequently, when he took his troops out for a lunchtime drink, whenever we were all in the office together, we staggered back well and truly smashed.

Morgan, an arch-survivor, used to keep his head down after these monstrous sessions, but the rest of us were less predictable. I was prone to rant and rave and threaten to throw a typewriter or two through the office window whenever I made a spelling mistake! These fierce boozing sessions took place in what was euphemistically called the City Golf Club, which was situated in an alley opposite our office and in the shadow of Fleet Street's own church, St Bride's. To beat the licensing laws of the time, it was allowed to stay open all day, presumably because it had an indoor practice golf range built in. But that soon disappeared in favour of round-the-clock drinking.

My guts were getting so bad at this time that I started to buy carry out cartons of a diabolical dark brown-looking liquid called Underburg from the nearby Old Bell Tavern and consume them in the office. Underburg was a German-manufactured 'hangover cure' and no wonder, because it contained about 90 per cent alcohol. While I was 'getting away with it' like this, it had not occurred to me to cut down my drinking. But something had to give soon and it did in spectacular fashion when my body suddenly jack-knifed and I keeled over in the office one afternoon. As I was being carted off to the sick bay, Arthur was shouting down the phone from Manchester to John Morgan to get me to finish my column first. If memory serves me, I was comically being billed by the paper as 'The Biggest Four-Letter Word In Sport' at that time, and like the biggest four-letter mug in the business I did struggle back to the typewriter and complete a few more agonised paragraphs.

The gall bladder which had left me in periodic bouts of agony for the past few years and had gone undiagnosed was suddenly useless and my body was poisoned with jaundice. I went green within minutes of arriving home in an office car and was whisked off to hospital, where I remained for the next 16 weeks. During that time I was marked down as 'nil by mouth' and my weight went down from 14½ stone to a skeletal nine. My wife was informed that I might have cancer of the liver and an emergency operation was carried out on the Saturday afternoon of 26 May 1979, when England beat Scotland 3–1 at Wembley. Heidi said when she came to visit me in intensive care, my first question was: 'Who won?'

Thankfully, I was still well enough loved in the office for a constant stream of colleagues, including the busy 'Grimbles', to visit me. But I was definitely not a pretty sight, with a bile bag hanging out of a hole in my stomach for all to see. When I was eventually allowed home, my ears were ringing with the worst possible news. The doctors had informed Heidi that my liver was shot to pieces and that under no circumstances was I ever to drink again. Such was my as yet undiagnosed alcoholic madness that throughout my long convalescence, I was consumed with just one thought – the horrible realisation that I could never again seek solace from a glass or a bottle. The prospect was almost as dreadful as the thought of death. At every opportunity I protested and pleaded with the hospital doctors to lighten my load, and eventually nagged them into agreeing to tell Heidi that three alcoholic drinks a day was to be my absolute maximum intake.

When I was eventually fit enough to return to work, 'Grimbles' was so delighted to have me back that he arranged with the management for me to be issued with the rarest of all privileges that Express Newspapers had to offer. This unbelievable perk was an air credit card, which meant that I could fly first-class with one companion to any and every part of the world, no questions asked, at any booking desk anywhere on the planet. It won't take a rocket scientist among you to work out that this card was to turn out to be my undoing on the paper, but that was still several adventures and a couple of sackings away.

The official reason for the card was that 'Grimbles' was taking me off the sporting treadmill to become his international scribe. His first ploy was to send me to Yugoslavia to cover the impending death of President Tito. That iron-willed dictator had been lying in an oxygen tent with a newly amputated leg for several days and had naturally declined all deathbed interviews. But my guv'nor, peerless Peter, reasoned that if anyone could crack this stubborn old nut, Batty could – presumably on the grounds that fools rush in where angels fear to tread.

Grimbles wanted me to do the job 'under cover' and so that the other papers did not tumble what I was up to, he suggested I went to cover a Manchester United friendly match against Hajduk Split and then make my way over to Belgrade. On the night after the match, I got into a long, drunken conversation with the top commissar in Split, who informed me that Tito was a soccer nut and that he had actually formed the Hajduk team himself from a group of war-time partisans. My tipsy comrade then reasoned that if I got the match ball autographed by the Manchester United players, that would indeed gain me access to the great man, no matter how close to death's door he happened to be. And then he topped this off with the kind of phrase I have heard repeated in almost every soccer-loving country in the world: 'Tito loves Bobby Charlton,' he assured me.

So I asked my mate Dave Sexton, who was the Manchester United manager at the time, to get the ball signed for me and to put a 'get well soon' message on it, too. Then, together with my photographer pal Stan Meagher, who accompanied me on this venture, I had to make a journey of several hundred miles by plane and taxis from sunny Split to snowy Belgrade. I remember that during the journey, Stan kept fantasising about getting Tito to nut the ball for him for his picture – conveniently forgetting that the dying president had only one leg and was in an oxygen tent.

Horror of horrors, when we eventually arrived at the hospital gates, the biro ink with which the ball was signed had been hopelessly smudged and made almost illegible by the blizzard we had been forced to negotiate because, like the idiot I was, I had carried the bloody thing under my arm all the way for safe keeping. Anyway, we made do and mended the situation by getting one of the president's doctors to pose with me and the ball, and we got his guarantee that the great man would 'indeed treasure this unusual gift'. 'Grimbles' seemed pleased enough with my story, though, and displayed it prominently along with Stan's picture on the main features page. President Tito died days later.

From Belgrade, Stan and I were dispatched immediately to Munich to cover some 'Common Market' tale about German car workers keeping cows in their back gardens. I must confess that I could not make head nor tail of what this story was all about, but to say I was enjoying my new lifestyle was an understatement. Stan and I had booked into the five-star Four Seasons Hotel in Munich and were living it up like a couple of Maharajahs. Stan, who has since died, had covered big stories all over the world on the *Express* but he reckoned this was the best number he had ever had and begged me to ask 'Grimbles' to make it a full-time post for him.

It all went pear-shaped back home, though when I began drinking more heavily than ever and getting pissed quicker than ever – presumably because my liver had gone. One night I wanted money in such a hurry that when I went to cash an advance expenses chit and found the cashiers closed, I bashed on the glass windows so violently that the security men thought there was a robbery underway and sent for the police. I was told later that I kicked up such a commotion that Jocelyn Stevens, the number two to the proprietor Lord Matthews and whose office was opposite the cashier's, dived under his table. My cause was not helped by the fact that there had been a robbery at the *Mirror* offices the week before in which a security man had been shot and killed.

Struan Coupar, the managing editor, was told to inform me that the only way I could keep my job was to undertake a 'cure' for my booze problems. So the company paid more than £700 for me to go to a clinic in Harrow-on-the-Hill, where I was to be an in-patient for a week. This turned out to be the worst experience of my life so far. The quack of a doctor there put me on antibuse tablets and then deliberately gave me whisky, which in turn induced an epileptic fit. Abstem, which I have taken since, has, I am reliably informed, been banned. And no wonder! On the third day of my course of these horrendous pills, Heidi was summoned to watch what was about to happen so that she would be under no illusions either as to the severity of my drink problem. She sat on the side of my bed while I drank three large scotches. In addition to the doctor being in the room, which looked like an operating theatre with bottles of oxygen and heaven knows what else in it, there was a nursing sister who helped the doctor to strap me down as the whisky took effect.

Heidi told me later that she had never seen me in a more pathetic state in her life. Apparently, my face went blood red, I could not get my breath, I began sweating and twitching so much that my arms and legs went into convulsions and I began drooling at the mouth. I was put out of my misery by a massive injection and did not wake up again for another 12 hours, when I felt light-headed but calm and collected. What I had endured was called aversion therapy and boy, did it work! I stayed on those tablets for months afterwards, too terrified to let a drink come within miles of my lips. Incidentally, I knew that both Jimmy Greaves and George Best had had this hellish stuff implanted in their legs, and my admiration for both of them grew tenfold.

When I took the trouble to read up on this invention from hell, I learned that it had been discovered in car factories in Scandinavia. Apparently, some chemicals in those factories affected the men who had alcohol in their blood so badly that it not only made them violently ill, it killed some of them. But those who were alcohol-free were totally unaffected by it. The big failing with this drug was that it only addressed the physical problem of alcoholism and did nothing whatever for the mental and spiritual state of the sufferer. This meant that you stayed sober on fear alone and were rendered a permanent clench-fisted, white-knuckled, teeth-scraping wreck. I learned much later at Alcoholics Anonymous that in this condition you are literally a 'dry drunk'.

I was to find out the hard way just how effective this drug could be when, shortly after my return to work, I took alcohol into my system accidentally. I was interviewing cricketing legend Geoff Boycott over dinner at a hotel just outside Manchester during an England Test match when there was a bomb scare. The meal was interrupted and all the guests were ushered out onto the hotel lawn for half an hour or so. My main course had been a dish which was normally cooked in wine, but I had requested the waiter to leave the wine out of it. This meal had been half-eaten when we scarpered and when they re-served it later, I had been so engrossed in my conversation with Geoff that I had forgotten to make that same request and second time round I got a meal which had been well and truly cooked in wine. Within minutes of going up to my room to study my interview. notes, I was shivering all over and had to keep asking the hotel housekeeper to bring me extra blankets and even an oil heater, despite it being a warm summer evening.

That experience put me off the pills for a while and turned me into a liar for the first time ever with Heidi, because I had promised her I was going to keep taking them *sine die*. For an agonising period of time, I started experimenting with them and found you could take a chance on a drink once they had been out of your system for about three days – although this calculation was sometimes touch and go and I would be violently sick when I sneaked a drink down me. I started a routine of drinking only when I went abroad and I would white-knuckle it on the pills until a couple of days before I was due to fly, then get steamed in on the plane, much to the horror of mates such as Reg Gutteridge and Colin Hart who were looking out for me.

Once, I remember going to a title fight in Reno, Nevada, and managing not to drink at all on the plane journey over there. On this occasion I had been on the pills for several weeks at a stretch and the desire for a drink occupied my every waking thought. We were staying at a huge hotel which had at least half a dozen bars in it, and I remember hiding away from Reg, Colin and company in one of them, ordering a large dry Martini and just leaving my tongue languishing in it for at least half an hour. It was bliss. But my trouble – like every other genuine 'alchy' I've ever known – was that one drink was never enough and once that booze hit my blood stream, the craving took over and I never knew where it was going to take me, except that the thought of the next drink and how and when I was going to be able to come by it was all-consuming.

Understandably, Heidi was beside herself with worry about me by now, but like most victims of the alcoholic, she too refused to blame the drink, preferring to believe my then sincere explanation that I was just a retarded teenager. With our own two elder children into their teens, Heidi had suggested that we get back upmarket in the housing stakes, because she saw that as our only possible chance of security. So we had moved yet again when I clinched the job on the *Star*. This time it was to Tunbridge Wells, where we bought a half-share in a mansion. I even threw in the luxury of a dalmatian puppy for my animal-crackers youngest daughter Caroline. That puppy, Lucky, turned out to be as mad as I was, but at least the kids got plenty of laughs out of her as she terrorised me on a daily basis by chasing me all over the place and nipping at my ankles whenever I was hung over, which was most of the time. I had kidded myself that I was always prepared to mortgage us right up to the hilt and beyond to keep Heidi happy, so long as I could keep my expenses as 'walking about money'. But I learned later that the truth behind all this moving – and there was plenty more to come yet – lay in my own constant restlessness. Practising alchies always subconsciously want to be on the move, but they neglect to remember that wherever they go they have to take their crazy heads with them.

And what a crazy head I took with me on a month-long trip to America to cover three big fights involving British boxers in March 1980. The first stop was to be Las

Vegas for the Alan Minter versus Vito Antuofermo world middleweight championship, then on to Maryland for Dave 'Boy' Green against Sugar Ray Leonard, and finally to Atlantic City for the world light-heavyweight clash between John Conteh and Mathew Saad Muhammad. My credit cards had long ago been cut up by Heidi because of my gambling debts, so I had to deal in cash or travellers cheques whenever I went on trips. On £50 a day, with hotels already found, I was carrying quite a large wad of dosh when we hit Vegas. We were staying at Caesar's Palace and after the 11-hour journey to Los Angeles, a three-hour wait for a connection to Las Vegas and another hour on the internal flight, during the whole of which time I was drinking steadily, I was in my usual 'jet-lagged' state when we arrived at the hotel.

Because there were so many high rollers booked in for the fight, most of the British press contingent had been allocated less than luxurious rooms.

Within minutes of arriving, I was taking a shower when, never very good with mechanical objects – so much so that I once took what I thought was a choke into a garage complaining that it wasn't working and the man told me, 'That's because it's a cigarette lighter' – I accidentally wrenched the old-fashioned shower handle off the bathroom wall and was left with what was left of a ripped pipe and a shower head in my hands. Fuming, I slung on a pair of jeans and went bare-chested and barefooted, with what was left of the shower, down 20-odd flights to reception. Anyone who has been to Caesar's will know that the long reception desk is situated on the same floor as the roulette wheels, the one-armed bandits and the craps tables, surrounded by cowboys in Stetsons hollerin' and hootin' at the dice.

The pretty receptionists are all lined up behind the

desk in their smart uniforms and one of them never took her eyes off me as I advanced, brandishing my dripping shower. This young lady must have sussed immediately that I was going to have a good old moan, but in an astonishing exhibition of American efficiency, she waited until I was still about 10 yards away and shouted: 'Fantasy suite.' Seconds later, a genial old black porter was whisking me back into the lift and installing me in a huge room with a sunken bath, mirrors in the ceiling and a king-sized bed. Before leaving, he politely informed me that my luggage would be arriving shortly, as would a bottle of champagne 'with the compliments of the house'.

After celebrating my good fortune, I got shaved, showered, suited and booted, and went downstairs to 'case the joint'. I was as high as a kite and consequently full of bravado. I promptly changed all my travellers' cheques into cash, with the intention of having a punt on the tables. But I stopped off at one of the bars and soon became engrossed in what must have been a totally nonsensical conversation with some fellow drinkers. One of them turned out to be an attractive lady who was almost certainly a hooker but told me she was a champion blackjack player. With that, I handed her my wedge – all one month's advance exes of it – and told her to have a go at the table just a few yards away so that I could keep an eye on my investment.

My befuddled brain told me that she was playing a blinder as everyone around her table was whooping her on and I began nursing dreams of avarice, but I happened to choose that precise moment to get into a scuffle with a loud-mouthed Yank at the bar over the respective merits of Minter and Antuofermo, and our altercation must have turned nasty because the next thing I knew I was being led away by a security man with a gun. As there are no clocks in Vegas casinos and I was not wearing a wrist watch, I had no idea what time it was, but presumed it must be bed time as this was the way I invariably went to bed when I was in Vegas. I was not too worried about the gun, but I was frantic about my money. My protests fell on the inevitable deaf ears as the security man opened my door with his pass key, ushered me inside and told me, on pain of death, not to leave my room for several hours until I had sobered up.

On this subject of bed time in Vegas, I had a quiet, guilty chuckle to myself only recently, as I read a tribute to Frank Sinatra by Patrick Collins in the *Mail on Sunday* in the week of Sinatra's death. Patrick told how a British press mate of his, whom he described as a pub singer of some repute, disrupted a live Sinatra performance in Vegas once by singing along with the great man to 'My Way'. And Patrick then went on to describe how his friend was led away by a man with a gun, who muttered something about the desert being a big place.

What Patrick did not know about, however, was the postcript to this unsavoury incident, which went like this: As cold fear usually sobers up a drunk quicker than cold water, I managed to strike up a conversation with my 'jailer' about dog racing and he marked my card about the dog track just outside Vegas, which he suggested would keep me out of the cabaret and out of this kind of trouble in future. And thereafter, on my frequent trips to 'sin city', I spent most evenings taking a bus trip out to a greyhound track. Talk about coals to Newcastle! And dog racing in the desert turned out to be an even bigger mug's game than it was back home, because there were eight dogs to a race to pick from instead of six.

But back to Minter–Antuofermo and when I awoke

from my sleep of the damned, I guessed I had not been spark out for long, because jet lag did genuinely wake you bolt upright after only a couple of hours' kip. I remembered that I had written a piece before I left England which would go into that day's paper, but obviously I needed to put myself about for the weigh-in that day. By the time I got downstairs, I had worked out a list of how much I could borrow from whom among the other press lads, but it was still going to be a nightmare hanging in there potless for a whole month. I noticed a couple of colleagues having breakfast. If memory serves they were Jim Rosenthal, who was then on radio, and another local guy. In desperation, I told them to give me five dollars each for their breakfast and that I would sign for their receipt. A roulette table was literally a dozen yards away I bought a 10-dollar chip and placed it on black 13. The ball spun, wobbled agonisingly over black 13 for a moment and then nestled softly into it.

I hollered louder than any cowboy and the weary-looking croupier said mechanically: 'That's a good start, sir.'

'And it's a fucking good finish, too, mate,' I roared as I made my way to the cashier's desk. I had won more than 300 dollars and I immediately put 200 of them on Alan Minter at 2–1, which I figured were ridiculously generous odds based on the Vegas bookies' convictions that all Limey fighters were bums. My good mate Alan won on points, becoming the first Briton to capture a world title on American soil since the fabled Ted 'Kid' Lewis 65 years earlier. Now I was so well and truly out of trouble that I even fixed myself up with one of those hotel cash deposit boxes to stash away my loot.

There was trouble of a different kind waiting for me in

Atlantic City, however. The stint in Maryland had been more or less free of any major memory-jogging incidents, apart from the spectacular left hook with which Sugar Ray Leonard floored 'Boy' Green. Dave himself admits that whenever he watches the video, he still says to himself: 'One of these days, I am going to get up.'

Well, when I woke up the morning after John Conteh's fight in Atlantic City, I was still fully clothed except that the front of my smart jacket had been burned almost to a cinder and there was the tell-tale scorch mark on my shirt and chest which told me that I had fallen asleep smoking again. But that was only the start of my problems. For I suddenly realised that the sledgehammer-style banging which was going on was not only inside my head, but somebody bashing on my hotel room door. It turned out to be John Morris, the man who is now the secretary of the British Boxing Board of Control, but was then one of the fellow sports journalists who used to keep an eye out for my welfare.

John was telling me that there was one helluva news story breaking because Conteh had, apparently, rampaged naked around the hotel and had had to be overpowered and sedated. Just as I was beginning to absorb this shocking news, I started to remember that myself and Hugh McIlvanney had been the last two people with John Conteh in the early hours of the morning, before I had obviously crashed out. And when I began to piece the night's events together, I was consumed with guilt about having to file such a destructive story about John, not least because he had his wife Veronica and baby son James in the hotel with him. And I knew I would feel like a Judas if I had to splash his shame all over the front page next day. But my guilty musings were soon shattered by the telephone call from my sports desk in England telling me that the agencies were full of the Conteh rumpus and that they were expecting a front page story from me..

What had in fact happened was this: John, who had been splashed all over the papers in the recent past because of his wild man behaviour, had been recovering from serious drink and drug problems before the build-up to the fight and was in no condition to give of his best against the formidable Saad Muhammad. In the worst performance of his otherwise glittering career, he was knocked down several times and stopped in the fourth round. After the fight, he had been drowning his sorrows with McIlvanney and me when, to use his own words, in the autobiography *I Conteh* which I ghosted for him a couple of years later, 'the press guys went off to grapple with their deadlines and I was left alone convinced that death might be a preferable experience to the way I was feeling.

'My last memory of what was to become a horrifying, living nightmare was of a young, smart Italian-American guy joining me at my table. Frank Sinatra, a big fight fan, was sitting close by, surrounded by a group of minders. I asked my new companion if he could fix an introduction and he came back and said: "Nothing doing." This made me feel worse than ever, so my new buddy suggested we "get the hell out of there" to a nearby disco. When I rolled back into the hotel, the sun was shining. That is all I remember of the rest of that day. I have to rely now on what I was told by Veronica, my manager Bobby Naidoo, my trainer George Francis and what I read later on the front page of most of the English newspapers. Apparently, I went berserk in the bedroom, tried to climb up the walls and windows, attempted to throw all the luggage into the street below and then rampaged up and down the hotel corridors naked. Bobby had our floor completely sealed off by security men and George bundled my family out of the room and locked the door on us from the inside. He said he was terrified of me, but managed to wrestle me to the bed, where I calmed down long enough for him to knot the bedsheets together and tie me down to the mattress. Bobby had sent for the hotel medical people to sedate me, but fortunately I sank into a deep slumber and they did not have to use the hypodermic.'

At first, I refused to write this story for the paper, saying that I couldn't possibly betray my drinking buddy this way. But I was told in no uncertain terms that it was either the story or the sack for me. And I was thoroughly ashamed of myself when I chickened out and wrote it. Ironically, John and I finished up in the same rehab clinic a few years later within months of each other. And I have to say that he managed to get sober and stay sober, a day at a time, much earlier than I did. To my knowledge, he still is and that, for me, is his greatest victory.

I returned from that trip to America to the shocking and, for me, almost tragic news that my beloved 'Grimbles' had been sacked. It had never really occurred to me until that moment that, for all my faults, I was a very loyal person, but Peter's departure made me realise that I could only be loyal to an individual I liked and admired and not to an organisation – no matter how much money or perks it showered upon me. Newspaper politics did not interest me. I always found that office politicking and the back-stabbing, brown-nosing, arse-kicking nonsense that went with it was much more exhausting and debilitating than actually doing the job you were paid to do. So it came as a great shock years later to read in broadcaster Derek Jameson's biography that, as editor-in-chief of the *Express* and the *Star*, as he then was, he was the man who axed 'Grimbles'. Both

Derek and Peter treated me with great kindness when I eventually found myself out in the wilderness. It was with much regret that I later learned that the two men have never spoken to each other since.

Still, life goes on, as they say, and it went on in spectacular fashion for 'Grimbles' when that adventure-loving lunatic got himself a job on a paper in Beirut at the height of the war there.

As for me, I had to try and settle for life under the new editorship of Lloyd Turner, an Australian sub on the *Express* who, I was told, had a major alcohol problem of his own to contend with in that he had been a big league whisky drinker, but had now sworn off the booze altogether and was white-knuckling it. This was to make him a perfectly charming but extremely unpredictable man, especially when he broke out occasionally and had a bout back on the champagne. Lloyd was to edit the paper from Manchester, where it was printed, and Brian Hitchen, another old mate from our days on the road together, took over as London editor. Brian was to go on to take overall charge of the *Star* and to edit the *Sunday Express*. I never had a cross word with him – even though he was forced to fire me twice – and he, too, was very generous towards me when I genuinely needed help later in life.

So when Turner took over, I knew I would have to redouble my so far pathetic efforts to stay off the sauce on a more or less permanent basis, if only for the fact that, as we all know, there is no one so fanatical as a recently reformed character, such as he was. Consequently, I had one of the most miserable months of my life covering the Moscow Olympics on Abstem tablets. At night I sat in my room brewing tea with a little electrical gadget and an old army tin mug which Reg Gutteridge lent me. Worse, I was the only press man who did not come back from there richer than when they went, because all the dodgy-money changing from the Russian currency spivs – yes, they had them there even back in the days of Brezhnev – took place in the bars and clubs, all of which I was afraid to set foot in for fear of succumbing to my non-stop craving for booze.

Fortunately, Turner became just as big a fan of my work as 'Grimbles' had been and he started to send me off on non-sporting assignments. He even had me writing features on the Labour party conference in Blackpool, and he dispatched me to the most emotional funeral service I have ever attended in my life, in Atlanta, Georgia. No fewer than 20 black children had been abducted and murdered on separate occasions in the past 18 months in that steamy city and I went to the funeral of the latest 13-year-old victim, where wailing women were being carried out of the church and laid on the sidewalk to expend their sorrow in helpless fits of grief. And all the while, the baritone voices of the black Baptist preachers and the angelic tones of the school choirs tore at your sensibilities, making it virtually impossible to quell the tears.

But in between sending me letters of congratulation, Lloyd had to keep summoning me to Manchester to answer the latest rumours about my drunken behaviour. The trouble with these little *tête-à-têtes* was that I could never stay sober on the train journey up there. One such confrontation will live in the warped part of my memory forever. The *Express* building is not situated in the most salubrious section of Manchester and as Lloyd was in the middle of bollocking me, he complained that my attention seemed to be wandering. Indeed it had been, but I had not got the bottle to tell him why. Through the window behind Lloyd's desk a couple of mongrel dogs were shagging away hammer and tongs on a piece of waste ground and my mind was rivetted by the heroic efforts of this canine male.

My own personal and family life was fast becoming a wasteland of its own, too. By this time, I had moved the family twice more, first to a rented house yards away from the Tate Gallery on the Embankment in London, and then to a five-bedroomed 'gaff' in Wimbledon. Heidi had chosen this latest home beause Wimbledon was so green compared to Vauxhall and, of course, it had *upmarket* Wimbledon Village and the world famous Wimbledon tennis courts. Again she had not twigged that it was also only a stone's throw from Wimbledon dog track. But I was so far gone by then that I wasn't worried where I did my boozing – up market or down. Some nights I would be pissing it up at the greyhound track and during the summer I would be getting smashed in the press bar at Wimbledon, where I covered the tennis on an annual basis.

It was to be another of my favourite annual sporting events, the Cheltenham National Hunt Festival, which eventually sent my world crashing around my ears again, however. I always mixed work and pleasure at Cheltenham, which was so crowded that I once shared a hotel room with my brother and no fewer than eight of his underworld associates. Every pickpocket and card sharp attended this, the world's greatest annual 'crack', as did almost every priest in Ireland, of course. But during the week prior to Cheltenham, 1982, I had committed some long-forgotten misdemeanour of such gravity that Turner had instructed Brian Hitchen to suspend me for a week – on full pay, but no exes.

Now, this should have been a licence for me to thoroughly enjoy myself at the races with no deadlines to fret over. But it so happened that I went to the Windsor race meeting on the eve of the Festival and fell into the company of Alan Ball, Mick Channon and a few other famous faces from world of sport and acting. I got rat-arsed, but as Alan and Mick drove me to Windsor station, they came up with a brilliant idea to get me to Cheltenham after all.

'Why don't you do a "Channon and Ball" column there?' said one or other or both of them, knowing that the subs would love the headline because comedians Cannon and Ball were all the rage at that time.

So, despite being banned on the previous Friday, I turned up bright and early at the office on Tuesday morning begging to be reinstated on the strength of this idea for a column. Yet even as Hitchen was weakening, there was still one more hurdle to cross. For when he phoned Arthur Lamb in Manchester, Arthur replied: 'If that big bugger is going anywhere, it will have to be to the Royal Albert Hall tonight to see this kid Frank Bruno fight.' It was the night of Bruno's professional debut, but I managed to talk my way out of that little snag by saying, 'Oh, big Bruno won't amount to much – he'll just be another flash in the pan.'

Anyway, I got my wicked way in the end, filled my pockets with advanced exes, got a first-class rail warrant and was on my way in time for the first race. I did not even have to write my first column until immediately after the last race on the following day. But I got so hopelessly pissed that first night that by the next morning I was a complete wreck. I made the mistake of trying to put myself right with a liquid breakfast and by the time Alan Ball eventually made his way to the press box to try to save me, I was out of it. Alan recalled later that he shook me by the lapels, slapped my face and begged me to write a column, only to have me reply: 'Leave off, I've got my living to get by backing horses.'

When the phone call from Hell finally arrived, via the sports desk, I was in no fit state to speak coherently, let alone write. My *Star* sports mate, David Emery begged me to let him tell the office that I was sick, but I grabbed the phone from him and told them I was 'pissed'.

This was, of course, a fuck-up too far as far as the paper was concerned and I was recalled and sacked. The National Union of Journalists, said that they would try to save my job on the grounds that I, at long last, owned up to my alcoholism and attended a therapy centre called 'Accept'.

Accept was situated in an old fever hospital under the shade of Chelsea football ground where, ironically, I used to get pissed with the likes of Peter Osgood, Charlie Cooke and Alan Hudson in the nearby 'Ifield Tavern'. I attended that clinic on a daily basis for six nightmarish months. It was only then that the true horror of my incurable addiction hit me. I could be helped to stay off the booze a day at a time, I was told, but I could never be cured. The illness could only ever be arrested.

The Batt family house in Wimbledon became a vale of tears as it sunk in that the *Express* were not about to give me my job back, nor pay me any redundancy money, and that we were skint and at the mercy of fate once again. Unbelievably, though, Heidi, who was working to keep us, found time for laughter, too, one night, when I caught her reading a book in bed entitled *Getting Them Sober*. When I asked her what was so funny, she replied: 'You are. There was I thinking you were unique – yet you are on every page of this book. About as unique as a pint of lager and box of matches.'

This was also the time of the Falklands War, so I

was able to bury myself away in that terrible conflict, morosely watching the casualties mount up well into the early hours of every morning on the box. But I soon had an additional 'wound' of my own to worry about. As I attempted to walk the quarter of a mile from the underground station to Accept every day, I found myself increasingly lame, until both legs were so numb that I could barely crawl. I panicked and telephoned Fred Street, the Arsenal and England physiotherapist, who aranged for me to go to Harley Street to be examined by the Arsenal consultant. I can only imagine that this was at that great club's expense, because I never received a bill.

Anyway, it turned out that I was suffering from Intermittent Claudication, a condition the medical profession calls 'smoker's leg'. My lifetime of chain-smoking had caused the arteries in the veins of my legs to fur up and insufficient oxygen was being pumped into my calf muscles. The specialist told me the good news first, not knowing that it would be extremely bad news so far as this teetotaller was concerned: 'A few nips of whisky will help your circulation a little,' he said, 'but you will, of course, have to give up smoking immediately.' He went on to warn me of the dire consequences if I did not and informed me that he might be forced to amputate one or both of my legs, just as he had done to that great old Arsenal, Middlesex and England footballer and cricketer, Leslie Compton, recently.

This news was enough to drive any man to drink, of course, and when I received a telephone call to say that, on hearing of my predicament, the boys and girls at both the *Star* and the *Sun* had had a whip round for me, my thirst knew no bounds. Thankfully, when their incredibly generous £600 was pressed into my hand, I did manage to hand it over to Heidi without making a dent in the wad.

I would love to be able to say that this was a rare heroic act of self-sacrifice on my part, but sadly, I fear it had more to do with the fact that I was now back on a daily double dose of the dreaded Abstem in the knowledge that therapy alone was never going to keep me sober.

Try as I might – and later, when I was financially flush again, I tried everything from electric shock treatment to hypnosis and acupuncture – I could not stop smoking. Meanwhile, I just had to settle for being a virtual cripple, except that I did learn the hard way that if I was prepared to walk through the pain barrier, the blood would flow again and the pain would temporarily ease. I have been doing that ever since, but at the age of 66 I now need the help of a walking stick. When I did manage some long-term sobriety and was given the option to either quit smoking or forego a life-saving heart bypass operation, I managed to compromise by switching to Nicorette chewing gum, which is just as addictive as cigarettes, but at least more socially acceptable.

Back in 1982, I was given a financial leg-up by *The Times*, of all papers, when another old friend, Norman Fox, paid me to write half a dozen by-lined columns for them, which chuffed me no end. But it was not until November that year, eight months after they had sacked me, that Arthur Lamb and Lloyd Turner finally offered me the chance to work for them on a freelance basis again. (This, I was told by someone close to them in Manchester, was because both of them had had a go themselves at writing a series on Geoff Boycott, but neither of them could hack it and they sent out an SOS to me in desperation.) So I was up and, even if not exactly running, at least on the go again. This time around, though, I decided to stick to one subject only: boxing. I had always had a guilty kind of love for this brutal but at times balletic sport and I particularly admired the men who were in it, knowing they had the courage to go where so many of the rest of us men feared to tread. In the old days when I was pissed, I would even be stupid enough to challenge world champions to fist fights, but fortunately they knew they had nothing to prove to me or any other man and would just laugh it off. Although I almost slipped up once at a boxing writers' dinner when I took the joke a bit too far with Alan Minter and his eyes flashed, for a brief second, as if he was going to wallop me. Craftily, though, I managed to save myself by whipping up my shirt and showing him my recent operation scar.

I also figured that if you could not write about boxing, you could not write about anything because it was a microcosm of life. But I had mental scars as well as physical ones to contend with, after the psychological battering I had taken in Accept, where I had been forced to indulge in that most painful pursuit of 'Who Am I?' – as if I was just 16 years old again – and had still not come with any truly satisfactory answers.

In February 1983 I experienced one of the most stressful single days of my life to date. I was in New England covering the Marvin Hagler versus Tony Sibson world middleweight title fight. The highlight of that trip so far had been to see that great country and western singer Johnny Cash at concert there. Ah, yes, what a stressful life, I can hear you say.

The stress when it came, though, was self-inflicted again. I had been on Abstem for the past year or more and although I wasn't drinking, I was as vulnerable and defenceless against booze as I had ever been. A couple of days before the fight, a group of the press lads decided to go for a slap-up fish lunch in Boston, some 50 miles or so from where we were based. I knew the situation was fraught with danger for me, but I decided to 'be a man' and join them. By the early hours of the following morning, I was more of a gibbering, physical wreck than I was a man, yet I had not touched a drop of booze.

If you happened to be a drinking man, this was one of those glorious, unscripted days when a lunch grew into an enormous piss-up. And inevitably, the half-dozen or so hard drinkers who set off for lunch soon had their number increased five or sixfold as word got around that one of those epic piss-ups was getting underway. The outing turned into a bar-hopping tour of Boston and it seemed that everyone who was anyone in boxing or from the planeloads of British fans who were out there, joined the happy throng. I was anything but happy, of course. Anyone who has ever stayed sober throughout a drinking session knows just how boring a crowd of piss-heads can be and what a load of old bollocks they keep spouting over and over. But I was not bored, I was terrified. I was absolutely gagging for a drink to put me out of my misery, but I knew only too well that if I took one, it would only lead to many and on top of the Abstem, this would not only send me into a fit, it would probably kill me. Naturally, I looked round for ways of escape, but I could not afford a cab for myself back to our hotel – it had required about five of us to share a taxi and the bill on the way out.

Just as I thought things could not get any worse, a snowstorm suddenly blew up which overnight was to turn into a blizzard, carpeting the whole of the Eastern seaboard in snow and grounding all aeroplanes for days to come. Trying to get my little group – all of them very well-known sportswriters – together was a nightmare. Rat-arsed pissed, they defied all my attempts to pour them into a cab by staging snowball fights and wrestling in the snow like a bunch of schoolboys. When I did eventually bully them into some kind of order, the taxi driver who took us on the long journey back up the freeway turned out to be total dummy, turning off at all the wrong exits and getting us stuck in the snow at what seemed like all points north, south, east and west of Massachusetts. By the time we reached our hotel, I must have gobbled up at least a dozen aspirins because when my head was in danger of exploding at moments like this, I popped them down me like smarties. I would not have given a shit if I was pissed, of course. And thereby hung my lifelong dilemma.

So, as soon as the necessary 72 hours had passed, I was back on the booze, for the first time in almost a year. This time I stayed on it, but now I began for the first time ever to try and make a secret of it. I would try not to drink in the office pubs such as the Old Bell, Popins, the Punch or the golf club, but would take my morning and evening tipple in the buffet at Waterloo station instead. This way, I reasoned, I would at least not embarrass myself by putting myself on stage in front of my mates, as I did in the old days when I sometimes caught one half of my mind in a kind of out-of-body-experience. I used to have this mental picture of those two old guys in the theatre box in the *Muppet Show* looking down on my 'performance' as I asked them what they thought of the show so far. And they shouted back, 'Rubbish!' But I still could not drag myself off the stage.

By now, Arthur Lamb had been promoted to assistant editor and the paper had acquired a new Manchester sports editor, a workaholic called David Balmforth. I don't think David ever knew that I was responsible for him getting his job on the subs' desk when I recommended him to Arthur after we had worked together for the *People* and Neville Holtham had told me he was the best young page make-up man in the business. Well, that's what I told myself when he eventually persuaded Lloyd Turner and Brian Hitchen to sack me again, for I reasoned that he surely could not have bitten the hand that had helped to feed him. But who knows?

Anyway, sacking me was the last thing he and Arthur had in mind when in the summer of 1983 they asked me if I could pull off an impossible dream for them and get an exclusive interview with Muhammad Ali, who was by now very ill and had not spoken in public for at least a couple of years. I came up with a round-about deal with the British promoter Mickey Duff which involved the paper paying for manager Terry Lawless to take Frank Bruno and Lloyd Honeyghan – both of whom later became world champions, of course – to go on a training and learning fortnight in the Catskill Mountains, where the legendary Rocky Marciano had regularly prepared 30 years earlier. In return, Mickey was going to try to get me that 'impossible' session with Ali and I was going to give that air card a belting which, for some strange reason, the *Express* had failed to confiscate the first time they sacked me and I had miraculously resisted the temptation to use by doing a runner to a Pacific island or some such paradise of a bolthole.

Incidentally, it was there in the Catskills that I listened to one of the most astonishing life stories I have ever heard, in a lifetime of listening to life stories. One of Frank's sparring partners was the number ten heavyweight in the world at that time, a young dude by the name of Jeff Simms. Simms first came to my attention when Bruno put him on the floor and I heard him growl: 'That chain gang slowed me down more'n I figured.'

Simms had been one of a family of umpteen cotton-picking children down in the deep south when he was imprisoned in his teens. He explained: 'Some dude stole my coat and shot me two times. When I got out of hospital and went to get my coat back, I shot him two times and that bad dude goes and gets himself killed by those two bullets of mine.'

Now, this is where this little story took its most bizarre turn. For those two bullets were still embedded in Simms – one in his head and one in his body – along with three more that he received in a subsequent shooting and more than 40 stitches from earlier stab wounds. Because of the extenuating circumstances of his early life, Simms received a jail sentence of only 15 years – seven of which were served on the chain gang.

Like so many American fighters before him, Simms took up boxing in jail and when he left prison he had 19 straight KO victories in the pro ranks before fate stepped in again and matched him with a world title contender called Kid Sampson.

'Our manager made us live together to save on expenses,' Simms told me. 'One night we got to arguing over who should do the dishes and shift the garbage and he shot me three times – in the shoulder, the ribs and the thigh.

'As I laid on the floor, I heard him reloadin' and I thought, "That son of a bitch is going to shoot me all over again."

'So I dragged myself up and jumped two storey out of the window, spraining my ankle. I was let outta hosital after three weeks with them three bullets still inside me, plus the two that were there from when I was shot as a kid.'

As far as we were concerned, even an amazing little story like this paled into insignificance, of course, when word came through to Mickey that Ali would be happy to invite us to his luxury home in Los Angeles. And within hours, Mickey and me and *Star* photographer John Dawes were winging our way, first-class, to the other side of the United States and to what surely deserved its billing in the paper as 'The Saddest Story Ever Told'. The *Star* splashed my interview with Ali and the accompanying pictures all over the front page and ran it as a series for four consecutive days. I spent a day at the home of 'The Greatest' and he looked and sounded as if he was at death's door. So much so that I pleaded with President Reagan to intercede on his behalf by providing the best possible medical treatment on behalf of the American people. My story went round the world and I went on breakfast television and various other TV chat shows to comment on it.

Ali was full of gloomy statements such as: 'I now live only for the afterlife – the life after death. I had all the luxury I want and it don't mean nothin' no more.' But his mood kept lifting temporarily each time he went into the next room to prostrate himself in prayer. He even allowed us to take pictures of this, and of him appearing to levitate six inches off the floor. In his playful moments, he kept picking up the phone and conning me that he was making multi-million dollar business deals with eccentric tycoon Howard Hughes and he topped it all off, as only someone with his essentially playful nature could, when he informed me: 'Since I last seen you, I learned to play piano, violin and saxophone. They're booking me up for the Boston Philharmonic.' At this, he sank back in his chair, allowing me to savour this astonishing piece of information. But suddenly, he conjured up a big, beautiful belly laugh and confided: 'Hell, I'm lyin' again, man.'

Unfortunately, because Ali kept sinking in and out of a deep slumber throughout our stay and because the world had no idea of the seriousness of his Parkinson's Disease at that time, I made the mistake of musing in print that he might have resorted to using drugs. That brought me a death threat from some of his old entourage back in the States because they maintained that, as a devout Muslim, Ali would never go against that religious doctrine, in which all forms of chemical substances are forbidden. On my next trip to Vegas, I stayed at the luxury MGM hotel, and within minutes of arriving, I was summoned to a meeting and warned that my articles, which had been syndicated across America, might have the gravest physical consequences for me. But after an hour or so of heavy talking, during which time I was all out to save my neck, I managed to persuade them that I had meant nothing by it.

Back home, this spectacular scoop meant that I experienced one of those honeymoon periods with the paper when I could do no wrong again. Lloyd Turner sent me an embarrassing congratulatory letter in which he called me a 'super star'. And I did, indeed, burn brightly again for a while. It was around this time that I was making regular trips to Clones, the Irish border town from which one of Ireland's all-time sporting heroes, boxer Barry McGuigan, had emerged. My fond memories are of the hospitality I and one of my best little mates, freelance photographer Roy Chaplin, received in the living quarters behind Barry's mum's grocery shop there. Teetotaller Barry would play the guitar while his dad, a singer who once finished third in the Eurovision Song Contest, and his brother, joined Roy and me in lusty sing-songs. Sadly, Barry's dad and brother and Roy are all dead now, so those memories are all the more poignant.

The year 1984 offered even more promise than '83 had done. The main cause for celebration, as far as I was concerned, was that I was drinking as much as I liked again and appeared to be getting away with it. Even better, the *Star* was being run more and more from London than Manchester, which meant that I was having to answer to my old mate Brian Hitchen, the London editor, more than to my northern bosses, who could be as aggressive as they liked down the telephone when they would surely have been a bit more careful if they had been sitting face to face as they attempted to bollock me.

Hitchen sent me on a couple of hairy but hilarious capers. The first was when hundreds of British lorry drivers were marooned for a week in the Alps because of a strike by French customs officials and he sent photographer Frank Barrett, myself and a glamorous model in a *Star* T-Shirt with a Harrods hamper to relieve our truckers. We got involved in a chase with the *Sun*, who sent a nine-strong team there, too.

We took a breathtaking helicopter trip from Geneva over Mont Blanc where we spotted the stranded drivers and descended with our hamper and our Star Bird, to much jollification and a lovely front page picture. Not only did we beat the *Sun* by almost a day, but when they arrived, the best they could come up with for the truckers was a load of Yorkie Bars – presumably because there was a popular TV advert at the time depicting lorry drivers and Yorkie Bars. The drivers duly told the *Sun* where to put their pathetic chocolate bars and Hitchen boasted later that he celebrated our triumph by sending a telegram to his rival editor, Kelvin McKenzie, which read: 'The trouble with those Yorkie Bars is that they ain't got no tits!'

Next, Hitchen had me invading France with another

load of Star Birds and hundreds and hundreds of British sausages, because of a French complaint to the EEC that our bangers were useless. A sucker for an adventure or two himself, Brian even accompanied us as we went in training for the D-Day style landing in a frighteningly high-speed Royal Marine Commando boat down in Dorset. But I was on my own with the Star Birds when we eventually 'liberated' Paris and I cooked British bangers on a primus stove on the Champs Elysées and offered them to puzzled passing Parisians.

Then, after a night when he was my guest at the annual boxing writers' dinner, where he shared a table with John Conteh, Chris Finnegan, Kevin Finnegan and my brother Jim and his 'oppo Les Burman, Brian invited Jim, Les and me to the Savoy for lunch the next day. There, he got the chaps to fix him up with a prison visit to Ronnie Kray and he went to see Ronnie himself in Broadmoor and wrote a centre-page spread on his exclusive interview.

Sadly, the rot began to set in for me again at the Winter Olympics, which were held in Sarajevo, Yugoslavia, that year. Normally, I would not have gone there because apart from the exploits of lunatics like 'Eddie the Eagle', there was not much for the tabloids to get their teeth into at the Winter Games. The big difference this time, though, was that the fabulous ice-skating team of Torvill and Dean were competing.

As had happened years ago at the *Evening News* when they forgot to book me into that hotel in Liverpool, the *Star* did not find any accommodation for me in Sarajevo. The result, as I remember it, was that I was laying my head wherever I could, which was mostly in all-night bars and restaurants – because even if I was warming myself up with a constant supply of schnapps and brandy, even a nutter like me was not going to kip rough in those blizzards. So this fortnight-long trip passed by in an almost permanent alcoholic haze. It did not prevent me from receiving a couple of 'herograms' from David Balmforth on the quality of my work, however.

My fondest memory of the whole befuddled escapade in this frozen city was of covering the British skating couple's gold-medal triumph with Frank Taylor, then of the *Daily Mirror*. Frank, who had been an even-time sprinter in his youth and had received crippling injuries in the Munich air crash, sat next to me as we tried to puzzle out what material Jayne Torvill's dress was made of. Was it chiffon or silk? we asked each other – then burst into laughter at the realisation that a couple of hairy-arsed old chauvinistic gits like us had been asked to cover such an 'effeminate' event as ice dancing.

Some time later, after sitting up all night to re-read Frank's book about the Munich crash which was entitled *The Day A Team Died*, by one of those strange quirks of fate I happened to hear on the radio that George Best had been the victim of an attack in a pub in which a glass had been thrust into his face. Filled with sadness, both from the book and this horrible incident, I telephoned Lloyd Turner and asked him if I could write the definitive 'fallen angel' tribute to Georgie. His reply was the worst thing I have ever heard from a newspaperman. He just said: 'The only time I ever want to see George Best's name in my paper again is when he's dead.' Some gratitude for all those column inches Besty had produced down the years.

Ironically, it was not long after this that Turner – with a good deal of elbow-jogging from Balmforth – decided that he never wanted to see my name in his paper again, either. This decision was based on my coverage of the Los Angeles Olympics of 1984, which I happened to think had been excellent. So either I was mad or else they were. Certainly Turner must have been mad to insist that I sign a formal declaration that I would not take one drink throughout my month-long stint in California – and I must have been bonkers to sign it. Hadn't I already sworn off the drink at least a dozen times before, even on 'my baby's life' and other such sacred oaths? Didn't I suspect that I possessed all the willpower of a snowflake, without yet knowing the awful truth that alcoholics have the willpower of tigers in that no power on earth can tear them away from taking a drink when they have set their minds to it?

At that time, I was just a shivering denizen of that evil old King John Barleycorn. And having signed that piece of paper, I made two more fatal errors. The first was to imagine that I was indispensable. The second was to use my air card to upgrade myself to first-class on the flight to the States.

I was not helped, either, when I got there, by the fact that my hotel room – which, judging from the decrepit, unkempt state it was in, must have been built at the time of the Pilgrim Fathers – was running alive with cockroaches. Whenever I woke up, these horrible giant roaches were in my shaving kit, my shoes – literally everywhere. So much for the high life! Afraid of past experiences of sitting up all night attempting to write columns, every one of the many thousands of words I came up with for this Olympiad I adlibbed straight into the phone to the copytakers at the other end, so that I could operate when I was half drunk most of the time. You can amaze even yourself as to how well you can do this kind of thing when you have had a lifetime's experience of phoning over running reports at football matches or from the ringside at boxing venues.

Indeed, so flush with success was I – or so deluded by alcoholic fantasies – that I went into the office on the morning after my return to England expecting to be received like a victorious Caesar returning to Rome and to be presented with a laurel wreath or two, at the very least. Instead, I was summoned to Struan Coupar's office, where that grim-faced managing editor of Express Newspapers presented me with a list of misdemeanours with which I was supposed to have disgraced myself. It started with the unanswerable ones that I had used the air card without first seeking special permission and that I had been observed drinking alcohol on numerous occasions. It went on to 'charge' me with singing 'Deutschland, Deutschland, Über Alles' whenever the ludicrously xenophobic Americans sang along with their own national anthem, and it alleged that I knocked over a television set in the press box when I danced too boisterously to the accompaniment of Lionel Richie's hit song 'All Night Long', which was played over and over again during the closing ceremony.

I flatly refuted each and every other one of the dozen or so accusations and was so furious that I appeared to have been spied upon and grassed up by one or other of my two colleagues who were with me in LA that I stormed out of Coupar's office saying that I would never darken the Express building's door again unless I received a written apology by first post the following morning.

Next day, I did receive a letter from him, but it was to inform me that I had been sacked yet again.

CHAPTER EIGHTEEN
CELEBRITY

This time around, even I, with my ridiculously unrealistic expectations of all the good things life usually had in store for us, had to admit to Heidi that we were well and truly in the shit. I was 51, unemployed and looking more and more unemployable. Jenny was at Bath University, Danny was taking his A-levels and Caroline was hoping to follow her older sister and brother into higher education.

We were, as usual, mortgaged up to the hilt. And as expectations so often turn out to be nothing more than resentments under construction, I was looking back at what at last seemed to be the end of my chequered newspaper career with much more bitterness than satisfaction.

Yet within 18 months, I was appearing as a minor celebrity on television as a guest of Terry Wogan on his top-rated chat show. This miraculous recovery was down to Heidi. She had read in a newspaper that the BBC was planning a new soap opera based on life in the East End of London, and she suggested that, as this cap appeared to fit me so well, I should write a letter to them applying for a chance to wear it. My luck was bang in again as within a week the show's creator and script editor, Tony Holland, was commissioning my first script and fixing me up with an agent. In late 1984, I wrote some of the first *EastEnders* episodes 'in the dark', with no actors even cast yet and nothing due to appear on the TV screens until early the next year.

I was getting paid handsomely and enjoying life to the full as a regular member of the scriptwriting team. And I began to enjoy it even more when filming started and I spent a lot of my time with the cast at the Elstree studios. Unfortunately, I was probably enjoying life a little too fully as far as my friendship with Tony was concerned, because I kept hearing on the grapevine that the producer, Julia Smith, was tut-tutting over the amount of drinking he and I were indulging in together.

I was never one to read the warning signs. My drinking got heavier instead of lighter and with so much time on my hands between scripts, I began indulging in my old gambling habits, except this time I was doing it 'showbiz' style by going horse racing by day and dog racing in the evenings. Wimbledon was the perfect geographical starting point for so many race tracks – Sandown, Kempton, Epsom and Lingfield were all within very easy reach and it was not much trouble getting further afield to the likes of Fontwell, Folkestone and Newbury. At all these venues, the same characters were present on an almost daily basis and the racing circuit became like a floating bar. There were bookies, trainers, sportsmen, actors and colourful turf aficionados like 'Jimmy the One' and 'Ronnie Racing'. Full of manic energy and scotch whisky, I would insist that one or other of my drinking pals gave me a lift to Wimbledon dogs to catch the last few races on the way home.

If you are wondering how I managed to get any work done, well, so did I, at times. Scriptwriting for me was a little creative miracle all of its own. Four of us would attend monthly script meetings and fight over the four episodes on offer, for this was in the days when there weren't that many episodes in a week. We were supposed to stick to the storylines which Tony had mapped out for us, but as far as I was concerned it mattered not one jot what the episode I had just been allotted was supposed to be all about, because nothing creative – absolutely nothing – happened until around five days after the script meeting and that was two days before we were supposed to deliver the first draft. Then, ritualistically, just as I was shaving on the fifth day, the characters would start talking and moving around in my head and I would have to throw down the razor, rush downstairs and start tapping at my typewriter. I would then type away, manically, more or less non-stop, until the script was finished. My script often bore little or no resemblance to what Tony had previously outlined because the characters all seemed to have lives of their own and to go their own way once they hit the paper in front of me, but a couple of days of rewriting soon put that right. So I was now in the happy position of earning a month's salary in roughly four days and nights.

It couldn't last, I thought, the bottom must fall out of this soon. It didn't just last – it got even better. One day at Elstree, out of the blue, Julia Smith asked me to go off and think of a comedy series for Penelope Keith, and my daughter Jenny, who happened to be home from college at the time, came up with the idea of making Penelope a National Hunt race horse trainer in a headscarf and green wellies, with a couple of dogs yapping at her heels. Julia thought this was such a great idea that within days I found myself being summoned to producer Gareth Gwenlyn's office and being commissioned to write a six-part series called *SideSaddle* in which Penelope inherits a rundown old stable called 'Beechers' from her impoverished old uncle. A veteran resident BBC writer, Christopher Bond, who had co-written Penelope's hit show *To The Manor Born*, was drafted in to show me the ropes and I decided to take advantage of my previous professional contact with leading trainer Jenny Pitman by inviting her to be the technical adviser for the show. Apparently, I was well pissed when I went to see her because after the BBC had offered her £1,000 per episode for her contribution, Jenny wrote a letter declining their offer, in which she said that this figure was way below what she was expecting. When my memory was jogged on the subject, I did guiltily recall telling Jenny something like this: 'You can forget all about having to train horses now, darling, this deal will make us stone rich. This time next year we'll be millionaires.'

Consequently, instead of Jenny I had to recruit my old mate, Brooke Sanders, who had herself become a trainer by now.

Again, I received handsome remuneration for my six episodes (which, incidentally, could never have been written without Christopher Bond's contribution). But it all came to nothing just before filming was due to start when Penelope pulled the plug on the project. A story and a picture of her on a donkey appeared in the *Daily Mail* previewing the show and Miss Keith, who I was told had an almost pathological hatred and wariness of the press, found out that I had been a newspaperman and thought I had leaked the story. Hand on heart, this story had not come from me. My old mate Reg Gutteridge had happened to mention it in passing when he was at a lunch with the *Daily Mail* showbusiness editor. Although why Penelope had objected in any case to such positive publicity, I could not imagine. Gareth Gwenlyn actually recommissioned the series again from me a few years later in the forlorn hope of making her change her mind.

Sadly, my newspaper background began to affect my standing on *EastEnders*, too. So popular did the show become that stories about it started to find their way onto the front pages of the tabloids. Ronald Reagan could be bombing the hell out of Gadaffi and Libya, yet that news would take second place to the latest *EastEnders* storyline revelation. Naturally, I was besieged by phone calls from old Fleet Street pals wanting me to fill them in, but I honestly did refuse every request. Julia Smith became so paranoid about her forthcoming storylines being revealed in the papers that she would sometimes alter them, at considerable cost and confusion, at the last minute, and I am sure the seeds of doubt about my integrity had been well and truly sown. So by the time I had appeared on *Wogan* to sing the praises of the show in April 1986, my survival instincts told me I should start looking for a new job again.

That came in the autumn of 1986 when Tony Smith, the sports editor of the *Sunday Mirror*, decided to make me an even 'Bigger Voice of Sport' than I already had been. Back I went onto the old treadmill of columns, but this time I had to come up with them only on a weekly basis. I say 'treadmill', but in truth I was never happier than when I was back rubbing shoulders with my old Fleet Street cronies. I loved working for 'Smithy', who was a great little pub raconteur. But he was also a self-confessed coward and, as I discovered to my cost some three years later, he was terrified of that old ogre Robert Maxwell, who owned the *Mirror*, and as the notorious 'Captain Bob' insisted on handling every contract personally, Smithy bottled out of putting his deal with me in writing. As I never really bothered my arse with contracts, I accepted his assurances that it didn't really matter anyway. And while Mike Molloy remained editor, as he was then, I am sure that Smithy was right.

Mike was a great editor in my book. So with him and Smithy running my life I figured I couldn't be in better hands, and so it proved.

The next few months were some of the craziest of my life. With two jobs – sports columnist and scriptwriter – money was coming out of my ears, but unbeknown to Heidi it was flowing either straight into the publicans' tills or the bookies' satchels. I was living like the playboy of the western world by drawing out a couple of hundred pounds in cash from the bank every day. And I was drinking like there was no tomorrow. The biggest miracle of my life was that with my liver supposedly shot to pieces, I had not fallen to bits physically just yet. I was told that the liver is the only organ which can regenerate itself. Mine must have been working overtime.

As the *EastEnders* scripts gradually fell away, though, I was operating on the *Sunday Mirror* more and more in blackout but managed to write my column with time to spare each week. These blackouts were so bad that I could remember going horse racing in the morning, studying the form over a few liveners in the buffet on the train and then placing what I imagined were relatively normal bets of around £30 to £50 a race for a while. I would also remember then going on to the dogs most evenings. With Heidi at work, there was no one to interfere with me and in the mornings I would almost always find my suit discarded on the bedroom floor and would go though the trouser pockets, which were invariably empty. No matter, though, there was always my gold credit card and the hole in the wall and, of course, my cheque book.

Just occasionally, however, my hip pocket would be bursting at the seams with a king-sized wedge. Mind you, I learned later that this was never quite as big as it should have been because if I had had it off the night before, I would, apparently, toss the bundle of notes up into the air and show off by growling at my younger daughter: 'Ere y'are, Curly, count this.' It was not until years later that I found out that 'Curly' used to weed large chunks of it out for her and her mum and brother and sister. But however much she weeded, she could not contain the endless harvest the bookies were reaping from me. Every morning I would attempt to fathom out the bets I had struck by reading the results in the paper, but I could seldom remember anything after the fourth or fifth race, which meant that I had been operating in blackout for most of the time and was putting on astronomical bets. As a result, I owed bookies money all over the place. Presumably because my picture was in the paper every week and my name was on the *EastEnders* scripts, my bookmaking friends must have thought I was rolling in it and they let me bet on credit. I soon ran up horrendous debts, some of which I would settle by cheque and some of which, I am ashamed to admit, I never did settle.

It took my bank manager ages to work out that the cheques were made out to bookies, rather than builders or decorators improving my house. And then he put the kibosh on me. But worse was to come for him when I used to go in there demanding money almost with menaces and he would either say to the cashier, 'Give him a couple of hundred to get rid of him,' or he would call the police.

But as I was being led away, I would invariably get the copper on my side by persuading him to agree with me what a hard old set of bastards bank managers were.

The most embarrassing moment I had as far as the bookies were concerned was when Portsmouth won promotion under Alan Ball and I arranged to meet him the next day at Salisbury races to interview him. When I got there he had not yet showed up. As I couldn't go anywhere near any of the bookies because of the size of my debts, I was hiding up in the stands having a few quid on the Tote when a message came over the tannoy loud and clear: 'Would Mr Peter Batt of the *Sunday Mirror* please report to the clerk of the course, as soon as possible.'

Naturally, blocked vein in leg permitting, I dashed down to his office as quick as I could only to find a couple of bookies' men waiting to try unsuccessfully to collar me for the money I owed their guv'nors. It turned out that 'Bally' had got so pissed celebrating promotion the night before that he was still in a country club in Hampshire somewhere and had got his mate Peter Osgood to ring the track and ask me to meet him there instead.

Obviously, by now, Heidi and the kids were fast losing whatever patience they had left with me. When the children were small I had enjoyed a good relationship with them because, as Heidi put it, I was just the fourth kid in the house. And in their eyes, I was the silliest kid in the house, too. So much so that they used to call me 'Kenny' after the retarded boy who featured in the children's TV series *Grange Hill* at that time. But now that they were all much more grown-up, they needed a sensible, mature, adult father, not an overgrown kid. And it was not as if I could claim to be 'Mr Nice Guy' anymore because my chronic drunkenness was making me more and more violent and unpredictable. My proudest boast was that I never laid a hand on any one of them, but Danny told me later that it would have been simpler to live with me if I had, because he would have known where he stood, whereas he never knew what sort of mood he would find me in. Maybe all this has something to do with the fact that Danny now works for the NSPCC.

I eventually ran into the buffers on New Year's Day, 1988. I was writing a column at the time and finding it increasingly hard going, with an inevitable hangover from the night before. The only thing for it, in my fevered imagination, was to pop over to the 'Stab' for a couple of 'swift ones' to help the flow. In reality, I had never had a couple of swift ones for the past 20 years or more. I was incapable of taking one or two drinks and then leaving.

For the past couple of weeks there had been pickets outside the gates of the *Mirror* every day, maintenance men and labourers who were in dispute with Maxwell over being laid off. About half a dozen of these young muscular guys were holed up in the Stab when I got there because the pub was open all day for the holiday. Naturally, one drink led to another for me and I kept putting off going back to the office to continue the column.

I happened to get into conversation with a couple of members of this little mob and discovered that they were all diehard Millwall fans. My instincts for trouble had been so dulled by the drink that I paid no attention when my colleagues kept telling me that bother was brewing and began urging me to leave the pub with them as they all gradually sloped off. Soon the bar was empty except for these half a dozen kids, myself and a few other strays. I was having what I thought was a lovely time telling a couple of these lads all about Millwall in the old days, when suddenly one of their mates shouted over from the back of the bar.

'Why do you keep talking to that old cunt? He's not just the Big Voice of Sport, he's the big Maxwell scab.'

Now 'cunt' I could live with, I had been called that enough times. No, it was the 'Maxwell scab' which did my brains in, so I walked over and took a swing at the loudmouth, sending him staggering back against the wall. Before I could make another move, the rest of them, including the two I had been chatting to, rushed me. They did not punch or kick me – yet – they simply rushed me in a group and their body weight took me off my feet and carried me right over to the other side of the bar and onto the floor. There was no chance of me getting to my feet before they began piling into me with their boots. One kick cracked my ribs, another broke the glasses in my inside pocket and a third cracked into my forehead before a couple of the young Aussie barmen leaped over the bar and broke it up. I managed to retain some kind of false dignity by telling my youthful assailants that their grandads would be ashamed of them and by promising that I would be back with a hammer, but that in the meantime I had to go back over the road to finish my piece.

Sleep was impossible for the next few nights as I kept fantasising about getting brother Jim and the chaps to sort this little firm out. But it would have been like sending for Dad's Army. Jim was rattling with pills and could barely get out of his chair, and Les Burman was on a walking stick. So I just had to swallow it and this drove me on the piss more morosely than ever.

The moment had to come when Heidi ordered me back on to the Abstem pills, with the threat of throwing me out of house and home if I did not take them and do what she ordered me to do for a while. But on the Sunday morning before Easter, as she stood over me at breakfast with the pills in her hand, I refused point blank, knowing that I had been spitting them out, without her realising it, for the past couple of days anyway. She went berserk and took a carving knife to me. I had the cheek to go upstairs and tell Danny and Caroline that their mother had taken leave of her senses, and actually expected them to take my side.

The outcome of all this was that I went walkabout for a couple of blackout days and nights during which I vaguely remember going to Folkestone races and attempting to bully Brooke Sanders into tipping me a couple of winners. When I eventually crawled home as skint and as depressed as a whipped dog, Heidi was waiting to tell me that I had been booked into the Roehampton Priory clinic by my mate Bobby Ball, who was, ironically, a manager at a brewery and had contacts at the Priory because so many of his employees had drink problems.

After detoxification, the first thing I discovered at the Priory was just how angry I was – and I was to stay that way for several more years. That anger, like all anger, stemmed from fear and this was the first time in my life that I was forced to admit that, like almost every other human being, I was full of subliminal fear.

Much to my surprise, my wife and children agreed to the Priory counsellors' request to attend a family therapy session there, and when each one of my kids spoke about me at the meeting, I could not believe what I was hearing. After they had finished unloading their home truths and left the building, I rushed after them and roared: 'It wasn't like that – that's not how I remembered it.'

They simply looked over their shoulders and calmly chorused: 'That's because you never listened.'

I wasn't listening much during my four weeks at the Priory, either. The trouble was that after we had attended group therapy all day and had been bussed out to AA meetings in the evenings, our group of addicts were free to do as we pleased at night, except to drink booze or take drugs, of course. We abused this freedom by meeting up in a communal part of the clinic and downing pot after pot of coffee together until the wee small hours, trying to outdo each other with our tales of drunken exploits. This was known in the therapy business as 'euphoric recall' and would have been a definite 'no-no' if we had been found out. The one thing the Priory did do for me, though, was to completely ruin my drinking for the rest of my life. Once the seed has been sown in your mind that you are – really and truly and very much to your chagrin – a bona fide alcoholic, carefree drinking becomes mentally impossible ever after.

Statistically, only a very small fraction of the people who attend rehabilitation centres get long-term sobriety at the first time of asking. And I had only been out of there a few days when Smithy sent me to the Liverpool versus Wimbledon Cup final and I relapsed that same night. Armed with hard-won hindsight, I now know that I had about as much chance of staying sober as Wimbledon had of winning the Cup. And what with Liverpool getting beat 1–0, there was no possible chance of a miracle of that magnitude happening twice in one day.

CHAPTER NINETEEN
HURRICANE

That year, 1988, was to turn out to be even more eventful for me than any of the previous 55 had been. Yet, I can remember silly little moments every bit as well as the more horrific ones.

For instance, a couple of nights after that New Year's Day fracas, I was having to pay off a debt to bookie Tony Morris at Wimbledon dogs and as I went to write out a cheque, I forgot what year it was and asked Tony. For some perverse reason, his reply still makes me chuckle! 'Eighty-eight, mate – two fat ladies.'

Well, one buxom lady who was to give me a particularly hard time then – though never to my face – was Eve Pollard, who had taken over from Mike Molloy as editor of the *Sunday Mirror*. I had known Eve when she was a voluptuous young girl who would josh with us sports hacks when she came to cover the fashions at Ascot. But word now came down from Smithy that she did not fancy too many pissy, old, hairy-arsed dinosaur sportswriters cluttering up the place, and even I had to admit that this was a pretty accurate pen picture of me. I now began to realise just how foolish I had been not to insist on a formal contract when I joined the paper.

So, after I recovered from that Cup final nightmare – a relapse which went on and on for a week or more – I decided I must do something really drastic about saving what was left of my life. I knew I had to stop fighting this losing battle with the booze and turn my life over to someone I could trust. I had heard about such a man when I was in the Priory. His name was Alan Lane and he ran the toughest treatment centre in the country down at Weston-Super-Mare. I located him and whined down the phone: 'When I look back at my life, it's as if I'm watching a film of someone else's. I can't believe that these things happened. There's no logic to it.'

He replied: 'Of course there's no logic in insanity, and alcoholism is a form of insanity.'

And this man knew what he was talking about because the booze had once taken him from being the proud owner of a huge garden with peacocks strutting in it to a straitjacket and padded cell. Like all successful counsellors, Alan had been to the places most of his patients had been to and worse. He told me to get my arse down to the seaside on the next available train. All the way down, I kept telling myself that it was just a missing key that I was searching for, that there must be a switch in my mind which would do the trick, if only he could find it for me. But Alan Lane had no magic wand. What he did have were eyes the colour of steel, a well-manicured moustache and the physical bearing of an army sergeant-major. The moment you looked at him you could sense that he had an inner drive and the strength of will that would make him one of the best at what he did. Yet, paradoxically, the same was true of so many addicts whom I would come to know better than my own brothers and sisters – only like me, they wasted all that determination and manic energy on maintaining their suicidal habits, long after reaching the point where they should have surrendered.

'Some of the most difficult people I have to deal with are priests and journalists,' Alan informed me as I faced him sheepishly across his desk. 'Priests because they think they have a direct line to God and don't like listening to mere mortals . . .'

'But why journalists?'

'Because you are all such a bunch of bloody know-alls, that's why,' he scolded.

I had half-expected to find a crew of red-nosed old pissheads as my co-inmates for the next 16 weeks, but I could not have been more mistaken. Most of my group were young enough to have been my sons and daughters. The men slept four to a room and when I crawled into bed that first night, I looked at the other 15 toes peeping though the sheets at me and cursed them for belonging to a set of no-good bums who were going to drag me down to their level. This again, I was to learn, was the typical attitude of the practising alcoholic. First, he assumed that he was the centre of the universe, and second, he was one of the few people in the world who could lie in the gutter and look down at the passers-by.

We were all given menial household chores to peform and – presumably because I was a big fella – one of mine was to carry the bags of new arrivals from the centre to the living quarters in another part of the town. Typical of my luck at that time, this resulted in me later having to undergo surgery for a misplaced hernia. Weston-Super-Mare then was known to addicts all over the country as 'Clean City'. It was full of treatment centres and hundreds of us met up at AA and Narcotics Anonymous meetings almost every evening.

'Normal' life as I had once known it had ceased to exist for me now, of course. We were all virtually schoolchildren again, even though our number included a middle-aged male opera singer, a property tycoon, an ex-millionaire from the clothing industry who was recovering from cocaine addiction, a prostitute, a couple of young ladies from the counties with cut-glass accents, several hardened drug-dealers, a clutch of teenage tearaways and a pair of tattooed Portuguese seamen. Local inhabitants had grown used to seeing this motley crew, with written homework slung over our shoulders in paper carrier bags, giggling as the lollipop man led us over the zebra crossing and into the sweet shop for an iced drink on a stick on our way home through town from the treatment centre to the recovery house. All our money and possessions had been confiscated and we had each been allotted £4 a day to spend on tobacco for roll-up cigarettes, and the lunch break from therapy.

One such lunch summed up most accurately just what the hell was wrong with me. My most glaring character defect, I was informed, was my grandiosity, Alan Lane said he had seldom seen such a prime example of the Freudian 'King Baby' syndrome, and as we left for lunch on this particular day, the therapist's last words to me were, 'Watch that grandiosity, Peter.' As many as 15 of us used to pile into a dirt-cheap cafe on the seafront for whatever items we could afford from the daily fry-up, and those words from Alan were still ringing in my ears when I verbally exploded on being overcharged a penny or two for my portion of baked beans. Such was the colourful quality of my language that the Greek-Cypriot proprietor called his entire family out from the kitchen to the counter to listen to it, and to witness the spectacle of my outraged veins attempting to burst out of my temples. This tirade was delivered at the top of my booming baritone voice and with so much clenching of fists that it presented some of the day trippers present with the opportunity to make hasty exits without paying their bills.

The theme of my abuse was that I had eaten oysters and lobsters in the best five-star restaurants in the world and that I'd be 'fucked if I was going to stand for them poncing an extra penny out of me for their poxy baked beans.'

When he phoned for the police, I suspect that it was not 'King Baby' which sprang into the proprietor's mind but 'Big Time Charlie'. And just to prove that as sure as God made little green apples, pride always came before the fall, the very next day I broke out of the clinic and relapsed.

My excuse for doing this was that Heidi had telephoned to say that Smithy had sent her an SOS explaining that he had kept Pollard at bay these past few weeks by telling her that I had back trouble, but if he was to save my job for me, I would have to come up with some words pronto. This was just the excuse I needed for doing a runner, of course, but only the devil knows how I managed to con £100 on a 'dodgy' cheque card from the local bank and leg it, without luggage, to Weston-Super-Mare station. I gibbed paying the train fare by taking half a dozen miniature whiskies into the loo with me and holing up in there. And then, just like a sick homing pigeon, I found myself at the Wimbledon dog track.

Heidi and Curly nearly fainted away when they opened our front door to see me standing there pissed as a parrot and potless. They were convinced I was knuckling down to it in Weston and well on the way to recovery. I had to find something on which to take out my anger and shame and chose the telly, foolishly kicking it after I had taken off my shoes and consequently dislocating my big toe. That night was spent with me sitting alone with the toe in a hot bowl of water, waiting desperately for morning and the chance to ring Alan Lane to beg him to take me back.

After giving me the mother and father of a bollocking, Alan agreed to let me return, but he decided that this time – because of the truly cripping nature of my debts, and for Heidi's sake rather than mine – I should write my weekly column while I was still in treatment. Smithy sent money for me to book into a local hotel on Friday mornings, where he fed me news of the week's sporting events over the phone and got me to take it from there. Those pretty bottles behind the hotel bar, though, still twinkled at me as seductively as ever.

Alan Lane had some fabululously original sayings and it was not long before I was playing a spot the quote game to give me and my mates a laugh. Each week I inserted one of his favourite phrases into my copy such as 'There's a fast train leaving tonight, be under it' and 'I've seen more life in a glass eye than I see in you.' Our group went *en masse* to do our washing at a launderette every Sunday morning, where we would buy the *Sunday Mirror* and giggle like schoolgirls when we read 'The Voice of Sport' paraphrasing our big bad counsellor.

Miraculously, I stuck it out at Weston for the remaining 12 weeks, writing every week without my editor having the faintest idea of where I was. I will never forget what Heidi said to me as we strolled hand-in-hand on the beach like a couple of young lovers before catching a train back to London.

'I feel just like a carefree kid, again – happy, joyous and free,' I told her.

She squeezed my hand and said: 'To me, you feel like a man at last.'

I, of course, wished with all my heart that I could live up to this most precious of compliments, but my head was soon to have other ideas. And although I try to resist the all-too-easy temptation to look for scapegoats for the mess I made of my life, it has to be said that on this occasion it was Tony Smith who planted those other ideas.

I had been back at work all of two days when he sweet-talked me into going to Jamaica. How can anybody need sweet talking to go to a tropical playground like Jamaica? I hear you ask. But when I say Smithy made me go to Jamaica, I mean it. I did make the rod for my own back, though, when I brought in an exclusive story from two pals of long standing – Frank Bruno and his manager Terry Lawless. Frank had just signed up for his first tilt at Mike Tyson's world heavyweight title and immediately before going into serious training he had decided to take his wife and children to visit his grandmother in Jamaica, so that Frank's grandmother could clap eyes on him for the first time since he was a young boy. The old lady suffered from cataracts and Frank had paid for her to have a successful eye operation at Moorfields Hospital in London. But he had been unable then to break training for his previous big fight against Joe Bugner and see her.

Smithy naturally told Eve Pollard all about it and she fancied it for the colour magazine. The plan was that we get exclusive pictures and interviews on a beach, with golden sand and a beautiful setting sun, etc. I was due to liaise in Jamaica with Micky Brennan, a freelance photographer who would be flying there from his base in New York. By coincidence, he and I had been sportswriter and photographer of the year together on the *Sun* in the same year and had worked and played together many times. A less happy coincidence, however, was that I had been told he was recovering from problems of his own and we both could have done without the temptations of a reunion. But Smithy almost went down on his knees and begged me to go, and then he mixed that tactic with the challenge: 'What use is stopping drinking if you can't do what you love best – getting exclusive stories like this?

As my flight was approaching Miami, where I was due to change planes for the West Indies flight, my self-congratulations about surviving the journey without resorting to a drink soon turned to panic when the pilot informed us over the intercom that a hurricane had struck that part of the world and that there would be no connecting flights to Jamaica for the foreseeable future. This 200 miles per hour wind, which had earned itself the meteorological moniker of 'Hurricane Gilbert', proved to be so ferocious that American clothes manufacturers later cashed in on it by bringing out a T-shirt emblazoned with the slogan 'I survived Gilbert'.

I succeeded in staying sober until I telephoned Smithy and he was obviously jumping up and down with excitement because I was the only journalist in the country who knew where Bruno was staying and at this stage it was impossible to tell if he was alive or dead. The fact that any form of communication with Jamaica was impossible and that there was no way in or out of there only made him more enthusiastic, because it meant that no daily paper could possibly get there before I did and that our story might hold until Saturday's edition time.

So my brief was to wait in Miami, however long it took, before boarding the first available plane to Kingston, try to make my way 70 miles across the ravaged island to where Bruno was supposed to be staying and then get a story and pictures back to London – 'phone or no phone, fair means or foul.' Personally, I just wanted to get to fuck out of there before I cracked and picked up a drink, but my only defence was to tell him: 'This will cost you an arm and a leg.'

He simply roared back at me: 'Money's no object. I will wire you all the cash you ask for and more.'

Instructions of that nature would have delighted me a few years previously, but now I knew I was doomed. There was only one thing left for me to do and that was to pour some 'fuck-'em-all medicine' down my throat and dive in at the deep end. Those four weeks in the Priory and 16 at Weston were about to be comprehensively wasted.

And boy, was that water deep. I booked into the most luxurious hotel on Miami Beach and soon found a horse racing track to take care of my boredom in the afternoons and a dog track for same in the evenings. My slurred voice over the phone told Smithy what was happening to me, but he had no alternative but to keep sending me as much money as I kept demanding and then to say his prayers. When the hounds of hell – or in this case Ms Pollard – were up his arse, dear old Smithy always did act now, then worry about it later.

With what I could only imagine was the devil's help, I managed to accumulate wads of winnings to go with my wedge from the paper, and by the time I did manage to board the first relief plane to Jamaica on the Friday, the pockets of my jeans were bursting with many more

American dollars than was good for my physical well-being – especially as there were rumours of machette-wielding looters roaming around Kingston. And when this mainly Red Cross plane did touch down, I found that apart from buying booze, my small fortune was useless to me. The foyers of the best hotels were like refugee camps, with frightened tourists huddled together on every available inch of floor space. With no electricity, telephones or public transport, and precious little water, the place resembled a scene from one of those horror movies about life after a nuclear explosion.

My attempts to cross the island that night with a taxi driver – who must have thought Christmas had come early when I flashed my roll of greenbacks – were thwarted by the immovable rocks and tree trunks which littered the main road. At great expense, the driver decided to take me to a guest house owned by a distant relative of his which had had its doors and windows blown away and was now wide open to the elements and, presumably, to the looters. I spent what up until then was the most anxiety-ridden night of my life alone in the pitch dark with spiders running up and down my legs and only a despised bottle of whisky as a Job's comforter. The fact that I had forgotten to advance my watch the necessary two hours turned this endless night into an even longer and darker one!

The road was made more or less passable the next morning, so I was able to make the journey to Negril where Frank and his family were, to discover that Bruno had become a local hero by sheltering his own and other people's children from the hurricane. He had used his massive frame to pin a bed to the floor while the children cowered beneath it. From the story point of view, this was now a hurricane and a half, but there was no sign of Brennan to take pictures and as I did not know the back end of a camera from the front, I persuaded Frank's wife Laura to take the pictures for me with her holiday box camera. When I got back to Kingston, Micky had just arrived at the airport on the next plane out after me, but our problem now was to get the story and the film back to England and as there were no telephones or wiring facilities available, that meant we had to get off the island somehow.

The trouble was, that was just what everyone else seemed to want to do. Montego Bay airport was absolute chaos. There were just three flights leaving that day, for Toronto, Puerto Rico and Miami, and they were to be the first ones out of there for nearly a week. They were all hopelessly overbooked. Micky was the possessor of a gold credit card so we tried, without luck, to hire a private plane. But the manager of this hire company put us in touch with a 'dodgy' airline official, who settled for a thousand dollars in cash and no questions asked to spirit a couple of bona fide passengers off the flight to Miami and put us in their places.

We would have settled for Toronto, Puerto Rico, or anywhere where there were communication facilities, and as we settled down for the flight to Miami I was beginning to wish we had, because the booze and the horses and the dogs were awaiting me there and I knew now that I was absolutely powerless over them. Once addicts have started 'using' again, they are powerless over their addictions – choice does not come into the equation because when the compulsion is upon him, a practising 'alchy' has no choice.

I became a hero again back in London when the still exclusive story and pictures were plastered all over the paper.

'Just like the good old days,' Smithy kept telling me down the phone. And then he hit me with the hook off the jab. 'Her ladyship, Eve, insists that you go back to Jamaica for the original magazine piece.' And he informed me that he would wire over another £700 immediately.

'Like fuck, I will,' I decided. I had enough notes for the grandma reunion story and my mate Micky Brennan, who I knew would not grass me up, could go back on his own. He didn't need me to hold his camera for him. I phoned a piece over from the hotel a few days later as if I had made the trip back to the West Indies as instructed – and set off on a trip to oblivion, all expenses paid.

For what must have been a week or more, I ignored all Smithy's and Heidi's pleas for me to come home and was only rescued by my oldest daughter Jenny, who is now a teacher but was then an air hostess with Caledonian Airways. She happened to be on a trip to Florida and was staying in a hotel about 50 miles away from mine. Out of the blue one morning, she arrived to bundle me on a flight back to London to experience, yet again, what I always dreaded most in life – facing the music then paying the piper.

CHAPTER TWENTY
WILDERNESS

Nineteen-eighty-nine was the first of my wilderness years. As with the previous year, it got off to a stinker of a start when I ruined my daughter Jenny's 22nd birthday party and got banged up in the police cells for a night as a result.

Heidi and I had agreed that Jenny and Danny could invite their college friends and have a shindig at our house, and that Caroline could bring some of her younger friends, too. I agreed to spend the night with Heidi in a nearby hotel. At that time, I was back on the waggon, attending AA meetings regularly again and, full of shame and guilt, was being understandably 'nailed to the cross' on a frequent basis by my long-suffering wife and kids. My children were particularly relieved to see me in this tame state because one of their main resentments towards me was that my regular drunken tantrums ruined their studies – even so, no thanks to me, they all went on to obtain university degrees – and, despite my protests, they said I didn't give a toss about their education. Once again they were proved correct when, to celebrate my oldest girl's graduation, I sent her a letter addressed to Miss Jenny Batt, BA, and it turned out she was a bachelor of science instead.

On the Saturday afternoon of the party, I began dreading the thought of booking into the hotel. Hotels and restaurants frightened me to death in early sobriety because I was terrified that I would not be able to resist the lure of a pint before dinner, some wine during the meal and brandy afterwards, which had always been a ritual whenever I did stop drinking long enough to eat. And the thought of gobbling up a dinner inside of an hour and watching television in the room afterwards was anathema to me in those still wild years.

Once these kind of rebellious longings start jostling for room in your head, they are soon running amok in a full-scale craving. There was nothing for it but to go upstairs, shut myself in the bedroom, lie down, breathe deeply and keep repeating the crisis mantra: 'This too shall pass . . .' Tragically, it didn't. Early that evening, I crept out of the house without anyone knowing it and went for a walk. On automatic pilot, my footsteps led me to the dog track and inevitably to several large whiskies between each race.

When I eventually lurched back to the house, the party was in full swing, and Heidi was beside herself with worry that I might have relapsed again. One glance was enough to tell her that her worst fears were confirmed and within minutes I had, in blackout, apparently set about ruining the party, cursing, swearing and niggling and goading Danny and his pals into an argument up to the point where half a dozen of them had to manhandle me to the floor and sit on me while Heidi called the police. This turned out to be the first of several times when

I was taken into protective custody and led away from my own home, under police escort, to be locked up in the local nick for the night.

The *Sunday Mirror* job had simply faded away by now. I filed perfectly readable columns but Eve Pollard declined to use them and Tony Smith went missing every time I telephoned to ask why. Things seemed to take a sudden and dramatic upturn, however, one summer Sunday afternoon. In between regular relapses, I was attending two and sometimes three AA meetings a day now at various venues all over London and the suburbs. I had just come off another short, sharp bender and was a shivering wreck when I got the impulse to share my problems. In a burst of self-pity, I blurted out all my financial problems to someone I met who introduced himself as 'Paul'. He suggested that it might be a good idea if I went bankrupt, and that he might be able to give me some advice on the matter. I hadn't revealed what I did for a living, but when I told him I was a journalist he then invited me to his house that afternoon. Knowing that I was still very unpopular at home, I decided to jump in his Porsche and accompany him.

His house turned out to be a lavish mansion in Esher, Surrey, complete with a swimming pool and tennis court. The first thing he said as we entered was: 'You'd better ring your wife and let her know you are OK. Oh, and tell her I want you to write a musical libretto.'

Not believing a word of what Paul said, I nonetheless relayed his message to Heidi thinking it was as good an excuse as any, and she said prophetically: 'It won't be long now before the men in the white coats come to take you away.'

Paul then led me into his lavish music room, which was full of modern electronic gadgetry. He said he was acting on an instinctive hunch that I would be able to write the definitive 'recovery' musical. 'Who better to write about addiction than an addict?' he reasoned.

When I told him that I had never written a lyric in my life and would not have a clue how to start, he hit me with this piece of logic: 'What are popular lyrics? They are nothing more than slogans and headlines, are they?'

I suddenly had a mental vision of all the pithy slogans which hung on the walls at AA meetings and realised that each one of them was indeed a cue for a song. And as a pub singer, I knew the lyrics of practically every popular song ever written during the years between my 15th and 30th birthdays.

As soon as he realised I was hooked, Paul revealed his credentials. His wife Jo was the widow of the late Gordon Mills, who had managed a stable of top singing stars including Tom Jones, Gilbert O'Sullivan and Engelbert Humperdinck, and Paul was now Engelbert's manager and also had a leading Austrian composer called Roland Baumgartner on the books of his own recording company. He then told me that Roland would compose the music for my libretto, which was to be called, appropriately enough, 'Jekyll and Hyde'. We shook hands on a deal and I went off home to start writing. To my astonishment, the words flowed out of me – and they were bloody good words at that. Heidi cheered up when she saw me working again and reckoned that the very least this lunatic project would do for me was to keep me sober for a spell.

A couple of days later, I received a telephone call from Paul telling me to go to London airport where an air ticket to Vienna was waiting for me and that when I arrived in the Austrian capital, Roland would be there to meet me with my accommodation fixed up and a couple of hundred pounds in expenses for me. Before ringing off, Paul added: 'On the way to the airport, buy a copy of the fairy tale *The Pied Piper of Hamlin*.'

This sent me into a swearing fit, protesting that I was already well stuck into 'Jekyll and Hyde'.

'You're in showbusiness now,' snapped Paul, 'and it's very unpredictable.'

In Vienna, Roland, who looked like a ringer for Joe Stalin when he was much younger, turned out to be the genuine article and had composed the theme music for several successful German television drama serials. He explained that he had been commissioned to compose a modern version of the 'Pied Piper' which was scheduled to open in a German theatre there the next year. He showed me the comfortable flat above his studio in Vienna where I would be writing, and then drove me off to his house in the mountains to meet his dancer wife and his two children. After supper, we went down into the basement, where he played an absolutely haunting melody on his piano and, there and then, I started to write my first song for the show – a ballad called 'He Loves Me'.

Roland hugged and kissed me and then raced upstairs to tell his wife that he had found a genius. But within minutes, the telephone rang and Heidi was on the other end of the line telling me that my beloved brother Jim had just died. She said she had rung Paul with the news and that he had arranged a flight back for me the next day.

I relapsed during the long wait for the plane at the airport, knocking back miniature schnapps after miniature schnapps, and then I rushed over to the stationery counter, bought a small notebook and pencil and wrote the theme song for the new show, which was to be called

'Rats' and was to feature junkies. The song was a big dance number for a group of young boys and girls who lived in a city squat and were waking up to the dreaded 'morning after the night before'. It took me about 20 minutes to write.

Some of the most respected men in Jim's fraternity were at his funeral, including Jimmy Nash, Billy Falco, Mickey Bloom and Les Burman. Jim had died under the anaesthetic on the operating table. While he was in hospital, Jimmy Nash, a bear of a man, sat with him and fed him with a spoon. Nash and his brother Johnny had also staged an auction in a north London pub to help Jim's widow Mavis and her three children.

A few years earlier I wrote a script for *EastEnders* in which a similar auction was held in the Queen Vic for the local hospital. Everything from a chicken leg to a bottle of beer is auctioned at these dos. In my script, Angie stood on the counter of the bar and offered her flimsy negligee for sale to the randy male customers. Dirty Den 'copped the needle', grabbed it off her and stormed off towards the stairs. That was meant to be the cliffhanger, but Angie topped me right up when she suddenly ad-libbed this fabulous line: 'And don't try it on, it's not your bleedin' colour.'

Naturally, I did not dissuade anyone from thinking that gem of a line was mine – I was more than proud to call it 'one of me own'. And that sounds like a fitting epitaph for my dear old brother, Jim: for I was more than proud to call him one of me own.

After the funeral, I returned to an empty house with just a table, a chair and a phone in the lounge and a bed in one of the five bedrooms. My family had left me at last and had left no forwarding address. I told myself that the reason for this was the terrible manic bender I had indulged in during the days between Jim's death and his funeral. But the reasons went far deeper than that – this was my paying-up time.

Lying in bed one night, I woke bolt upright, shaking with fear. I heard a loud gurgling noise and felt myself being sucked down the bed into what I imagined was a horrible, huge wastepipe. From Caroline's old room came the most piercing scream I had ever heard in my life. It took all my strength to pull myself up and out of bed, but before I managed this I noticed that my body had literally moved many inches down the bed and that while it was doing this, I had been convinced that I was going to die if I allowed myself to be dragged down that dreadful gurgling pipe.

I rushed downstairs and prayed for sobriety. Sobriety, sadly, lasted just a few hours until the off-licence across the road opened and I scraped enough money together to buy half a bottle of Scotch. As I was drinking, a burly, bearded man arrived, announcing that he was the bailiff, and a young man with him immediately began to change the keys on the front door. I snapped, put my fist under the bailiff's nose and said: 'I have been saving this right hook up for years, someone has got to cop for it and I can't think of a better candidate than you.'

To my astonishment, this big man started whining: 'Go on, hit me,' he said, 'everyone wants to hit me – especially the man next door when I'm evicting an old lady.'

Obviously, this took the wind right out of my sails and I turned on my heel and sloped off to look for someone from whom I could borrow a fiver for the next drink. That night, I slept on Wimbledon Common. It was early September and the weather was not too bad. The following morning, I had a brainwave and rang my oldest newspaper pal, Colin Hart. He contacted Peter Evans of the Newspaper Press Fund, a benevolent society for down-and-out hacks to which I had contributed on an annual basis. On condition that I got sober and stayed sober, Peter arranged for his organisation to pay for my accommodation at the YMCA in Surbiton, Surrey, for a limited period of time. Before I booked in there, though, I made a check call to Paul and he dispatched me straight back to Vienna to continue my stint with Roland. The YMCA promised to hold a place for me, which meant that I at least had the security of a roof over my head whenever I returned from Austria.

Roland put me back to work in his flat, where I made a Herculean effort to stay sober and, despite some horrendous withdrawal symptoms, managed to achieve this state for a fortnight while I typed away, working at irregular hours during the day and night. By some miracle, I wrote 17 songs and a powerful libretto during that time. But the moment I had crossed the last 't' and dotted the last 'i', I legged it out of that flat and got steamed into the local schnapps. Roland, who had been informed by Paul about my drinking problem from the start of our association, was very disappointed to see me in this state but he let me stay in his flat for another week because I was alone there, anyway.

When I came back to England again and booked into the YMCA in Surbiton, my main ambition was to try to win Heidi and the kids back. But I knew it would be a long, uphill struggle and that I had no chance unless I sobered up permanently. This I achieved in white-knuckled agony for almost the first week, but – wouldn't you know it – disaster soon struck when out of the pub across the road from the YMCA one day staggered Ann Pacey, my old film critic croney from the

Daily Herald days, and another drinking mate, George Ackland, once of the *News Of The World*. The pub, the Victoria, turned out to be their regular watering hole and it was full of other eccentric old piss-heads like them who liked nothing better than a communal sing-song. Both Pacey and George were more than ready to finance my next relapse – out of love, not perversity. So it was not long before I became a regular customer at their expense.

When Paul got to hear about my latest breakout, he bollocked me rigid and said that if I was not sober by the time 'Rats' was due to be staged in 1990, I could forget about my glamorous new career as a budding Tim Rice. So, somehow, I managed to resist my old mate Pacey's siren calls to drink ourselves to death, and survived a sober Christmas and New Year in the YMCA, where many of my co-residents were young practising heroin addicts and the night porter was an old AA mate named Eric. By the time 1990 arrived, Heidi had begun visiting me and lending me the odd tenner to pay my bus and train fares to AA meetings, but she refused to tell me where she lived.

For several months, I managed to stay sober through AA meetings and even began going upmarket by attending some Chelsea meetings, which seemed to be full of film stars, pop singers and glamorous models. But I was happiest back among my own kind, the one-time down-and-outs of Wimbledon. I was reminded of one of my old man's favourite pissy songs which was called: 'We all came in the world with nothing – and we can't take anything out.'

It was during one of Heidi's visits that she told me that Danny had gone to Purdue University in Chicago for a term as an exchange student and that Hugh McIlvanney, who was based in America at that time, had very generously invited him to stay with him for a few days. Hughie and I were friends with each other's families, wives, children, mums, brothers and sisters – the lot. And I had another McIlvanney to hero-worship in Hugh's equally talented brother, the author Willie, whom many good literary judges regarded as the best living writer in Scotland. I used to love it when Willie and Hugh sat over a drink with my brother Jim and his mates, comparing the hard men of London and Glasgow. I am not sure why Hugh, Willie and I had this fascination with hard men, but it must surely have had something to do with our backgrounds. Willie immortalised his upringing with a couple of great books, *Docherty* and *The Big Man*, which was made into a film starring Liam Neeson.

Anyway, I was inordinately proud when Heidi told me that Danny, who refused to speak to me for four more years, revealed that in New York, Hughie had taken him to Costello's bar, a famous watering hole for international journalists, and that he had listened to 'Batty' stories all night. He had told her: 'I had no idea the old bastard was so famous.' I just thanked God he had found something positive to say about me at last, no matter how hollow it was.

Then, in high summer, Reg Gutteridge came up with an almost carbon copy of the Seventh Cavalry rescue act he had staged with George Walker some 12 years previously. This time, I had just been watching Paul Gascoigne crying his heart out on our communal YMCA television set during the World Cup in Italy when I received a phone call from my old minder Reg. Again his news was that a wealthy man was inviting me to lunch in the West End to put a business proposition to me. This one was a fight fanatic named Steve Davies, whom I had seen but never spoken to at many of the big boxing scenes around the world.

Over lunch, Steve explained his background to me. He was, apparently, a one-time trade union official who had become a very successful entrepreneur and had just sold his technical business to the big industrial company Blue Arrow. He had, he told me, even written speeches for Margaret Thatcher. As someone who still thought I was the centre of the universe, my interest in his conversation started to fray at the edges and I found my concentration being dangerously grabbed by all those seductive bottles behind the restaurant bar. So much so that I rather rudely asked him what all this had to do with me. He then said that he wanted me to write a television play about boxing and that he had checked me out with top boxing people such as Jarvis Astaire and Mickey Duff, who had very flatteringly told him that I was a genius, no less.

Assuming that he was some kind of a nutter, I then came up with a phrase that I had deemed was too grandiose for even me to use before.

'You'd better get in touch with my agent,' I said, thinking I had brought the meeting to an end.

At this juncture, Steve said: 'I don't want to bother with all that old bollocks' and suddenly pulled a wad of notes from his pocket – £2,000 in fifties. 'How does this suit you?' he asked.

Bearing in mind that I was down to poncing cigarettes and bus fares by now, I could only stammer: 'Very nicely, thank you,' and trouser the proffered wedge a bit lively.

He then followed this up by asking: 'How long will it take you to write it?' Plucking a figure out of thin air, with my eyes by now rivetted to those bottles of booze behind the bar, I ventured: 'Oh, about 12 weeks, I suppose.' And with that, this new benefactor plonked another £250 in fifty-pound notes into my hand and said: 'That will be your wages every week while you're working on it.'

I was already scraping my chair back as if I was adjusting my starting blocks for the dash to the nearest bar, when he suddenly added ominously: 'Reg tells me you've been sober for 16 weeks now, is that right?' I confirmed that it was, fearing, even as I said it, that this happy state was due to last about another 16 minutes, when he added: 'This money I am paying you depends entirely on you staying sober, of course.'

Delighted by this turn-up for the book, Heidi brought my typewriter round and in a few sober but manic days I had the play finished. Steve proclaimed himself 'well pleased' with it and then turned up outside the YMCA in his Rolls-Royce. Having had his card marked by Reg, he then inquired where the rest of my life's work was – such as musicals, film and comedy scripts – and I pointed to an old black bin bag and a couple of Tesco carrier bags. Steve carted the whole lot off to his big, posh house in Berkhampstead and then whipped me up to some showbiz solicitor in Soho to sign a deal with him.

He may have been an expert in company law and something of an academic, too, but when it came to negotiating with people, bespectacled Steve was an out-and-out Rottweiler. He went to war with Paul and Roland, and he sacked my TV agent. Then he set about getting the musical recorded himself, at great expense, using high-class demo singers and the best studio equipment. The trouble was that the more he played it back to me, the more excited I got by it and the inevitable relapse, when it came, was such a humdinger that he stopped paying for my accommodation at the YMCA – which he had taken over from the Newspaper Press Fund – and I found myself sleeping on Wimbledon Common again.

We then endured a crazy relationship in which we drove each other mad, with me in and out of the YMCA like a yo-yo, in and out of AA like a spinning top and kipping with drunks in squats in Wimbledon.

I had managed to reach the point where I sobered up for a couple of weeks when, in 1991, I got news that my mother was dying. At the age of 94, she had decided to give up the struggle when Jim died, making it five out of seven children which she had survived – Louise had died in South Africa a few weeks earlier – and Mum had succumbed to a stroke and was in a coma. She had always been a God-fearing woman and she was so afraid of dying that she reminded me of those other old manipulators, Winston Churchill and President Tito. I sat with her every day in the hospital in Enfield and prayed her into the arms of Jesus.

Then I took myself off to a Christian home someone in AA had told me about. This place was in deepest Kent and it was a charity for male drunks and drug addicts. One of the houses there was for young men who were even further down the list of last-chance saloons than prison. These really were no-hopers and never-wassers. I declined the chance to live with them and plumped instead for the offer of joining a set of old men in another house who were literally waiting to die. I found myself chopping pallets into firewood every day there, just as I had done with my brother, all those years ago and delivering it to the local greengrocer. Obviously it was a strict dry house and we were required to attend a Bible reading every evening and church every Sunday.

Somehow, I managed to stick it out for six weeks until I broke out and traversed the five miles of country roads to the nearest station in the pitch-black November late evening, carrying my suitcase and limping on my gammy leg. To this day, I don't know how I stopped myself from stepping in front of the headlights of a passing car and ending it all. I feel the same way about the number of mornings I had stood on Surbiton station longing to throw myself beneath the wheels of an express train – I think it was simply the terror of going to the Hell I had read about in my youth that kept me alive.

I did not have a penny to my name, but I managed to fare-dodge my way back to Wimbledon and into the Alexander pub next door, where I ponced enough money off my old drinking mates to get pissed before closing time. The horrible thing about these constant relapses was that I was pissed in no time at all. The first drink always tasted like nectar from the Gods, the second put me in that omnipotent state I described earlier, but by the third, the spiritual blinds had descended and I was a terrified, raging, dangerous animal.

At the back of my mind throughout this latest nightmare was the knowledge that I had discovered the address of the flat that Heidi and Caroline were renting in Wimbledon Village. And after the pub shut, I dragged myself up Wimbledon Hill to the second floor of a Thirties-style block. No matter how hard I banged on the door and begged through the letter box, Heidi would not let me in. She must have telephoned the police, because I had a rock from the garden in my hands and ready to throw through her window when a copper grabbed me. A woman constable then went upstairs to talk to Heidi and then came down and gave me the mother and father of a bollocking for being the 'disgusting, drunken old chauvinist pig' which I undoubtedly was by now.

They were driving me to the nick when I suddenly remembered Mick the Brick's gaff and asked them to be kind enough to drop me off there. They waited until Mick poked his head out of the window and agreed to let me in before they drove off – without pressing charges.

Micky Morgan, an ex-bricklayer, was a well-known Wimbledon practising alcoholic with a heart of gold who kept open house for half the down-and-out drunks in Wimbledon. Incredibly, he lived with his nan, who was more than 100 years old, half blind and half deaf, and described herself as a 'white witch'. The monstrous, mangy black cat she kept did nothing to dispel this description. The miracle of Mick was that, although he was drunk every day of his life, he never failed to stagger home to cook his nan's dinner.

He and I were members of the 'over 50s' club, which must be one of the biggest in England and consists of single men, mainly divorced, all unemployed but working on the black economy as cowboy builders and the like, and all desperately lonely. Club members spend all their spare time in the pub and pool whatever money they earn or ponce on the sedative of alcohol. Mick's was open house for 'club members' and certainly a bit upmarket from the squats and the gutter.

Mick was one of the many thousands of middle-aged drunks who had not the slightest intention of getting sober. Physically as hard and wiry as a nail, he had been married an incredible five times and astonished me once, by showing me a picture of his handsome son on the front page of the *News of the World* with his arms around glamour girl Samantha Fox, next to an article in which he was described as the 'latest hunk' in that lady's life. I often wondered what Samantha would have thought if she had visited her boyfriend's dad and great-grandmother for tea.

I lived with Mick until January 1992 and paid my way there by doing pieces for the *Daily Star* again, where, for old time's sake, Brian Hitchen helped me out financially and turned a blind eye to my drinking as long as it never took place in the office. But by now, newspaper offices were so different to the old Fleet Street days that no one drank in them anymore, anyway. The *Star* was now housed in the new Express Newspapers building on Blackfriars Bridge, and as soon as I entered that place, I knew the old magic was gone forever. The big room was as silent as the grave, with everyone staring into computers and seemingly locked into a lifeless world of their own. The floor was carpeted and the noiseless atmosphere was about as intoxicating as a stroll round John Lewis's furniture department. When Hitchen invited me into his office, the drinks cabinet with which editors always entertained their guests remained closed – assuming there even was one. And I knew then that there was nothing here to crave anymore except dangerous memories of the old days.

This realisation should have kept me sober, but it didn't. I took to drinking on the Waterloo station buffet again, and by now my system was so far gone – what with not touching any food whatever at Mick The Brick's or indeed in the pub – that the only thing I could keep down me was Pernod. I even became known by the bar staff there as 'Pernod Pete'.

I remember that the stunt I dreamed up for my Christmas earner that year was to go down to trainer David Elsworth's yard and stick a Santa Claus hat on his fabulous grey steeplechaser Desert Orchid, who was competing in his favourite race, the King George at Kempton on Boxing Day. David, an old racecourse companion, was so delighted with the picture I arranged that he turned it into a Christmas card. He also tipped me a horse for me and my other down-and-out mates' Christmas money, but typically the going changed overnight, the horse got beat, we all 'did our bollocks' on it and didn't have a penny on when it won next time out.

That particular Christmas Day turned out to be the worst of my life. Mick and I caught flu, and all the pubs were closed except, we had been told, the Dog and Fox in Wimbledon village. We walked the two or three miles from South Wimbledon to the village only to find that this pub, too, was as dark and bolted shut as the rest of them. On the long walk back, we passed house after house with twinkling lights and Christmas decorations, and I wept silent tears of despair for my lost family and my long-lost innocence.

There were more tears to come, however, when a letter arrived at Mick's via the Surbiton YMCA telling me that I had to appear at the High Court in the Strand for my bankcruptcy hearing. This was another of life's full circles, considering that I used to take shorthand notes there when I was with Snell and Son. The VAT people had caught up with me from my freelance days and instituted proceedings against me for non-payment. When I came out of the court, it was raining heavily and I had holes in my shoes. So, instead of walking round to report to the Official Receiver in Holborn as I was instructed to do, I went straight over the road from the Law Courts and got smashed on Scotch in one of my old Fleet Street pubs. But this bankruptcy hearing turned out to be something of a blessing in disguise when, during the course of it, I suddenly wondered if I had any kind of pension to come – after all, I had paid into several pension schemes in my time, including during my days on the *Herald*, the *Sun*, the *Evening News* and Express Newspapers. So the next day, I took my hangover to the *Express* pensions department and, to my surprise and delight, was informed that

I did indeed have few quid owing to me. Within a week, I was the possessor of a cheque for more than £6,000. It felt like six million to me. I still had Heidi's telephone number, so I rang her and asked what she wanted me to do with it, and she advised me to go to my nephew Martin and his wife and young family in Australia.

That was about the only place in the world I could feel loved and safe anymore. They were Pentecostal Christians and after my experience in South Africa, I thought the only Power that could help me now was Jesus and the Holy Spirit. So after telephoning Martin and being told his family would welcome me with open arms, I caught a flight to Perth and from there another one to Geraldtown, a little seaside paradise on the west coast of Australia.

CHAPTER TWENTY-ONE
RESTITUTION

Martin, his wife Kim and his two children, Leila May and Caleb, could not possibly have been any more Christian and charitable towards me. Martin, who was my oldest sister Louise's son, had stayed at my mum's flat many years before when he was a young man and Jim used to take him clubbing at the Astor. But now he was a teacher and the devout leader of a group of unorthodox Pentecostal Christians who held meetings in his comfortable house, which had fantastic panoramic views over the sea. He fixed me up with a caravan in his back garden, where I lived like a Gipsy King and even entertained his children and their friends.

I tried, oh how I tried, with all my mental strength, to embrace their happy, clappy style of worship and even agreed to be ducked in a swimming pool and baptised by a visiting minister as a born-again Christian. But almost every time I worshipped, I kept remembering what an AA old timer, 'Guardsman' John, had told me: 'Jesus saves your soul, but AA saves your arse.' (Another little bit of perceived AA wisdom went 'Religion is for people who are afraid of going to Hell. AA is for people who have been there.') Sadly, within days of that sacred ceremony, I was cheating by having a lager or two on the terrace before Martin and Kim, who was an occupational therapist, collected the kids from a friend's house and returned home from work in the evenings. Like everyone else of the dwindling band of people who still cared about my welfare, a condition of their loving shelter was that I stayed sober.

So it was with both a heavy heart at letting them down and the thrill of a false sense of freedom that I left them after a couple of months and checked into the best seaside hotel in town. It had a lovely sea view and in the vicinity was a betting shop which, because of the time differences in that vast country, featured race meetings from dawn to dusk. Most of my new-found betting mates were Aborigines, while my evening drinking companions were the cream of Geraldtown society, such as it was. I managed to hold out until the first week of March when my six grand had all but evaporated and I booked myself on a flight back to London after a tearful farewell to Martin and his ever-loving family.

When I got back to England, I checked into a little hotel in Wimbledon Broadway, called the Wayfarer and continued drinking like a lunatic. I instructed the porter there to put my 'tank' – what was left of my cash – into a locked drawer behind his desk where I couldn't get at it too easily, but when one morning he informed me that I had got so pissed the night before that I had spent most of it on telephone calls to Australia, I could only wince at what I must have been saying to Martin and Kim in blackout, and decided to end it all that night with a couple of bottles of brandy and a bottle of pills. When I awoke from this little debacle, most of the brandy was gone, the bottle of pills remained unopened and the manager was demanding that I pay for my accommodation and my bar bill or he would call the police. I made an SOS call to another very close and fabulously generous AA mate, 'Boxer John', who settled my bill and lent me the money to check into a nearby bedsit. Yet despite all John's charity, I clung to the belief that the time had come when it was right for me to drink myself slowly to death, and I was soon thrown out of the bedsit, which was a hell-hole anyway.

It was around this time that I committed one of my very worst public nuisances. The greyhound derby finals were staged at Wimbledon dog track and sponsored by the *Daily Mirror*. As I was known by the gatekeepers there and the restaurant manager as a *Mirror* man myself, I managed to gatecrash the posh, dinner-suited top tables section dressed in an open neck shirt and jeans and make an absolute drunken pest of myself. I lurched from table to table borrowing money – from Keith Fisher, the *Mirror* sports editor, Harry Lloyd, the paper's dog racing expert, from John McCririck of Channel 4 and, worst of all, I waylaid Jarvis Astaire as, in a splendid white dinner jacket, he made his way down to present the trophy to the winning owner; but not before I had put the arm on him for a tenner.

It was back to sleeping under the stars on Wimbledon Common until I crawled back into AA yet again and one of my very oldest AA pals, an ex-builder named Phil who had once had his own business and had, coincidentally, first got sober in Australia, invited me to stay with him and his two young children in New Malden, where the council had provided them with a house, Within weeks, the pair of us had relapsed and Phil had lost the house and was back on the streets begging while his kids had to be looked after by relatives, and I wandered around in a ludicrous pair of shorts which I had worn in Australia – poncing, drinking and waylaying Heidi in the summer evenings as she arrived home at Wimbledon station from her full day's work in Notting Hill. When she told me how ridiculous I looked in those shorts, at the age of 59, I didn't tell her that I wore them because I kept pissing my trousers now after the first couple of pints and would rather the urine ran down my bare legs. This was because I did not want to blot my copybook with her and spoil my chances of one day winning her back. But worse was still to come.

I lurched into an AA meeting one night and slagged them all off for being all talk and no action and challenged any one of them to give me a bed. Ted, an atheist, who has since relapsed and died after around 20 years of sobriety, became a truly Good Samaritan and put me up on the couch of his little flat in a big council block in Roehampton. But even with his iron-fisted help I could not stop drinking and one night I was watching the 1992 European Championship final on a pub TV when I started hankering for the old days and something inside my head snapped again. Breaking my sacred vow never to bother Heidi at her home again, I staggered up to her flat in the village, where it turned out Danny happened to be staying at the time, too, and I began punching in the glass front door with both fists. The police were called again and I was carted off to Wimbledon police cells, dripping blood from both arms. By now I had come to be regarded by them as one of the local drunk nuisances and was kicked out again next morning without charge and told to go to casualty and get my wounds stitched up.

Then it was back to Wimbledon Common again, from

where I managed to crawl up to the AA headquarters in London, and in a basement flat beneath their building, a counsellor I knew from the Chelsea meetings promised to try to get me into a treatment centre called St Joseph's, which was situated in a hospital run by nuns in Haslemere, Surrey. The only problem was getting my local council to come up with the funds, because treatment centres were being closed by the Tory Health Minister, Virginia Bottomley, right, left and centre, until there was almost nowhere to get de-toxed any more.

This counsellor asked me if there was anyone, anyone in the world, whom I could now turn to for help, and I remembered that an old drinking pal, Steve Whiting, who had been chief sports sub-editor during my days on the *Sun* and was then a cricket writer for the *Sunday Mirror*, was now a born-again Christian who had tried to help me in the past.

Steve, the nephew of George Whiting, one of the greatest boxing writers this country ever produced, suffered from multiple sclerosis, had just been rendered a widower with the death of his beautiful Australian wife and had a delightful four-year-old daughter to bring up on his own – yet he still found time to worry about me. He put me in the emotional care of a couple of Christian ladies from his Baptist church and he drove me down to Portsmouth, where I managed to get a day-patient place in the Nelson Hospital there – one of the rare hospitals which still specialises in alcoholism.

I had borrowed some money from my last remaining brother, George, for this final, do-or-die fling at recovery, and as he handed me the money, George, to my astonishment, quoted Omah Khayam at me: 'The moving finger writes and having writ, moves on.' Then he said: 'Your trouble is that you live in the past, you are full of nostalgic longings for the good old days that never really were. You used to sit in the kitchen for hours on end when you were a kid, persuading the old lady to tell you stories about her old life in Stepney.'

The money which George had given me – he had always been a sucker for my hard-luck stories – I used for a cheap night's kip in a 'low-life' bed and breakfast gaff in Southsea and then, as soon as Steve had driven off home, would you believe, the craving hit me as hard as ever and I got as drunk as a skunk in the seafront pubs that night. Weeping alcoholic crocodile tears of shame again at what I had done to Steve and George, I found myself at dawn on the beach where a statue commemorates one of the starting points for the D-Day landings and, full of drunken bravado, I waded into the sea, fully clothed, with the intention of ending it all. Pathetically, I soon found myself treading water, then swimming back to shore – well and truly fucked.

My Higher Power intervened again, however, as when I went back to get my bag from the B and B, one of the other dole types there tipped me off about a 'spike', a down-and-out dry house for tramps and ne'er-do-wells in Southsea where I could get board and lodging down to the local DSS. I spent the next fortnight there, attending the Nelson Hospital every day for detox until word came through that I was one of the luckiest men in the world and had got my precious place at St Joe's.

My last drink had been on 6 July, the night before the pathetic dawn suicide attempt, and I thought, this time, that this would turn out to be the last one of my life. I was a month past my 59th birthday by now and reckoned that even I would surrender at last. I spent 10 weeks in St Joe's where they put me to bed with a Teddy bear every night and told me to find my inner child. I was also encouraged to gaze at myself in the mirror for 10 minutes every morning and could not believe some of the self-pitying reflections I found. The main cause of this was that despite all my lady counsellor's efforts of writing to and telephoning Heidi, my wife was adamant that she was going to divorce me and told the counsellor that she had already begun proceedings to this effect.

During my stay at St Joe's, where I underwent similar psychotherapy to what I had previously experienced in Accept, the Priory and Weston, I developed high blood pressure and had to be woken up every morning by a nurse from the hospital wing to have tests. These had been arranged for me by the head of the clinic, who was a middle-aged male doctor and not a psychotherapist like the rest of the staff. He surprised me by telling me that psychotherapy was a waste of time for someone like me. He reckoned I was a manic depressive and should have been on a mood-altering pill instead. This diagnosis infuriated the psychotherapists and I took their advice and stuck with them instead. But this doctor's opinion was to have a strange postcript some years later.

On my release, I was transferred to a half-way house called Arch House in Brighton. This place turned out to be a bit of a nightmare in that some of the the inmates kept relapsing, so weakening my own resolve. Most of the residents were ex-jailbirds who surprised me by knocking all kinds of shit out of me at Scrabble. Apparently they had played it on a regular basis for years in the nick and were past masters at the four and three-letter word big points scorers.

But I soon had more than relapses to worry about when in the middle of one night, after I had been reading – of all things – the Book of Revelations in the New Testament,

I was awoken by what turned out to be a massive heart attack.

I had been sleeping in a tiny single boxroom and managed to drag myself, naked, across the landing to the even tinier lavatory. I had this strange recollection about having once asked a man who had suffered a heart attack how you would know if you were having one or not, and he had simply replied: 'You'll know!' And there was no mistaking what this was that was happening to me now. The pain was becoming unbearable when I slid down the lavatory wall and put one of my knees out, too, a relic from those dodgy cartilage operations I had in my boyhood. As I was slumped there, I knew that I would soon be slipping into unconsciousness and I felt I had had more than enough of life, anyway. I wanted to go out like John Wayne with a cry of 'Fuck 'em all' on my lips, and I yearned for a bottle of whisky to put me out of my misery. Instead, in a voice that did not seem to be mine, I heard myself whispering over and over again: 'Jesus, save me. Jesus, save me.'

At that point, a little red-headed Scotsman who had cooked us a diabolical curry dinner earlier that evening came in for a piss. I can remember him standing there looking flabbergasted and repeating over and over: 'That's no' the drink you're suffering from. That's definitely no' the drink . . .' I wanted either to kill him or get him to send for an ambulance, but I found I couldn't speak.

My red-headed mate must have alerted the caretaker down in the basement and they must have carried me back to my bed, because the next thing I remembered was lying face down while a needle was stuck into my arse and the voice of a lady doctor was saying: 'What you have just witnessed, gentlemen, is a classic heart attack.'

I seem to remember, too, the medics getting up to all

sorts of life-saving antics in the ambulance and a doctor in casualty even cutting into my chest and stitching something into it. And all the while, I was still softly murmuring to myself: 'Jesus, save me.' He obviously did, because some time the next day, I woke up in the cardiac unit of the East Sussex Hospital with my wife and three children gazing down at me. I was overwhelmed with gratitude at the sight of them, but it was no Hollywood-style reunion. They left after a couple of hours to walk out of my life again.

They kept me in hospital for a couple of weeks, where my old *Evening News* guv'nor Peter Watson and his wife Sheila came to visit me from their home in Eastbourne. I knew that Arch House was not a stable enough dry house for me to return to, and an AA mate in Brighton turned up one day with a couple of young ladies who interviewed me for a place in their halfway house in another part of town. The first thing they told me was that under no circumstances was I call to call them 'darlin, luv, pet, precious or dear heart'. They insisted they were Ms's and told me not to forget it.

When I went into their care, I found myself sharing the house with half a dozen shaven-headed, tattooed characters who were not too sympathetic about me having to do very little exercise for the next six weeks or so and seemed more interested in my swollen knee, which I treated by sticking packets of frozen peas on it, than my dodgy ticker. Either way, they were not going to let me get off my share of hoovering and lavatory cleaning, and my frequent pauses to spray my anti-angina treatment under my tongue cut no ice whatever with them. I was to stay in that house for the next couple of months, attending therapy sessions every day and AA meetings most nights. But because I was not allowed to walk any great distances,

I had to keep begging lifts from AA members, which must have made me something of a pain in the arse.

Then one day in town I bumped into Ellen Jameson. She and my old guv'nor Derek had their own nightly radio show now and they lived in a lovely house on the seafront at Hove. They came to the recovery house to pick me up and drive me there to tea on several occasions, generously bunging me some tobacco money, too. The visits of these two celebrities caused quite a stir with my lady counsellors and they began to wonder what I was playing at. I began to get even more visitors when *Sun* editor Kelvin McKenzie published a piece about my heart attack on the sports pages of his paper. Reg Gutteridge and Steve Davies turned up and then Peter Grimsditch drove all the way down from Manchester to inform me: 'There will be no more cardboard boxes for you.' With that, he drove me to a slap-up lunch in Brighton and asked me to start writing sports pieces for the *Daily Sport*, which he now edited from Manchester.

This lunch, fortunately, was a sober one for me, unlike the one I had enjoyed at the *Daily Sport*'s expense several years earlier. At that time, I was approached by Bobby Moore to become his regular 'ghost' when he was appointed as sports editor and sports columnist of the new paper, which was still on the drawing board then. The pair of us kicked off by going to one of Bobby's favourite Italian restaurants in Clerkenwell and knocking out our first dummy column over several bottles of delicious wine. I had drawn £100 in advance expenses from the paper for that purpose. But the editor, an old hack named Mike Gabbert, whom I knew from our *People* days together when he had made a name for himself by leading the investigations into the infamous football bribes scandal of the 1960s, kept sending messages to

Bobby begging him to return to the office. Bobby was having none of it because he knew the ludicrous reason why Gabbert wanted him so desperately. The paper was appearing in court that day to answer questions about some such nonsense as a nipple count in their upcoming tits-and-bums paper, and they wanted the World Cup-winning England captain to give them an air of respectability by disclosing to the court that he was their new sports editor.

Needless to say, by the time the wine had stopped flowing my services were no longer required, so I had lasted precisely one day. But I got another earner down to the *Sport* owner, porn king David Sullivan, when I featured him and in his luxury mansion in the *Daily Express* Saturday morning colour magazine some years later.

But back to Brighton and the halfway house. I had by now come to believe that all living there could teach me about recovery was how to exist with half a dozen other headbangers, and did not fancy one more day of it. Again, the problem was taken out of my hands when Steve Whiting's Christian lady friends invited me to Sunday lunch at one of their homes in Hampshire and accidently served me trifle with wine in it. When I shared the news of this accidental wine intake in group therapy the next morning, the two Ms's gave me 24 hours to get out for good – weak heart or no weak heart.

Steve Davies came to my rescue again by paying for me to stay at the YMCA in Watford for a couple of weeks, but after one piece on Lester Piggott for the *Daily Sport* – which they printed underneath a monster headline proclaiming 'Batty is back!' – I had to jack in Grimbles' latest job, because I knew that in order to maintain this long period of sobriety, I would have to attend at least three AA meetings a day.

I was stuck out in Watford because it was near Steve's Hertfordshire home and because he wanted to keep an eye on me again. He even persuaded me to arrange for us to go down to Hove to play the musical to Derek Jameson, who was an opera buff, and who just might have had contacts willing to put up the necessary few million quid to stage it in this country. Derek pronounced the first few songs – the music for which had been written by Roland – as the best he had heard since *West Side Story*, but he was not so keen on the other melodies which Steve had commissioned. And as I had lost touch with Paul and Roland, both 'Rats' and the Jekyll and Hyde libretto had gone on the back burner while I concentrated on staying alive.

Steve helped to finance my railcard day tickets which conveyed me to meetings in the city every lunchtime and afternoon and on to Chelsea and sometimes even as far as Wimbledon and Surrey in the evenings. But he warned me that he could not continue to pay for my accommodation for more than a few more weeks.

It was then, at a City meeting, that I was offered the chance to live with an AA member who was caretaker of a block of flats in Petticoat Lane. So those ever-decreasing circles of mine were still decreasing at a rate of knots, to Brighton and the scene of my evacuation and now back to the very edges of my birthplace in Stepney. I moved in with Martin, who was separated from his wife and two young sons, and slept in a child's bunk in what had once been the boys' room.

The meetings in the East End were something else again. I had already been downmarket to the big Sunday morning meeting at the Oval and the headbangers' meeting at St Martin's Lane, but some of these meetings, at the seamen's mission in Chadwell and the Salvation

Army hostel in Whitechapel, were a TV documentary producer's dream. The seamen's mission meetings were attended by a group of leathery-jowled park bench old-timers that even Hollywood would not have been able to cast. And with not a white coat of a therapist or a doctor in sight, they shared their innermost feelings and searched for spirituality with facial expressions and revelations which those TV people would have given their eye teeth to become flies on the wall for.

When I had been sober for around six months, Heidi, who had dropped those divorce proceedings by now, agreed to meet me after work and treat me to the cinema occasionally. And as soon as I got bits and bobs of freelance work on the *Star* again, I was able to return the treat and even take her for a meal, too.

But it was one of those *Star* pieces which was to lead, indirectly, to my ruin again. I did an exclusive Christmas spread on an 'at home' with hard man footballer Vinnie Jones, for which I was to receive £1,000 – half of which was to be handed over to Vinnie or Steve Davies, who was by this time advising Vinnie on his off-field career moves. Christmas and the New Year in Petticoat Lane and the City were a nightmare. It was utterly deserted and unreal around there all through the holidays, and the days were hanging over me like so many vultures. I had stopped counting the Christmases during which I had been away from house and home now, and was missing my family dreadfully.

The money from the Jones article was due the first week in January and when I rang up Steve to tell him about it, he had gone off on holiday to Florida. The inevitable happened when I drew that grand and got it cashed. 'Guardsman' John had warned me that money would do me a lot more harm than good, and he was right. I got suited and booted and went into the lounge of a posh hotel, where I ordered a pot of tea. I got on the phone to Heidi at work – I still did not have her new home address or number – and unsuccessfully begged her to take me back. I abandoned the teapot for the hotel bar and several large whiskies later, as if by magic, I found myself at Wembley dog track, where I kicked off by backing a 10–1 winner and adding to my wedge.

That night found me in a bed and breakfast near Paddington station and the next found me at Wimbledon dogs, where I met up with a couple of well-known characters there. One was Derek 'the Ghost' who was a compulsive gambler and lived alone in some squalor in 'the buildings' near Waterloo station, and the other was Alan 'Wheels', who used to drive Jimmy White, the snooker player, around. I treated the three of us to a three-day bender, during which I bought a mattress in Petticoat Lane in order to kip down on the Ghost's concrete floor. But when we went to collect my clothes, Martin was too scared to open the door and shouted through it that he had thrown my clobber away, anyway.

So there I was with no permanent roof over me again and only the clothes I stood up in. Me and my two running mates had a couple of slap-up 'pissy' lunches in the Tower Bridge Hotel and then spent the afternoons in a Petticoat Lane pub and a nearby betting shop. Soon, I was feeling too ill to leave the pub for the betting shop and got Alan to run my wagers. When we were all but skint, I booked Alan and I into the Grosvenor Hotel at Victoria station, with the intention of making my way down to hospital in Brighton again to have my heart checked over. I guzzled brandy all night on credit and then had to get Alan to call an ambulance as I suffered another heart attack in the hotel room in the early hours of the morning.

The ambulance whisked me off to Westminster Hospital where I was detained in their cardiac unit. Later, I was put into the Marie Celeste ward where I was to undergo various tests with a view to heart surgery – but as the hospital doctors knew of my homeless plight, I think they took pity on me and unofficially let me have a bed there until I was much fitter.

I was told much later by Bob Driscoll that when he rang Hugh McIlvanney and said: 'Guess where Batty has finished up this time?' and then told him it was the Marie Celeste ward, McIlvanney thought for a moment and then gave one of his famous one-line replies. 'Well, if it wasn't the Marie Celeste ward, it certainly is now.'

The days ran into weeks at Westminster Hospital, during which time my mental condition deteriorated into full-blown psychotic mania. When I asked a lady doctor why I had gone mad, she said: 'A horse would have gone mad if it had been abused as much as you have abused yourself.'

When I was admitted to the Westminster in January 1993, it was on its last legs, much the same as I was. This condemned old building was due to be demolished and, after talking to the hospital social workers and establishing that I was now a vagrant with no fixed abode and no income – not even dole money – the heart surgeon was persuaded by my Australian lady doctor to let me fade away along with the hospital.

The only thing wrong with this charitable plan of hers was that something inside my head refused to let go quietly. Each night, I stood on an outside, glass-covered bridge linking the Marie Celeste ward with the X-ray department. It must have been one of the dankest, dreariest, most Dickensian-looking bridges in London. By day it was the last refuge for heart patients who still wished to smoke themselves to death. Two large, ugly ashtrays furnished the bridge, spewing out a carpet of cigarette ends which I lit and smoked when I ran out of patients and their visitors to ponce fags from.

This was during the depths of a very cold winter, yet I was so hot that I could almost feel smoke coming out of my arse. That could have had something to do with the fact that I was hallucinating and was convinced that the Second Coming was going to occur on the roof of the Criminal Investigation Department building which was the main view from one side of the bridge's grime-covered windows. But while I was waiting for Jesus to descend in all his glory, I would perform solo sing-songs which owed more to songs from the shows than any psalms or hymns. Other patients would holler for me to shut up, but I would just shout back, 'Bollocks!'

Obviously this made me such an all-round pain in the arse that I was right when I suspected that the doctors and nurses were plotting to get rid of me and toss me out into the street again. Especially when the very lovely, leggy Australian lady doctor told the visiting psychiatrist that I had tried to pull her into the bed with me for some nooky. The psychiatrist just nodded sagely and said something about this being perfectly normal behaviour for a psychotic. But when my condition deteriorated to the point when I became hysterical at night because I could, almost literally, feel my ribs being torn from my chest and screamed with pain and fear at the sight of what I thought was the Devil grinning at me from the fires of Hell, they had to start injecting me with what I now know to be largactol – known in the jails of England as the liquid cosh to quieten violent prisoners.

Totally off my head by now, I was transferred to the nearby Gordon Hospital in Vauxhall which, in old-fashioned terms, was the nut house. While I was there, I was visited one day by Vinnie Jones and Steve Davies and thought they had come to claim their money, which I had done this runner with. But they both told me later that they were absolutely horrified to see the condition and circumstances I was in. I could still see the funny side later, though, when they told me that as the nursing staff crowded around Vinnie for his autograph, I kept protesting: 'It's him you want to lock up in 'ere. He's the headbanger, not me.'

When I was eventually discharged, I was still foaming at the mouth on a regular basis and was full of drugs they had given me and told me to continue to take. The best thing to come out of this latest hospitalisation, though, was the letter they gave me which turned out to be my passport into the mysterious world of the Department of Social Security and all its infuriating workings. All I had to do was plonk it on the counter and foam at the mouth to at least get someone to pay some attention to me. Youngsters seemed to know how to get dole money – I had never yet mastered the intricate art of talking my way round the counter clerks. I had not even known – or maybe I was just too proud to bother to find out – that I could have got the State to pay the interest on our mortage a few years earlier, and so have prevented that terrible eviction and maybe even the bankruptcy.

But all that was just so much spilt milk so far as my present plight was concerned. The few times I had hitherto tried my luck at the dole offices, I found that if you were a lone male in your late fifties, you could forget about it as far as they were concerned. Still, I could hardly complain as I had got more than my whack out of the Health Service when it came to hospital treatment – and there was to be more to come yet.

The hospital letter which was to prove so helpful later went like this: 'Riverside Health Authority, Mental Health Unit, Gordon Hospital, Bloomburg Street, London SW1V 2RH. Private and Strictly Confidential: March 11, 1993.

To Whom It May Concern: Mr Batt was admitted to the Westminster Hospital on January 13, 1993, following a heart attack (he had a previous major heart attack in September 1992 and was admitted to hospital in Brighton). After his admission to the Westminster he became unwell with a hypomanic illness, probably complicated by his history of alcoholic dependence and abuse. As a result of this, he was seen by a member of the psychiatric team and transferred to the Gordon Psychiatric Hospital on February 9, 1993. As a result of his heart condition, past history of alcohol abuse and vulnerability to mood disorder, he remains extremely vulnerable, although he is complying with medication and attending AA groups regularly. I think it would be helpful for him to be placed in a flat in the Wimbledon area. An ex-journalist, he has quite a few supports in the community in Wimbledon, including his estranged wife.

Dr Hilary Scurlock, Locum Senior Registrar to Dr Paul Robinson Consultant Psychiatrist.

Thank God, Colin Hart used this letter to persuade Peter Evans's Newspaper Press Fund to pay for accommodation for me at Wimbledon YMCA, but only for two weeks. On the morning those two weeks were up, I found myself sitting in the breakfast room at the YMCA, rattling with pills, still foaming at the mouth and beside myself with anxiety. The only place the letter succeeded in getting me into this time was one of the most notorious hostels in London, where the inmates regularly attacked the cooks with knives and many of them were pissed around the clock. I knew damned well that I was not fit enough, either physically or mentally, to cope with this kind of environment.

Luckily, a young Jack the Lad, who was the 'daddy' of all the other displaced kids in the YM at that particular time, came over to ponce 'a snout' from me and asked me what the long face was all about. In desperation, I flashed him my letter and told him the name of the hostel I was heading for. His face went white.

'You'll get killed in there,' he said. 'Just wait here for an hour or so while I get you fixed up.'

Jack the Lad soon returned with another man in a car, who introduced himself as Merlin. He stuffed my battered old suitcase, containing all my worldly belongings, into the boot of his motor and drove me off to his house, which was only a couple of hundred yards away. The whole world might have felt like Hell to me at that time but Wimbledon was, without doubt, my spiritual home now, so I was not complaining about this 'abduction'.

Merlin's turned out to be a residential care home of sorts, which he ran through State handouts for all his 'patients'. I stayed there for three months and my companions were half-a-dozen senile old boys who were refugees from a properly supervised care home, complete with nursing staff, which, along with hundreds, maybe even thousands of others, had been closed down under the infamous Care In The Community scheme. As two of these unfortunate old chaps shat in their trousers every morning at breakfast – which, incidentally was a gargantuan fry-up – I took to eating alone in my room.

Out of the weekly sickness benefit which Merlin claimed

for me, he allotted me £15 a week for tobacco, and I could walk to the AA meetings in Wimbledon. To say I was depressed would have been an understatement. This was even more like having one foot in the grave than the Christian care home had been. But I was, nonetheless, extremely grateful to Merlin, even if he was making money out of me. My one ray of hope this time was that although I was mentally still very ill, Heidi met me regularly for a cup of coffee in the evenings after she had finished work.

And although I did not know it then, I have come to thank God a million times over for that spell in the nut house and all the consequences of it, because that desperate experience did turn out, at long last and miraculously, to be my almost unreachable rock bottom. Despite numerous temptations and sporadic periods of insanity, I have never raised glass or bottle to my lips since then. And that means that the first and last decades of my life so far are the only ones in which I have not taken alcohol into my suspect system.

Another saviour was to enter my life in Merlin's. A young, extremely dedicated, local GP, Dr Chris Baillie, made regular visits there and so took me onto his books. He traced my long lost medical notes and has kept an eagle eye on me ever since. And as I shall explain, I owe my continued existence to him. Dr Baillie describes me as his 'miracle patient'. If that is so, there is no doubt that he was my miracle worker. Under his constant monitoring of my mental and physical condition, I was able to move into a Wimbledon bedsit on my 60th birthday and live under my own steam, with the daily help of AA. Yet again, I had the Newspaper Press Fund to thank for paying my deposit. For another booby trap the DSS puts in the path of those of us who are forced to live on income support is that you have to have a bona fide landlord in place before you can claim rent, and secondly you have to pay your own deposit. As no landlords I ever encountered would take you in without a deposit, there was more often than not only a cardboard box, the pavement or the more upmarket Common as alternative accommodation.

Six months later, the Press Fund helped me yet again by providing the deposit for a little one-bedroom flat where, for several months, I learned the important difference between loneliness and solitude – the difference being that solitude can be very pleasant. And I reached the much longed-for state where Heidi felt safe enough to take me home.

CHAPTER TWENTY-TWO
REDEMPTION

During the wilderness years, it transpired that Heidi's stepfather had died and had left her mother enough to buy Heidi a little terraced house in Wimbledon, where we now live.

So, under my wife's loving care, I was able to sign off the sick and try to get some bits and bobs of freelance work with which to supplement the monthly wage from her nine-to-six full-time job. An old and much loved friend, Sandy Williams, fashion editor of the *Standard* and *Star* when I worked for those papers, contacted me to say that she was now commissioning editor of the *Daily Express* colour magazine. In the small world that newspaper people inhabit, I found the *Express* was being edited by Eve Pollard's husband Sir Nick Lloyd, who had sat next to me during our days as reporters together on the old *Sun*.

Sandy transformed my life again by getting me to do regular features on the magazine. To my bewilderment, I found myself taking tea with and writing about the

Duchess of Bedford, Lady Herries and the Marchioness of Blandford – and to cap it all, I received a letter on headed notepaper inviting me to submit my personal details for entry into *Burke's Peerage* (whether this was a piss-take or not, I never did find out). I even managed to get back on to 'exes' again with a trip to South Africa to interview golfer Ernie Els for the mag, and I cashed in on my old life by writing pieces about *EastEnders* and another article on actor Michael Elphick. A few years earlier, when we were both raging alcoholics, Michael and I had spent a few days on the piss together as I wrote six story-lines for a television newspaper series entitled 'The Bingo Boys'. Our proposed partnership was broken up when he got the call to go off and star in the long-running hit series *Boon*, so 'Bingo Boys' never saw the light of day. But one of my story-lines did when it appeared on television years later dressed up as 'Harry' in another series Michael was doing. When I got in touch with him to tell him that I was not too pleased about this, Michael held his hands up and said: 'I thought you were either dead or in a cardboard box.' And like the gentleman he is, he arranged for me to be paid for my trouble.

All these nice little earners made it possible for me to help pay for my eldest daughter Jenny's wedding to Peter Reynolds, who had been her brother Danny's best friend since boyhood. Peter, a solicitor, is the son of a judge, no less.

This latest career of mine was dramatically cut short, however, when severe chest pains forced me to pay a visit to Dr Baillie's surgery one morning in September 1995, where he immediately called for an ambulance to take me to St George's Hospital in Tooting. There, I underwent life-saving quadruple heart bypass surgery. And for good measure, Dr Baillie threw in a double hernia operation which was performed by fancy new lasers. All I need now is another 'op' on my gammy leg and I'll be as right as ninepence.

After I had regained my strength, Heidi and the kids persuaded me to apply for a place as an adult student at Roehampton University, and a friend who is a lecturer at that college helped me to get accepted as a freshman in English Literature and History. Sadly, some of my old defects resurfaced at college when I rediscovered just how averse I still was to accepting authority and instruction – especially from women – and I soon began to argue with the female lecturers. I spent a long time agonising over why I was like this until I remembered that Alan Lane had once told me in Weston: 'You treat women like woodlice.'

As I was now living full-time with two women again in Heidi and my youngest daughter Caroline, I decided to do something drastic about this unacceptable behaviour, and that was to abandon my selfish pursuit of knowledge at college and put all my efforts into attaining a more mature and balanced sobriety. I knew there was only one place and one way to do this and that was at AA meetings, and it meant attending on a twice-daily basis again. So after a year, I jacked it in at Roehampton and threw all my energies into AA.

This time around, I had the added help of Prozac, the sunshine drug, which had been recommended to me by one of the young students at Roehampton – talk about 'out of the mouths of babes', because I have to confess that Prozac has done more than anything to restore my equilibrium.

But what AA does is to teach me what I want to do with that new-found balance and how to use it to help others as well as myself. Naturally, I did not become a saint by the very next Thursday, but at least I am working on my defects on a daily basis now.

Incredibly, I do seem to have found that elusive peace which passes all understanding – at first it came in brief lightning flashes, but now it can sometimes last for days on end and, even when I find myself disturbed or distressed, I can make the effort to change my day round there and then.

None of us is issued with a manual at birth explaining how to negotiate life's ever recurring ups and downs, but most people I encountered seemed to have more instinctive knowledge of how to cope with them than I did. So I was forced to accept Arisotle's ancient advice and agree that the unexamined life is not worth living.

But when Prozac began to make me feel so much better, I remembered what the doctor at St Joseph's had told me about my need for a mood-altering drug and I was tempted to curse the fates and reason that, for all those nightmare years, all that had been wrong with me was an unlucky chemical imbalance. This was so much bollocks, of course. For what had been so disastrously wrong with me was that I was self-will run riot, which meant that I had to find a way of handing my will and my life over to God as I understood Him, Her or It.

At one of my first AA meetings, all those stubborn years ago, I had heard someone saying that the need for a belief in a Higher Power was so imperative that it did not matter if you chose a parrot, a hatstand or a number nine bus – just so long as your Higher Power was not your own crazy thinking, the best of which had brought you to this woeful point of your existence. Well, being the obsessive alcoholic I am, I naturally went through the cards in my spiritual search, embracing at different times Christianity, Buddhism and Hinduism. And I am delighted to report that I now have a Higher Power in which I have complete faith and trust. This naturally does not mean that I can guarantee that my own ego will not rebel and sabotage everything by persuading me to pick up a drink and fuck up again.

But I have vowed that, on a daily basis, I will ask my Higher Power not to let me take a drink, even if my arse falls off.

INDEX